Washington at Work

★ ★ ★

WASHINGTON
AT
WORK

Back Rooms and Clean Air

RICHARD E. COHEN

Congressional Reporter, *National Journal*

Macmillan Publishing Company
New York

Maxwell Macmillan Canada
Toronto

Maxwell Macmillan International
New York   Oxford   Singapore   Sydney

Editor: Bruce Nichols
Production Supervisors: Charlotte Hyland and Ann-Marie WongSam
Production Manager: Linda Greenberg
Text and Cover Designer: Eileen Burke
Cover illustration: Gus Szabo
Except as noted, the photographs for this book were taken by Richard A. Bloom.

This book was set in Times Roman by V&M Graphics
and was printed and bound byArcata Graphics/Fairfield.
The cover was printed by New England Book Components, Inc.

Macmillan Publishing Company
866 Third Avenue, New York, New York 10022

Macmillan Publishing Company is part of
the Maxwell Communication Group of Companies.

Maxwell Macmillan Canada, Inc.
1200 Eglinton Avenue East
Suite 200
Don Mills, Ontario M3C 3N1

Library of Congress Cataloging-in-Publication Data

Cohen, Richard E.
    Washington at work : back rooms and clean air / Richard E. Cohen.
        p.   cm.
    Includes index.
      ISBN 0-02-323190-4 (pbk.)
      1. Air—Pollution—Government policy—United States.   2. Lobbying—
United States—Case studies.   I. Title.
    HC110.A4C64   1992
    363.73'92526'0973—dc20   91-27505
                                        CIP
Printing: 5 6 7   Year: 3 4 5 6 7 8

To Milton and Charlotte Cohen,
for their life-long encouragement

To Lyn Schlitt, for her support
and for taking care of Lily

Contents

PREFACE ix

NOTE ON SOURCES xiii

1 "IT'S TOUGH TO GET THINGS DONE" 1

2 EARLY CLEAN-AIR POLITICS 10

3 THE REAGAN YEARS: DEFINING THE LIMITS 25

4 BUSH BREAKS THE LOGJAM 45

5 CRUMBLING COMMITTEES 64

6 THE SENATE LEADER TAKES OVER 81

7 SPECIAL INTERESTS AND INFLUENCE 99

8 BEHIND CLOSED DOORS 113

9 MAKING ALTERNATIVE DEALS 133

10 REACHING COMMON GROUND 151

11 CLEARING THE AIR 167

INDEX 181

ABOUT THE AUTHOR 191

Preface

This study is designed to explain how the 1990 Clean Air Act Amendments became law. In choosing the extended title for the book, I have sought to highlight three themes:

Washington at Work: What Washington does may not be pretty, but the way that it works tells us a lot about ourselves as a nation. Few citizens understand what really happens in our nation's capital. This book attempts to offer a corrective.

Back Rooms: Congress and the White House conduct very little of their most serious work in public view. That is good, bad or irrelevant, depending on your perspective. But readers may be surprised to learn just how little of their maneuverings lawmakers allow us to see.

Clean Air: Despite growing interest in environmental quality and growing concern over deteriorating local conditions, many environmental issues have been surrounded by haze. Public officials and business leaders have failed to explain the extent of our ecological problems or the cost of their cleanup. Properly understood, the extended effort invested in the latest clean-air law clarifies those issues and choices.

I have focused on the specific 1990 law because the handling of the bill exposed important aspects of how Congress operates. This book has been written neither to glorify nor to criticize the institution or its players. It eschews the "Perils of Pauline" step-by-step approach of some legislative case studies. Instead, it focuses on the way that Congress transacts the public's business, on the issues that forced the most protracted and prominent disputes surrounding the clean-air bill, and on the key players who drove the process. My goal has been to demystify and to provide a larger framework for studying how Congress functions under internal rules that have changed radically since 1970, when Congress passed the first major clean-air law. Although there were some unique features in the handling of the 1990 law, which one Senate participant called "the bill from hell," many major bills have recently been enacted in ways that have not fit simple models. I believe that both seasoned and naive Washington watchers need to consider the Clean Air Act as an example of a major modern legislative departure from past practice. In addition to Congress's internal changes, I have also sought to convey how the executive branch and lobbyists influence lawmaking.

Previous stories about Congress either have become dated or are too narrow to offer meaningful, broader lessons. In particular, three books written in the past two decades have most often been read for insight into how the institution operates. Eric Redman's *Dance of Legislation* (Simon and Schuster, 1973) became a classic for undergraduates because it gave a first-hand view of the making of a bill. Although it studied an obscure bill creating a national health-service corps, which was out of the legislative mainstream, the book has been popular because it added a human element to the Capitol scene. Unlike Redman, who later became a Seattle attorney far removed from public understanding of Congress, T. R. Reid took a journalist's perspective when he wrote *Congressional Odyssey* (W. H. Freeman and Co., 1980). That book, based on his reporting for *The Washington Post*, was a blow-by-blow account of the modestly successful effort to increase user fees on the nation's inland waterways, a law that otherwise has aroused little public interest. Redman and Reid both wrote in the 1970s. Jeffrey Birnbaum and Alan Murray, Washington reporters for *The Wall Street Journal*, turned their newspaper accounts on the enactment of the 1986 Tax Reform Act into a book, *Showdown at Gucci Gulch* (Random House, 1987). Their superb reporting of the many perils facing a complex piece of major legislation wove the essential elements of the debate into a fast-paced chronology. But even since 1986, much has changed in Washington.

Two other books about Congress have given special attention to early clean-air laws, although they did not take a traditional case study approach to all the players and issues. In *Clean Air: The Policies and Politics of Pollution Control* (University of Pittsburgh Press, 1975), Professor Charles O. Jones reviewed the enactment of the landmark 1970 law, largely from the perspective of one city, Pittsburgh, attempting to address its local problems. Journalist Bernard Asbell, in

The Senate Nobody Knows (Doubleday, 1978), examined two years in the legislative life of Sen. Edmund S. Muskie, with a heavy emphasis on his sponsorship of what became the 1977 Clean Air Act.

The how-a-bill-became-law genre of books attempts to add spice to political scientists' often dry and impersonal study of how Washington works. Political intrigue, much of which is typically understood by only a few insiders, prevails in Washington. But real issues and tales of personal power lie beneath these conflicts. Critics might say that this approach gives Congress too much credit for rationality and being "on the level." Admittedly, this tale of the 1990 Clean Air Act shows that the federal government does not work smoothly, but it also shows that occasionally the government eventually gets the job done, for better or worse.

Acknowledgments

In addition to the many persons who have provided me with details of the fight over clean-air legislation and have shared their knowledge about Congress, I thank my colleagues at *National Journal.* Their support and stimulation have been instrumental in expanding my understanding of environmental policy and the often mystical ways in which Washington works. Rochelle Stanfield and Margaret Kriz, who both covered the clean-air bill for the magazine, offered especially helpful suggestions and reactions. Larry Haas and Burt Solomon provided continuing insight on the intrigue of government and on the fundamentals of good writing. And Richard Corrigan, who aided me as an editor, was an enterprising pioneer two decades ago in reporting clean-air policy. Dick, regrettably, died suddenly in January 1991. *National Journal* editor Richard Frank and publisher John Fox Sullivan also supported this project and, as usual, accommodated my work habits. Finally, I express special gratitude to Bruce Nichols of Macmillan Publishing Co. for encouraging me to develop this proposal and to navigate the rigors of book-writing. His helpful suggestions and questions also revealed shrewd insights into both the legislative process and the creative process for writers. I, of course, take full responsibility for the text.

Note on Sources

I first gathered details of how the 1990 clean-air bill became law in my weekly writing for *National Journal*. As someone who is especially interested in how the institution of Congress operates, I was fascinated by the range and impact of the bill's many issues and occasionally perplexed by how it was being drafted. The idea and the decision to write this book came only in the final weeks before Congress finished drafting the bill. Although I have missed some advantages of intensive contemporaneous reporting, I believe that both readers and I have been better served by my decision to return to the major players and, with the perspective of hindsight, to reconstruct the major parts of the chronology. By doing so within a year or two of most of the major events surrounding the bill, I also have encouraged my sources to take a fresh look at the often murky details of the legislative process. All quotes in this book are taken from my own interviewing, unless otherwise indicated.

I express thanks to the dozens of people who have provided me so much of their time and expertise on environmental policy and congressional politics. They included most of the individuals chiefly responsible for writing the new law. Among them are (in alphabetical order) Sens. Max Baucus of Montana, Tom Daschle of South Dakota and Dave Durenberger of Minnesota; Senate Majority Leader George J. Mitchell of Maine; and Reps. David E. Bonior of Michigan, Jim Cooper of Tennessee, John D. Dingell of Michigan, Dennis E. Eckart of Ohio, Philip R. Sharp of Indiana, Gerry Sikorski of Minnesota, Al Swift of Washington, Mike Synar of Oklahoma, Tom Tauke of Iowa and Henry Waxman of California. Helpful current and former congressional staffers included Phil Barnett, Jeff Biggs, Diane Dewhirst, Mark Dungan, Brent Erickson, Shelley Fidler, Linda Finley, Dennis Fitzgibbons, Ruth Fleischer, Mike Gillette, Louise Hilsen, Bob Hurley, Kate Kimball, Chuck Knauss, George Kundanis, Peter Levine, John Orlando, Jimmy Powell, Ed Senn, Mike Shields, David Strauss, Greg Wetstone and Jim Whittinghill. I am especially grateful to House aides Dave Finnegan and Phil Schiliro. Despite initial reservations about opening the door to their back rooms, both were generous and patient in sharing their detailed knowledge about clean-air policy and legislative politics. From the Bush administration, I was assisted by Roger Porter, Boyden Gray and Bob Grady at the White House; Bill Rosenberg, Rob Brenner, Jeff Clark and Joe Goffman at the Environmental Protection Agency; and Linda Stuntz at the Energy Department. Helpful lobbyists and others from the private sector included former Sen. Edmund S. Muskie, Dick Ayres, Barbara Bankoff, Bill Becker, Bruce Bertelson, Leon Billings, Frank Blake, Leslie Dach, Terry Dean, Brenda Day, Dan Dudek, Chris Farren, Bill Fay, Ned Helme, Bill Klinefeltner, Rob Liberatore, Peter Lincoln, Terry Maguire, Howard Paster, Bob Rose, Bill Samuel, Russell Train and Dan Weiss. Without the assistance of these people and others, some of whom requested anonymity, I could not have written this book.

1

"It's Tough To Get Things Done"

After a decade of trying to write a new clean-air law, House and Senate conferees completed their work on Oct. 22, 1990, at a congressional hearing room. They were exhilarated, and exhausted.

At 2:30 p.m. on Oct. 22, 1990, several dozen members of Congress convened in Room 345 of the Cannon House Office Building, one of the largest meeting places on Capitol Hill. Their purpose was to vote on a compromise between separate versions of a clean-air bill that the House and Senate had approved earlier that year. The final deals to resolve their differences already had been cut behind closed doors, and this meeting was no more than a formality. But the session's organization and its mood offered hints of the myriad but little-known ways in which the nation's laws are written.

At one end of the room, seated at the two-level platform where House members often conduct hearings, were the key House and Senate members of the conference committee who had worked to resolve differences between the two versions of the bill. The principal players were mostly Democrats, mirroring their party's control of Congress. Scattered along two long rows of tables that extended like arms from the main platform were members of the House committees that played secondary roles in the handling of the bill. Behind those tables were dozens of aides, most of them young, who advised their bosses and helped to draft the final document. At the far end of the room were scores of lobbyists, most of them interested in narrow slices of the bill's total pie. To one side were television cameras and reporters recording the event for the first draft of history.

Sen. Max Baucus of Montana, who was about to mark the biggest achievement of his 16-year legislative career, presided over the meeting. As chairman for less than two years of the Environmental Protection Subcommittee of the Senate Environment and Public Works Committee, Baucus had had a crash course in the intricacies of the nation's most far-reaching and expensive environmental law. The drive to finish the bill had forced him to curtail visits to his home state in the previous several weeks for what he had earlier feared would be a close re-election contest. But he partly compensated for that problem by hiring a Senate Democratic camera crew to tape his comments at the meeting, which were transmitted by satellite and broadcast that evening on local news programs across Montana. "At times, [the debate] was contentious," said Baucus to the meeting and the cameras. "Most times, it was congenial and cooperative." In fact, less than 12 hours earlier, when the doors had been closed to the public, he had threatened to kill the entire bill if the House insisted on retaining a section that would have tightened restrictions on air pollution in national parks, all of them located in western states like Montana.

Seated next to Baucus was Rep. John Dingell of Michigan. Dingell's face was lined with fatigue as he covered his weary eyes with his hands. After fighting to block efforts during much of the prior decade to toughen the nation's clean-air law, the veteran chairman of the House Energy and Commerce Committee had seemingly turned full circle, spearheading the complex negotiations to fashion the most far-reaching overhaul since the 1970 dawn of the environmental movement in Congress. Now, a string of late-night sessions to hammer out the final compromises had left Dingell so tired that he could barely read his brief statement. But he could be satisfied that he had protected his power in the House by meeting the demands of Speaker Thomas S. Foley and others to finish a bill in the 101st Congress. At the same time, he felt that he had done his best to satisfy the tens of thousands of automobile workers and executives in his Detroit-based district who feared the impact of additional federal controls on their economic future.

Other major players briefly added their comments. Rep. Henry A. Waxman of California, the chairman of the Health and Environment Subcommittee, who has devoted much of the past decade to an often uphill battle to strengthen the clean-air law, praised the bill and the efforts required to achieve it. He graciously credited President George Bush and Senate Majority Leader George J. Mitchell of Maine, two of Washington's most powerful officials, for extending the support that moved the bill past previous obstacles. "It has been a long, winding uphill road but the result has been worth it," responded Mitchell, who had labored unsuccessfully during the 1980s to craft an acceptable bill at the Senate Environment Committee but then adeptly used his newly gained leadership post to make it happen.

Finally, the voice-vote approval by the conferees echoed like an afterthought. Only Rep. William E. Dannemeyer, a California Republican strongly opposed to federal regulation of the economy, registered a "nay" vote. Five days later, after swift House passage, the Senate took the final legislative action on the bill, approving it 89–10.

The House and Senate votes, like the earlier pro forma meeting of the House-Senate conferees, were the customary clasping of hands at the end of a long, bitter fight. They masked the thousands of decisions that were part of the bill, the often bitter conflicts between powerful private interests and between various regions of the nation, and the costly steps that would be required of businesses and individuals to comply with the new law. As they groped to reach the end of their legislative work and to prepare for an election two weeks later, members of Congress lacked the energy or perspective to focus on the significance of their achievement. They were simply relieved that they had finished their work and could go home.

If the role of government is to improve the quality of life for its citizens, the Clean Air Act of 1990 embodied a truly landmark piece of legislation. Amid other legislative preoccupations and conflicts spawned by war, taxes and congressional ethics, in 1989 and 1990 a relatively small group of senators and House members persevered. They drafted legislation that would have a direct impact on the lives of nearly all Americans. That proposal was designed to improve the quality of the air we breathe. It would have wide-ranging impact on health, transportation and the economy. It would affect sources of electric power, the cost and availability of consumer products, and countless other features of workplaces and homes. As even its strongest opponents conceded, the law marked a serious effort by government to address major national problems.

The first legislative move to clean the air since 1977, the new law has several major parts. It continued what many consider the unduly slow but relentless progress in reducing automobile tailpipe emissions that pollute the air. It detailed important steps intended to improve air quality, especially in smog-ridden urban centers like Los Angeles and Houston, where local officials have resorted to controlling such routine pollution sources as dry-cleaning shops and charcoal grills. It placed the first major restrictions on Midwest industrial pollution from coal-fired burners that has entered the air, traveled east and dropped its deadly poisons—acid rain—on many lakes and forests in New England and Canada. It listed 189 toxic chemicals for which the Environmental Protection Agency must set public-health standards to reduce their pollution of the air. And it took the first steps to deal with issues such as global warming and the growing hazard of high-altitude ozone depletion posed by chemical CFCs (chlorofluorocarbons)—problems that were unknown, even by scientists, when Congress had last passed a clean-air law.

The handling of this bill, in many respects, displayed Congress at its best and in its most hands-on style. It involved players both legendary and pedestrian—from savvy veterans pushing the levers of power to relatively junior members helping to make the process work. Some worked for their constituents' often narrow interests, others tried to advance the national well-being. At the heart was the seemingly simple notion of cleaning the air that we breathe, but the issues surrounding that notion posed questions and solutions of mind-numbing technical complexity that did not easily translate into legislative language understood by members of Congress, let alone by ordinary citizens.

Demonstrating the choices that constantly confront a legislative body, the bill pitted public and private interests as diverse and wide-ranging as the nation itself. Among these major clashes faced by lawmakers and their constituents was a contest between the suppliers of grain and of natural gas, which are major sources, respectively, of ethanol and methanol, two competing sources of alternative fuel. Another clash pitted automobile manufacturers against gasoline-station operators over the cleanest way to pump gasoline into cars. And the Senate nearly scuttled the bill because of a dispute about unemployment compensation for Appalachian coal miners who might be put out of work because of the new law. These and many other disputes eventually were resolved in a package that filled 102 pages, in small type, of the *Congressional Record*.[1] All this to achieve the ostensibly simple goal of cleaning the nation's air!

The 1990 Clean Air Act was not simply a statement of national environmental policy. It also was an important lesson of how Congress, our nation's chief rule-making institution, functions, and of the changes in the exercise of power during the previous two decades. Individual effort and sheer force of personality often outweighed older and more formal patterns of authority. The crumbling of traditional power centers has left a system where, as the clean-air debate showed, members can achieve leadership only if they understand and respond to the will of the rank and file.

How else to explain the impact of the intellectual brilliance, physical endurance and political control of Senate Majority Leader Mitchell? He determined that the only way to pass the bill would be to abandon important parts drafted by a Senate committee on which he had been a major player, and to force the dozens of combatants into his office a few feet from the Senate floor. There, they hammered out, over a grueling month, a deal acceptable to President Bush and a cross-section of the Senate. In the House, debate was marked by constant tensions between Reps. Dingell and Waxman. These two masterful legislative tacticians identified with the needs of their competing constituencies, Detroit's auto industry and Los Angeles's auto users, but they often had serious problems in dealing with each other as they sought a legislative consensus. Their decade-long war, according to other House members, forced a battle so brutal that, in the end, these two leaders sometimes needed House Speaker Foley as an intermediary to help them communicate. But Dingell and Waxman also held many private sessions where, with some help from others, they made deals settling critical details of the new law.

Many aspects of the battle presented Washington in a less than flattering light. Most of the new law was written in the Capitol's back rooms outside the public eye, despite the supposed increase in public demand for open government. Much of it was crafted by anonymous staff aides like David Finnegan and Kate Kimball. Their long experience and technical familiarity with clean-air issues made them indispensable in drafting the details of the 1990 bill. And their operating style and the changing work practices on Capitol Hill meant that they sometimes carried as much influence as has traditionally been wielded by the most senior senators and representatives. Most members of Congress barely understood large chunks of the bill—even members who served on the committees that drafted the legislation. Debate on the Senate and House floors was mostly a formality, largely to the relief of lawmakers who wanted to avoid choosing sides in votes that might please one interest group or set of constituents and anger another.

That the new law was a decade overdue added to the familiar congressional pressure to "do something." But it also intensified the conflicts and posturing among the many private groups with a stake in the clean-air law. Members of Congress were well aware that the lengthy debate was marked by a maze of legal complexities and political conflicts often impossible to decipher or resolve. The sweeping scope of the bill had produced many well-intentioned but often narrow-minded zealots, both on and off Capitol Hill and from all views. Because no single person could understand the ramifications of each issue, most participants focused on their relatively narrow interest. On one side, environmental lobbyists and their congressional friends were convinced that the polluters were resisting every reasonable proposal to foster clean air. On the other side, industry lobbyists and their congressional allies were equally convinced that new government mandates would disrupt businesses' best efforts to improve the nation's dirty air. Most members facing this no-win dilemma wanted to pass something that they could proudly call a strengthening of the nation's clean-air law while keeping their hands off the difficult task of deciding the actual details.

Polling data have consistently shown that most of the public view the institution of Congress with contempt but are more tolerant of their own local members. Some of the hostility derives from citizens' lack of comprehension of how Congress operates; also, they have little opportunity to track the progress of important measures through Congress. The progress toward the 1990 Clean Air Act, for example, produced a mere handful of stories on the three television networks' evening news programs in 1989–90. Coverage in *The New York Times* and *The Washington Post*, the major newspapers for the nation's intelligentsia, was sporadic, dealing with small parts of the story without filling in the larger picture. Even with the impressive growth of C-SPAN, which provides, via cable TV, admission to the House and Senate galleries for more than 54 million homes, the public's awareness of Congress remains shallow.

Generations of students have learned about the legislative process from publications like "How Our Laws are Made," a Government Printing Office document available in most congressional offices. But the formal description in this primer has become so irrelevant that it verges on the ludicrous. Anyone familiar with the 1990 Clean Air Act, for example, could not seriously accept the self-serving official depiction of debate on the House floor: "Our democratic tradition demands that bills be given consideration by the entire membership with adequate opportunity for debate and the proposing of amendments."[2]

Nor can today's emerging political scientist receive much guidance from many of the traditional, often-cited textbook classics. In Woodrow Wilson's *Congressional Government*, the landmark 1885 study written when he was a graduate student, he asserted, "Congress in its committee rooms is Congress at work."[3] That characterization may have been apt from 1885 through the early 1970s. Since then, however, a more enterprising spirit has swept through Congress and the nation's politics. The desire of individuals to gain a piece of the action has left many of the old rules in tatters and placed greater demands on leaders to prevent full participation from deteriorating into chaos. The tendency of congressional scholars is to theorize from afar while largely ignoring members' actual interactions. Members, lobbyists and reporters have recognized that these personal and parochial aspects of legislating are often the most vital but they rarely explain the full story to the public.

To achieve passage of the Clean Air Act, long-standing feuds between influential members who barely spoke with each other had to be carefully managed. Before they could make their artful deals, politicians were forced to decipher often peculiar differences in business practices and natural features among states. It was significant, for example, that Michigan electric-utility power plants had made far more progress in modifying their ability to control exhausts than had their neighbors in Illinois and Ohio. Likewise, the question of who should pay the costs of unemployed mineworkers in West Virginia was a major sticking point. Responding to these real-world dilemmas is a critical facet of modern-day legislating.

Although the players, issues and moods in today's Congress may evolve, certain facets predominate. Several of these themes emerge repeatedly in the tale of the 1990 Clean Air Act. Perhaps the most striking and least-understood change has been the increased power that has flowed to Senate and House leaders at the expense of committee chairmen. Although most members still prefer to operate under the regularized committee procedure in which Congress functions most smoothly, many committee and subcommittee chairmen have shown that they are simply incapable of responding to increased organiza-tional demands. Important bills are handled in informal groups and task forces, both partisan and bipartisan, that feature ad hoc relation-ships and power-sharing. Most of these meetings occur behind closed doors so lawmakers can escape pressures from lobbyists and reporters, who have made it more difficult for them to handle business "in the sunshine." This procedure was an integral feature of the 1990 Clean Air Act: virtually none of its major sections resulted from votes on the Senate or House floor. These changes are an obvious consequence of the breakdown of the once-dominant role of seniority. That legacy of the 1970s has rendered the chairmen no longer the automatic masters of their domain and has given junior members the opportunity to be-come informal deal-makers. In the resultant legislative chaos, elected party leaders often must intervene to assure progress on important legislation. To be sure, this committee breakdown is most visible on major bills. But those big bills are the acid tests for a legislature.

These altered relationships ultimately stem from the conflicts and tension inherent in a politically divided government. Control of Con-gress and the presidency has been split between Democrats and Repub-licans since 1981 and has been unified for only 14 years during the past four decades. The unprecedented length of this division of power has made the handling of major legislation more difficult. The ten-dency of the major players to blame each other in cases of deadlock has weakened the notion of accountability that is critical to legislative and political success.

The relatively few major bills approved by Congress in recent years have become increasingly complex and lengthy, in terms of both their substantive issues and legislative maneuvers. The panoply of interested groups, both on and off Capitol Hill, the new procedural complications and the longer periods that elapse before existing policy problems are addressed have all conspired to make the legislative process a test of Charles Darwin's principle of the survival of the fittest. As has become dramatically clear on issues like the federal budget and the Clean Air Act, the most abiding rule on major legislation is that there are no rules. This tendency toward congressional "ad hoccry" has meant that on many bills, conventional committee action has hurt more than helped in achieving final House and Senate action.

"There are some issues that are complex and controversial and they take time for Congress to deal with," said Sen. Mitchell in looking back on the handling of the 1990 Clean Air Act. "Persistence is an important attribute. It's easy to get discouraged when an attempt to solve a problem stretches over nine years. If someone is impatient and loses interest at the first setback, it's tough to get things done."

The Clean Air Act Amendments of 1990 is a law of profound significance to every citizen. Our review of its enactment will illustrate its policy impact. More important, it should provide a glimpse of how the nation develops a democratic consensus when thorny issues and complex procedures impose formidable obstacles to reaching agreement.

Endnotes

1. *Congressional Record*, Oct. 27, 1990: H13101–13203.
2. *How Our Laws are Made*, House Document 101–139 (Washington: Government Printing Office), 23.
3. Woodrow Wilson, *Congressional Government* (Cleveland, Ohio: The World Publishing Co., 1956), 69.

2

Early Clean-Air Politics

Former Sen. Edmund Muskie applied hard work and political influence in 1970 as the architect of clean-air legislation. He witnessed
major changes in Congress during the next two decades.

The 1962 publication of Rachel Carson's best-selling *Silent Spring*, which chronicled the threat posed by pesticides to life cycles, helped to create environmental consciousness.[1] Concerns about population growth and industrial expansion, which had been of interest chiefly to nature-lovers, became a national movement triggered by the deteriorating quality of life in both urban and rural areas. The public began to realize that belching smoke stacks and automobile tailpipes posed a health hazard. Across the nation, Earth Day rallies on April 22, 1970, including a rock concert at the Washington Monument grounds, attracted millions of participants.

In Congress, which—above all else—is sensitive to public opinion, environmentalism became a virtual Holy Grail. Before the 1960s, citizens and public officials had barely understood the causes of, let alone the solutions for, pollution. The federal government's activities had been housed at a low-level research-oriented division of the Health and Education Department. Leaders of this obscure Public Health Service office said during the 1960s that it was nearly impossible for them to gain attention, or decisions, from top government officials.

The initial clean-air debate was framed during a turbulent era. The civil rights revolution and the divisive Vietnam War of the late 1960s and early 1970s had fueled a political and social activism that demanded a more aggressive role for government. President Lyndon B. Johnson's "Great Society" produced the most significant domestic legislation since the Depression. As for Congress, which was on the verge of major changes in its operations, the ruling coalition of Republicans and Southern Democrats that had often stymied Democratic presidents had largely broken down. But moderate-to-liberal Democrats remained hampered by House and Senate rules and traditions as they sought to seize power from the old guard.

Into this unfocused jumble stepped Sen. Edmund S. Muskie, a Maine Democrat. An ex-governor who refused to abide by the Washington convention of "go along to get along," he had exercised little power during his early Senate years. He was stymied as a freshman in 1959 because he refused to pledge allegiance to then–Majority Leader Lyndon Johnson of Texas, who ruled the Senate with an iron hand. Relegated to minor committee assignments, Muskie decided to launch his own initiatives as a member of the Public Works Committee. That panel had been known mostly for its support of local economic development, such as highways and harbors, and for other forms of federal pork-barrel aid. Then, at his urging, it created in 1963 an Air and

Water Pollution Subcommittee, from which Muskie, as chairman, authored what became the nation's first air-quality laws.

Muskie directed his first attack at water pollution because he had focused on that issue while governor of Maine during the 1950s. "Air pollution was initially regarded as chiefly a California problem," he said during a retrospective interview in his Washington law office. "None of us knew very much about air pollution. We educated ourselves in the subcommittee's hearings." The initial result was three vaguely worded air-quality statutes in the mid-1960s. These early laws, which would soon become a forgotten prelude to the 1970 law, increased federal research, but they placed the burden largely on state governments to achieve a 50 percent reduction of air pollution by 1970.

Meanwhile, the Senate Interior and Insular Affairs Committee, chaired by Sen. Henry M. Jackson, a Democrat from Washington, sought its own piece of the environmental action. In 1969, Jackson sponsored a significant reorganization of federal antipollution activities as part of the landmark National Environmental Policy Act. That law created the White House Council on Environmental Quality and required federal agencies to show greater sensitivity by issuing "environmental impact statements" for most federal projects. Jackson separately set into motion a government-reorganization process that allowed President Richard M. Nixon to consolidate all federal antipollution efforts into a new Environmental Protection Agency. These initiatives, at least as important as Muskie's actions, helped to spur bolder action because Muskie resented the attention and influence they gave to Jackson, whose Interior Committee chairmanship often made the two of them bitter Senate rivals for influence.

Those initial laws were an early demonstration of two important features of clean-air legislation: (1) Clean air became a goal whose public backing brought it close to motherhood in popularity, and (2) the number of congressional players with a hand in drafting the new laws was quite small. The 1960s statutes had a relatively limited impact. Their chief feature was to give state and local governments small amounts of money and power to combat dirty air. The federal government's role was chiefly advisory, limited to steps such as calling for conferences with local officials or recommending pollution studies. Even Muskie was slow to give the federal government a more aggressive role. In 1967 he opposed the Johnson administration's efforts to set national standards to limit industrial emissions. Instead, Congress that year followed his approach of setting criteria that the states might follow.

When Congress addressed clean-air legislation in 1970, the lawmakers initially planned to make the type of incremental changes that characterized their efforts in the 1960s. But they were prodded to take bolder action by Nixon, who made environmental issues the domestic focus of his 1970 State of the Union message to Congress. "The great question of the seventies," Nixon said, "is, shall we surrender to our surroundings, or shall we make our peace with nature and begin to make reparations for the damage we have done to our air, to our land and to our water?"

Nixon's policy concerns may well have been prompted by the political goal of reaching out to young, middle-class voters. "The White House was very sensitive about Muskie as a 1972 challenger," said Russell Train, a long-time Republican lawyer whom Nixon picked as the first chairman of the Council on Environmental Quality. Muskie gave a similar retrospective assessment. "Nixon saw me emerging as a potential presidential candidate and he knew of my interest in environmental issues," Muskie said. "So, he created the EPA. He tried to pre-empt the issue from me." Nixon was clearly trying to steal the thunder of the environmental movement away from Democrats like Muskie and Jackson. Whatever his motivation, he became the first president to place the environment high on the national agenda.

Muskie responded cautiously by calling for stronger federal authority to administer the existing federal/state mechanism in order to protect public health. But his initial proposal was less sweeping than was Nixon's recommendation to set stricter standards and enforcement procedures for automobile and industrial emissions. "In this first round, at least, the president emerged as a prime supporter of strong legislation in a field generally conceded in the past to his adversary [Muskie]," political scientist Charles O. Jones wrote in his review of the early sparring.[2]

Several factors stripped away that caution and produced one of the most far-reaching laws ever passed by Congress to regulate the domestic economy. At least as vital to the outcome as Muskie's views was his influence in both the Senate and national politics. He had become a national celebrity following the chaotic 1968 presidential election. Although unsuccessful that year as his party's vice-presidential nominee on the ticket with Hubert H. Humphrey, Muskie's homespun New England character gained in appeal in his first appearance on the national political stage. He became the early favorite for the

1972 Democratic presidential nomination. That standing was enhanced by the swirl of negative publicity surrounding Sen. Edward M. Kennedy of Massachusetts. Mary Jo Kopechne, a young woman who had been an aide in the ill-fated 1968 presidential campaign of Robert F. Kennedy, died when the car Kennedy was driving went off a bridge and sank at Chappaquiddick on Martha's Vineyard, an island off Massachusetts, in July 1969. The collapse of this erstwhile frontrunner enhanced Muskie's stature. He became a senator with whom his colleagues and Republican President Nixon dared not trifle. As would occur two decades later, a conservative but pragmatic Republican president was pressured into backing major environmental advances by a liberal, consensus-seeking Democratic senator from Maine.

Muskie, known in the Senate for his short temper, may also have been provoked by a negative appraisal of his record in a 1970 book, *Vanishing Air*. This harsh assessment of federal efforts to reduce air pollution, which was prepared by consumer advocate Ralph Nader and his staff, was especially tough on Muskie. It focused on the limited approach and enforcement of earlier environmental laws, including Muskie's interference with federal steps to clean up the heavily polluting paper industry in his home state of Maine. "The Senator must be credited with seizing the issue earlier than most of his colleagues and providing some leadership and attention in those early days when the words 'air pollution' still had an exotic ring," according to the report. "However, Muskie's leadership has wavered significantly over the last several years. The recent lessons learned by the public concerning air pollution have been largely self-taught."[3]

Nader had put Muskie on the defensive at a time when he was attempting to burnish his national reputation. Muskie vigorously rejected what he termed a personal attack. "Nader did make me angry," Muskie later said. "But I don't think that he affected what I did. I am a middle-of-the-roader. When he attacked me, that put me in a good position and I looked good to the right wing." Muskie's most effective refutation, in the end, would be to produce legislation that resolved doubts about his commitment to clean air.

The House forced Muskie's hand by passing on June 10, 1970, a clean-air bill that strengthened current law and was modeled on Nixon's proposal. Proposals setting more stringent auto-emission standards were rejected. Now, in the Senate, Muskie could prove that he was Mr. Clean Air and, at the same time, enhance his standing in Congress and his opposition to Nixon. After extensive discussions among his subcommittee members, Muskie settled on a strategy to attack automobile exhaust, the primary source of air pollution. His plan called for the auto industry to make a 90 percent reduction in its total emissions by January 1, 1975. That figure was set after Leon G. Billings, Muskie's chief environmental aide, asked John Middleton, HEW's antipollution boss, how much auto pollution would have to be cut to reach the earlier requirement that states cut their pollution by 50 percent. Muskie added an escape clause permitting federal regulators to give the automakers a one-year extension. "Everyone understood that the goal could not be reached with state-of-the-art technology," Billings later said. "But the debate was not over the 90 percent cut. It was over what could be done if the automobile industry could not meet the standard. Muskie's theory was that a bureaucrat would always extend the deadline, so he wanted to require Congress to make the decision."

Muskie held lengthy private discussions to give his panel members more confidence in the bill. Earning the nickname "Iron Pants" because he could spend countless hours without leaving his chair, he kept his subcommittee working day after day to create the strong bipartisan support vital to enhancing the measure's credibility. This collegiality was marked by a greater participation by senators and less of a staff role than would prove to be the case in the Senate two decades later. As a result, Muskie's bill passed the Senate, 73–0, on Sept. 22. When the House-Senate conference committee sought agreement during a lame-duck session after the November election, House conferees were outgunned by Muskie's political strength and his superior understanding of the issues. The final deal, embracing Muskie's deadlines for major cuts in auto emissions, so offended the Nixon administration that the president reportedly considered a veto; then, his aides refused to invite Muskie to the White House signing ceremony. The Maine Senator's bold determination and persistence had turned him from villain to hero of the environmental movement.

In retrospect, it may be surprising that the automobile industry, the chief target of Muskie's bill, mounted relatively weak resistance. Muskie later speculated that some industry leaders "could see what was coming" and gave limited cooperation. "The industry then saw environmental issues as a hindrance and a cost it did not want to pay from the profit margins of its executives," a business lobbyist said two decades later. But a hindrance is hardly the same thing as a catastrophe. The industry's passive attitude on Capitol Hill was explainable partly by the industry's strong financial position at a time when imports represented only 13 percent of all U.S. auto sales and partly by its weak lobbying operation; by 1990, imports would exceed 26 percent of all U.S. auto sales.[4] Lobbying was still a relatively small business in Washington in 1970, when there were fewer than 4,000 persons seeking to affect federal policy, compared with about 14,500 in 1990.[5] General Motors, for example, did not establish a Washington lobbying office until 1969. Although the automobile was still part of the American dream, the industry's localized geographic base in the Midwest meant that it had a relatively narrow range of support in Congress. Many other politicians viewed the industry as arrogant and unresponsive.

The 1970 Clean Air Act was, in many respects, a legislative marvel. Congress required an industry to make major changes in its product, which would surely increase costs for consumers. In acting primarily to achieve a health standard, legislators overrode opponents who said that the needed technology was not available. Congress acted with some scientific basis but even more faith that the automobile industry would meet the 1975 deadline for the law's standards by developing catalytic converters for their engines that would reduce tailpipe exhausts. The legislation was "technology-forcing," in the sense that it required scientific advances not yet achieved in laboratories. Lawmakers justified this unusual approach by arguing that the auto industry's lack of economic competition and the marketplace's inability to regulate itself left government as the only tool to force managers to improve their product.

"Three fundamental principles shaped the 1970 law," Muskie wrote 20 years later. "I was convinced that strict federal air pollution regulation would require a legally defensible premise. Protection of public health seemed the strongest and most appropriate such premise. Sen. Howard Baker [a Tennessee Republican] believed that the American technological genius should be brought to bear on the air pollution problem, and that industry should be required to apply the best technology available. Sen. Thomas Eagleton [a Missouri Democrat] asserted that the American people deserved to know when they could expect their health to be protected, and that deadlines were the only means of providing minimal assurance."[6]

In addition to the reduction of automobile emissions, the 1970 law had several other important requirements, some of which were not achieved on schedule. It directed the EPA to set air-quality standards across the nation. The EPA also was required to place restrictions on industrial use of toxic pollutants and to establish national limits for emissions from new stationary sources, such as factories and power plants. Each state was required to establish a state implementation plan (SIP) to limit its pollutants, subject to EPA approval.

As innovative and aggressive as that clean-air law was, however, it had limitations as an environmental statute. It dealt directly only with smog caused by automobiles, the largest source of dirty air but hardly the only one then known. Although it set deadlines, the 1970 statute gave the automobile industry no incentive or advice on how to achieve the goal. And it was far less forceful in cutting pollution generated by other industries such as steel and electric utilities, many of which were nationally based and therefore had more friends in Congress than did the auto industry. The 47-page statute appeared to assume naively that Congress could simply set a wide-ranging rule and expect compliance, regardless of the consequences.

Muskie's work on the Clean Air Act, however, had only begun. As difficult as it may be for members of Congress to come together and agree on an idealistic goal like clean air, it can be even more difficult to enforce regulations in the private sector. Not surprisingly, the auto industry quickly complained that it could not meet the tough new standards. It won approval, first from the EPA and later from Congress, of requests to extend the deadlines until the 1978 model year. Although environmentalists claimed that the automakers had developed the requisite technology, the industry heatedly disputed that it could meet the 1970 Act's standards. It escalated its threats of a national calamity in 1977 by storing at a Michigan fairgrounds thousands of new cars that could not be shipped to dealers unless the law was modified.

By the mid-1970s, however, the industry was better organized in Washington: the politics of environmental control had begun to shift. As business began to feel the impact of the 1970 law, the number and sophistication of corporate lobbyists increased greatly. The new EPA aggressively defined problems and staked its share of the policy-making turf, not always in sync with environmentalists. Perhaps most important, greater public concern over the aftermath of the 1973 energy "shock" caused by the Arab-Israeli war and then the 1974–75 recession distracted attention from environmental passions. In addition, Muskie's abysmal failure in his 1972 Democratic presidential campaign dimmed his national political luster. Although he intensified his efforts and regained some stature on Capitol Hill, Muskie would painfully discover his clout reduced once he was no longer at the forefront of presidential politics. His earlier identification principally with environmental issues was also diminished when he became chairman in 1974 of the newly created Senate Budget Committee, where his attention and time shifted to the rigors of disciplining federal spending.

Crafting the next clean-air law proved so controversial that it extended over three years and two presidents. In 1975, Muskie and his renamed Environmental Pollution Subcommittee began work on extending the 1970 law. They confronted a conflicting mass of evidence on the effectiveness of, and compliance with, that law. In ordering a 90 percent pollution reduction, Congress in 1970 set limits on the three chief sources: hydrocarbons, carbon monoxide and nitrogen oxide. The first two were cut relatively easily. Detroit's biggest problem was reducing its so-called NOx emissions. That pollution unfortunately tended to increase as the result of Washington's separate demand—in the wake of the 1970s fuel shortages—for more fuel-efficient vehicles, which produce both more heat and more nitrogen oxide fumes. The 1970 requirement to cut the poisonous NOx from 3.5 grams per mile to 0.4 grams was nowhere in sight in 1975, with the auto manufacturers struggling to reduce their emissions to 2.0 grams. Muskie proposed modifying the 1970 law, reducing NOx emissions to 1.0 gram per mile for 1980 models.

Muskie's plan, with its 1980 deadline, passed the Senate on Aug. 5, 1976. In September, the House passed a weaker version, which did not demand compliance with the 1.0 gram NOx standard until at least 1982. The House version, which had strong support from the auto industry, was sponsored by John Dingell, who had become a growing power in the House. After heated negotiations, Senate-House conferees agreed to a compromise that, not surprisingly, split the difference by setting a 1981 deadline. But the whole package collapsed because freshman Sen. Jake Garn, a Utah Republican, exercised his right to talk the bill to death with a filibuster. He objected to a separate provision barring further deterioration of federal air-quality standards for relatively clean areas. Under the Senate's procedures of unlimited debate, any Senator may stymie action on a bill unless 60 senators affirmatively vote to force a vote. Sen. Robert C. Byrd, Democrat of West Virginia, who was about to become majority leader, administered the final blow by calling for final adjournment of the 94th Congress, rather than challenging Garn's filibuster. Byrd's motion passed, over Muskie's strenuous opposition, by 36–33.

When Congress reassembled in 1977 with Jimmy Carter as the new president, some observers expected the entire battle to be refought. But the more environmentally conscious Carter temporarily bolstered the clean-air lobby's influence. He made a key decision, angering Dingell, to agree to back a version similar to Muskie's earlier plan. Dingell, however, again managed to pass an amendment on the House floor. He had gained additional strength since 1976 because of intensified support from the United Auto Workers, which had joined the industry-led fight because of its fears that increased auto imports posed a grave threat to jobs in Detroit.

With the Senate holding firm behind Muskie, the final outcome was similar to the 1976 conference agreement setting a NOx limit of 1.0 gram per mile. Despite this loosening of the original 1970 law, environmentalists did score a win, giving the EPA authority to limit construction of new industrial sites in areas that had not met its air-quality standards. And the law included a modified version of the "non-degradation" provision to prevent significant deterioration of air quality in relatively clean regions, which Garn had successfully opposed in 1976.[7]

The three-year battle was noteworthy partly because of changes since 1970 in the House committee handling clean-air legislation, which was then called Interstate and Foreign Commerce. The emergence of many ardent environmentalists from the large number of activist Democrats in the "Watergate class" reshaped the political landscape. (That group got its name when the mostly liberal Democrats were elected in 1974 in the wake of the Watergate scandal.) Among those with unconventional backgrounds for legislators at the time were Reps. Andy Maguire of New Jersey, an expert on urban development; Toby Moffett of Connecticut, who had been part of Ralph Nader's network; Philip Sharp of Indiana, who had been a professor of political science at Ball State University; and Timothy E. Wirth of Colorado, a former aide to HEW Secretary John Gardner. Although they lost some clean-air fights on the House floor, this group of firebrands created a counterforce at the Commerce Committee. One result was to strengthen the hand of Dingell's chief nemesis, Paul G. Rogers, a Florida Democrat, who chaired the Health and the Environment Subcommittee. With Rogers, the Watergate class tipped the congressional hand to Muskie who, with Carter's encouragement, achieved the 1977 amendments to the Clean Air Act.

The difference between the 1977 and the 1990 amendments chronicled in this book was huge, in terms of congressional makeup and handling. The power of committee chairmen declined. Rank-and-file members became more assertive. Ad hoc decision making replaced committee procedures. The 75 House Democrats in the 1974 Watergate class helped to achieve many of these important long-term changes in how Congress operates. The sheer number of this group solidified the efforts initiated by reformers several years earlier to make committee chairmen more responsive to the Democratic Caucus. Such reform efforts that are intended to bring in additional players are common among those who lack votes in restricted arenas like committees. In 1974 the reformers scored many procedural gains. The aging conservative Democratic committee chairmen, many of them Southerners, found their high-handed tactics in running their committees tempered by rule changes imposing more accountability on committee chairmen and expanding the influence of subcommittees. The most jarring attack on the seniority system was a series of Caucus votes in January 1975 ousting three of the most autocratic "barons." Filling the void were not only new chairmen but also an array of informal party groups and issue-based caucuses of varying stripes, all seeking to shape legislative policy. The "new breed" Democrats sent a message to the House's elite, present and future, that if they wished to retain their influence they must respond to the shifting views of the party's majority. Since then, the Caucus has displayed its willingness to use that power, as shown by the December 1990 ouster of two aging, unresponsive committee chairmen, 75-year-old Frank Annunzio of Illinois and 77-year-old Glenn Anderson of California.

The Senate, for its part, had earlier begun to disperse power among its members. The 1961 selection of Mike Mansfield, a Montana Democrat, as majority leader, after Johnson was elected vice president, had made the Senate far more open and encouraged all senators to express their views without fear of antagonizing party leaders. Where the domineering Johnson had sought to control much of the Senate's power, the professorial Mansfield viewed the Senate as 100 equals. But the Senate did not go so far as the House's 1974 changes of replacing committee chairmen and enacting new rules for party discipline.

The switches in party control following the 1980 and 1986 Senate elections made most senators more aware of the need for party cohesiveness to encourage election success. Independent committee chairmen, as a result, saw their effectiveness curtailed. But not all of the committees responded to the pressure for partisan discipline. In some cases, such as Muskie's former Public Works Committee, chairmen proved unable to meet the political challenge or the issues proved too complex for one committee. The frequent result was that party leaders were forced to take control of major issues and to resolve them in the more time-consuming and procedurally difficult forum of the Senate floor. The eroding influence of once all-powerful Senate committees and their bosses also prompted the creation of more ad hoc committees and party task forces to develop legislation.[8]

These changes, as a whole, often resulted in a Congress held hostage by individual members not on the committees and by the views of relatively narrow public and private interests. One unintended consequence was that the legislative process became more cumbersome. To some extent, that may have been desirable. The constitutional framers had intended to guard against hasty action by building a system of checks and balances to restrict the power of each of the three branches of the federal government. In particular, President James Madison wrote in *The Federalist Papers* that "factions" should attempt to cooperate in Congress so that the institution could promote national consensus, to any extent possible. "The causes of faction cannot be removed," Madison wrote. "That relief is only to be sought in the means of controlling its effects."[9] The framers, in creating a bias toward the status quo, also fashioned a system encouraging stability, in which public passions could be cooled. But the reforms of the 1970s may have exacerbated this tendency, making it more difficult both for Congress to break deadlocks and for presidents to win approval of their programs. Increasingly partisan and negative election campaigns added to the nervousness and instability in Congress and to the difficulty of achieving bipartisan cooperation.

At the same time that Congress was becoming more fractured, another political development hampered expeditious policy making. The growing pattern of Republican Party control of the White House and Democratic control of Congress produced an unprecedented period of "divided government." Before 1956, this had occurred during only four presidential elections in the nation's history. Since then, it has been the rule in six of the nine contests. The heightened conflict has in many cases preempted serious policy debates and efforts to build cooperation between Congress and the president. During the 1980s this trend extended to long-standing conflicts over the federal budget deficit and U.S. aid to the Nicaraguan Contra rebels fighting the Sandinista government.

The weakening of congressional consensus-building mechanisms was accompanied by closer communication between many members of Congress and their constituents. This communication took the form of both direct contact by lawmakers with and through their staffs in their home areas and grass-roots lobbying campaigns organized by national special-interest groups. The inclination of most members to respond to local views was fueled by better access to information and staff expertise. The House payroll nearly doubled from 4,055 in 1967 to 7,920 in 1986; the Senate had a comparable increase during that period. And during those two decades the annual budget for the legislative branch jumped from $198 million to $1.78 billion.[10] More consistent attention to the home base has meant that incumbents, especially in the House, have been reelected in record numbers, maintaining Democratic control of Congress and hence bipartisan fracture in the government.

During the Reagan years, clean-air policy provided a dramatic example of the perils of divided government, as we shall see in the next chapter. Even in the most politically cohesive times, the issues attached to clean air would make agreement difficult. In the 1980s, it was impossible.

Here is a brief summary of the often complex and highly technical clean-air issues, which would preoccupy dozens of Senate and House lawmakers from 1981 to 1990 and ultimately become the core of the 1990 amendments. Enactment of any one of these sections would have constituted major environmental legislation.

Urban air quality. The continuing failure of over 100 metropolitan areas to meet the air-quality standards set by the 1970 law, as amended in 1977, left those areas in "non-attainment" of the deadline, which was extended to 1982, and for some pollutants to 1987. Particularly nagging has been the inability to address the public-health hazard caused by exposure to ground-level ozone, which results from the interaction of hydrocarbons, nitrogen oxide (from cars and factories) and sunlight. This problem is troublesome in many cities during the summer, when those ingredients yield a mix that can cause serious respiratory problems. According to a University of California study, decreased air pollution in southern California could save nearly $10 billion in annual health-care costs and increase agricultural yields. But the problem of dirty air has not been solely regional: Congressional studies report that 150 million Americans live in areas that failed to meet either the carbon monoxide or ozone standard set by the EPA, pursuant to the 1970 law. As a result, Congress more aggressively sought to reduce pollution from stationary sources, such as industrial sites and consumer products.

Mobile sources. The cause of 90 percent of carbon monoxide and half of the ozone non-attainment has remained a continuing problem with emissions from mobile sources: automobiles, trucks and other vehicles. Despite the improvements that Detroit has made to its products since 1970, the 69 percent increase in motor-vehicle registration since then has reduced the impact of cleaner cars. The total number of vehicle miles traveled doubled from 1970 to 1990. In addition, the early hopes of Congress to reduce the 0.4 grams per mile nitrogen oxide (NOx) standard for tailpipe emissions have been unrealized. Environmentalists have been forced to seek other ways to limit auto exhaust, including federal inspection and maintenance programs, improved and alternative fuels and reduced vehicle use.

Acid rain. Since 1977, scientists have learned that pollution from NOx and SO_2 (sulfur dioxide) can travel hundreds of miles through the atmosphere and return to earth in rain and snow as nitric and sulfuric acids. These have damaged lakes and streams and high-elevation forests and are suspected of causing harm to human health, especially in the northeastern United States and southeastern Canada. The chief source of these acids is power-plant and industrial exhausts, which result from the use of certain forms of coal with a high sulfur content.

Toxic pollutants. Although the 1970 law required the EPA administrator to establish standards for "hazardous air pollutants," the agency has moved very slowly, issuing federal rules on only seven of those pollutants. EPA officials have cited the law's flexibility to defend their cautious response. But environmentalists and their congressional allies have sought ways to force the EPA to act by setting statutory deadlines for emissions standards that would apply to close to 200 toxic pollutants from both existing and new sources.

CFCs. Scientists have raised growing concern in recent years about destruction of the earth's ozone layer, which is the main protection against the sun's harmful radiation. This has been caused by the growing public use of chlorofluorocarbons and similar manufactured substances, whose destructive chemicals are released into the ozone layer. Although CFCs have been banned in aerosol cans, for example, they are actively used in other consumer products and manufacturing processes, such as refrigeration, air conditioning and insulation.

Permits and enforcement. Since the Clean Air Act of 1970, Congress has closely monitored implementation of federal regulations to ensure that U.S. industry takes steps despite the cost to meet the new requirements. But many factors have frustrated those goals, including disputes within and between the executive branch and Congress, resistance by the private sector and different interpretations of how to achieve the complex standards. As a result, compliance became an issue in itself. Among the key procedural issues facing Congress have been proposals to restrict the operating permit required for major sources of air pollution. In addition, Congress considered expanding federal penalties as enforcement tools.[11]

Endnotes

1. Rachel Carson, *Silent Spring* (Boston: Houghton Mifflin, 1962).
2. The best discussion of how Congress passed the 1970 Clean Air Act is provided by Charles O. Jones in Chapter 7 of his book, *Clean Air: The Policies and Politics of Pollution Control* (Pittsburgh: University of Pittsburgh Press, 1975).
3. The Ralph Nader Study Group Report on Air Pollution, *Vanishing Air* (New York: Grossman Publishers, 1970), 292.
4. 1991 Market Data Book of *Automotive News* (Detroit: Crain Communications, 1991).
5. Arthur C. Close et al., editors, *Washington Representatives 1991* (Washington: Columbia Books Inc., 1991), 3
6. Edmund S. Muskie, "The Clean Air Act: A Commitment to Public Health," *Environmental Forum*, January 1990: 14.
7. For a thorough discussion of the 1975–76 efforts to amend the Clean Air Act, chiefly from Muskie's perspective, see Bernard Asbell, *The Senate Nobody Knows* (New York: Doubleday, 1978). For a more general overview of the 1977 law, see Chapter 6 of Norman J. Ornstein and Shirley Elder, *Interest Groups, Lobbying and Policy Making* (Washington: Congressional Quarterly Inc., 1978).
8. Some of the discussion in this section is adapted from my essay, providing an overview of the institutional changes in Congress for *United States: A Handbook,* scheduled for publication by Facts on File in 1992.
9. Jacob E. Cooke, editor, *The Federalist* (Middletown, Conn.: Wesleyan University Press, 1961), 60.
10. Norman J. Ornstein, Thomas E. Mann, and Michael J. Malbin, *Vital Statistics on Congress, 1989–90* (Washington: Congressional Quarterly Inc., 1990), 132, 140.
11. The extensive reports by the congressional committees with jurisdiction over clean-air legislation have been useful research tools. See in particular House Report 101–490, Part 1, "Clean Air Act Amendments of 1990," by the Energy and Commerce Committee; and Senate Report 101–228, "Clean Air Act Amendments of 1990," by the Environment and Public Works Committee.

3

The Reagan Years: Defining the Limits

President Ronald Reagan and Senate Democratic Leader Robert Byrd were at the center of the stalemate that frustrated the writing of a new clean-air law in the 1980s. Once they left their posts, the game was over. (White House photo)

If Ed Muskie's activism symbolized Washington's clean-air politics during the 1970s, then Ronald Reagan's indifference set the tone for the 1980s. Posturing by all sides. Intensified problems. Missed opportunities. Half-hearted attempts at compromise. And, in the end, deadlock.

In 1981 the circumstances for writing a new clean-air law were less than auspicious. As often happens, changing political dynamics had an important impact on how Congress crafted policy. A Republican president had taken office intent on undermining existing regulatory statutes, either directly through new legislation or indirectly through lax enforcement. Despite his often-professed love for the outdoors, Reagan made his most famous comment on the environment during the 1980 campaign when he suggested, only partly in jest, that trees cause pollution.

Unlike his strong and clearly-stated calls to cut federal taxes and spending, which he convinced Congress to implement during his first seven months in office, Reagan did not, during his 1980 campaign against President Carter, publicly frame environmental issues as a major goal. He consequently had minimal long-term impact on environmental policy other than to delay decisions. Ironically, his lack of interest eventually resurrected public support for stronger enforcement. The president's initial top appointees for dealing with those problems displayed a visible contempt both for existing environmental policies and for Washington's political culture. Environmental activists targeted these officials, chiefly Interior Secretary James Watt and Environmental Protection Agency chief Anne Gorsuch, for ridicule and critical public-relations campaigns. If the Reaganites had done more to enforce the existing law, there would have been less pressure for a new law.

Revising the clean-air law may have been a practical impossibility during Reagan's presidency, given the sharp policy differences among powerful players. In lawmaking, presidents do matter. "We learned in the Reagan years that we could not pass a bill based on bits and pieces from different people," Dingell said retrospectively. But that did not prevent a fractured Congress from addressing the issues in several different ways. Some influential lawmakers, including the Senate leaders from each party and the chairman of the House committee with control of the bill, sought to work with the Reagan administration. Other, more junior chairmen tried to ignore the president's views. And some members simply assumed that they could cut a deal when the moment of truth arrived.

The inherent difficulty of enacting almost any major legislation was never more apparent. The elements were destined for gridlock. The president never showed much interest in the subtleties of the legislative process. On the other end of Pennsylvania Avenue, Congress was split between a Democratic-controlled House and a Republican-controlled Senate during the first six years of Reagan's presidency. When Reagan rallied a coalition of Republicans and conservative "boll weevil" Democrats to support his spending and tax-cut programs in 1981, he achieved his major campaign goals and his most important legislative victories. But he so poisoned the well for leaders of both parties that he could not effectively restore that coalition on a sustained basis during his remaining years in office. His few other congressional achievements, such as social-security and tax reform, required the cooperation of Democratic leaders on less ideological issues.

The tensions of divided government, which had become common since the 1950s, were exacerbated by the Republicans' poor performance in congressional elections during the 1980s. In 1980 they won 192 of 435 House seats, their highest total since their 1953–54 majority of 221. That number fell to 166 seats in 1982 and during the remainder of the decade they struggled to raise it above 175, a total that usually was inadequate to build a majority coalition with conservative Democrats. As for the Senate, Republicans held a slim majority of 53 to 55 of the 100 seats from 1981 to 1987, giving them little margin for error in that increasingly partisan chamber. In their disastrous 1986 election and the two subsequent campaigns, Republicans fell back to the minority with either 44 or 45 seats.

Thus ensued long periods of paralysis in Washington mixed with occasional bursts of activity. Democratic congressional leaders and committee chairmen used devices such as press conferences and hearings to focus on what they hoped to portray as the shortcomings of the Reagan administration. Perhaps the best example was the decision by House and Senate Democrats in 1987 to investigate the Reagan administration's Iran-Contra affair, which already had generated detailed public inquiries and criminal-law investigation. The White House responded that Congress was aiming to weaken the president and to enhance its own power. In the end, relatively few voters were swayed by these spectacles and the chief result may have been an increase in public cynicism toward government. These squabbles dramatized the difficulty of legislating without consensus among the president and key congressional leaders.

With hindsight, the prospect that the key players during the Reagan era would ever have agreed in the clean-air debate seems bleak, given the sharp policy differences among powerful players. When the administration displayed its antagonism toward environmental legislation, the other side usually had a counteraction. But members of Congress were not and could not have been so certain of an unsuccessful outcome at the time. Lawmakers, after all, are elected to address the nation's problems—in short, to make laws. For members who sincerely believe in the correctness of their view and the need for action, politics often gets pushed aside. They scheme on how to pass a bill now, not two years later when unforeseeable changes will have taken place in the attitudes of the public and the legislators who represent them. Advocates often are so convinced of the intellectual wisdom and the political soundness of their ideas that they cannot imagine their colleagues will fail to see the light. Compromise often seems more attainable before the battle has begun. And none of the adversaries could safely assume how the other side would respond.

Partisanship is not the sole or even the dominant factor that shapes many congressional debates. Efforts to control the environment, for example, can divide members along geographic lines. When Henry Waxman, the liberal Democrat from Los Angeles, filed his proposal to reduce smog in urban areas, his chief co-sponsor was Rep. Jerry Lewis, a leading conservative Republican. Like Waxman, Lewis represents pollution-plagued southern California. Steps to control the use of smoky coal, likewise, pitted coal-state senators from the Appalachian region against Northeastern senators who represented constituents choking on power-plant exhaust. At other times, legislative outcomes are determined by more informal factors, such as committee assignments or friendships among lawmakers. When members of Congress are uncertain how to vote, they may rely on a respected colleague's opinion.

As proposals concerning the Clean Air Act were introduced, supporters and opponents formed sides. Arguments were articulated and debunked. And deadlines, both real and self-imposed, were missed. "All of our efforts probably had no chance," said Rep. Al Swift, a Democrat from Washington who served on the Energy and Commerce Committee. "But you need to wear away each other, even though you know you have no chance of getting a final bill." In effect, Swift said, success in the legislative arena requires time, sometimes years, to identify which issues and alternatives are worthwhile and which should be set aside. A Senate aide who spent several years working on the complex bill said that the educational process ultimately allowed the players to feel more comfortable about their final decisions. "Although the debate often was frustrating," he said, "it was good politics to push."

The legislative maneuvers during the Reagan years centered chiefly around four Democrats: Dingell and Waxman in the House, Byrd and Mitchell in the Senate. In public statements and actions, they usually remained far apart. Operating in 1988 largely unknown by the public or their own colleagues, however, these "four horsemen" came close to reaching a private agreement, which would have had a good chance of winning enactment. Even though the advocates did not shake hands on a deal during the Reagan era, their ability to narrow their differences allowed them to set a framework that finally produced a new law in 1990. The story of those efforts provides an important backdrop to what followed after Bush entered the White House. It also fueled a spate of second-guessing that Dingell and Byrd, in particular, may have ill-served their blue-collar constituencies by not pushing more aggressively to close a deal in 1988.

Because so much of the decade-long conflict in the House was a struggle between the two powerful and savvy House Energy and Commerce Committee members, there is a natural inclination to frame this story around their two personalities. But the reality is that Dingell and Waxman, whose skills and ongoing antagonism have lent them a larger-than-life quality, became symbols of much larger political and economic forces in Congress and the nation.

To understand Congress one must first understand its members, their personalities and their roots. John Dingell's home district lies on the southern and western outskirts of Detroit and once was the home of more than 80,000 auto-industry jobs. It includes such renowned sites as Ford Motor's giant Rouge plant, an industrially integrated facility built by Henry Ford in 1910. Besides autos, the district contains huge facilities for producing related products such as steel and shock absorbers. Dingell's second wife, Deborah Insley, was an heiress to the family that founded Fisher Body Corp., which General Motors Corp. purchased in 1919. She worked before and after their 1981 wedding as an executive in GM's Washington office. But a congressional wag commented that the marriage did not change Dingell's relationship to GM or the auto industry as a whole. "John Dingell was married to General Motors long before he was married to Debbie."[1]

Dingell is also a son of Congress. In 1955, when John D. Dingell Sr. died, his young lawyer son won the vacant seat. The elder Dingell had been a prominent architect of the New Deal, especially federal banking laws, during his 23 years in the House. As a child, the son lived in Washington and served from 1938 to 1943 as a House page. Like many veteran members and others who have grown up around the Capitol, he loves the House and has considered himself a student of its often complex rhythms and interactions. Dingell also has taken pride in his ability to get what he wants, even if it requires flaunting his imposing physical presence. When *The Washington Post* profiled him in 1983, Rep. Ed Madigan, an Illinois Republican, had this to say about his committee chairman: "Sometimes I think he is an arbitrary and capricious son of a bitch, and other times I think he is a great parliamentarian. . . . Dingell is formidable not because he has more friends than anyone else, nor because he is more skilled—there are others as skilled as he is. His strength comes because he takes the skill he has and combines it with good staff work, a thorough knowledge of the issues and a bulldog determination not to let go. He is the most tenacious member of Congress."[2]

In 1981, when President Reagan's popularity and prowess were riding high, Dingell had serious concerns. The once-powerful automobile industry, in the midst of the nation's worst recession since World War II, had hit hard times. Chrysler was on the verge of bankruptcy. GM and Ford were laying off thousands of workers. And the 1977 Clean Air Act, with its costly requirements to reduce tailpipe emissions, was about to make things worse. As the new chairman of the Energy and Commerce Committee, Dingell was well positioned to come to the rescue of his industrial constituents.

Conveniently, the Reagan administration was ready to oblige, though for different reasons. Its top officials contended that federal regulations had gotten seriously out of control and were imposing too many rules on economically battered industries. Working with a White House task force chaired by then–Vice President Bush, the administration planned to overhaul federal regulations to give them a more market-oriented approach. Their goal, according to Reagan critics, was nothing less than repeal of the Clean Air Act and its effort to use government to force industry to cut pollution. Dingell quickly realized that this relief could help Detroit's prime industry and he joined forces with Reagan. But he took a more direct approach than did the administration's authors of economic cost-and-benefit studies by asking, what was the best way to save jobs?

Enter Henry Waxman, nearly a foot shorter and much softer in tone than Dingell, but every bit as tenacious. After helping Rep. Rogers to defeat Dingell in the 1977 clean-air fight, Waxman launched an unusual bid to succeed the Floridian, who retired in 1978 as chairman of the Health and the Environment Subcommittee. In the contest, which was waged among Energy and Commerce Committee Democrats, the brash Waxman defeated the much more senior Richardson Preyer of North Carolina. Waxman skillfully used three assets: his strong contacts among the junior Democrats, some strategically useful and legal channeling of campaign funds to other members and an attack on Preyer's ardent support of his home-state tobacco industry. Waxman won the post after his allies defeated Preyer, on a 21–6 vote, gaining the House's attention and deepening Dingell's enmity.

Dingell was troubled not only by Waxman's disrespect for seniority and desire to push his aggressive environmental agenda; to Dingell, who sometimes exaggerated his case, Waxman represented the wealthy and trendy glitterati of Los Angeles' fashionable Rodeo Drive, who drove foreign cars and looked down their noses at Dingell's blue-collar voters. Dingell also believed that Waxman's views and his constituents, who thought nothing of driving an hour to work each day, had exacerbated southern California's pollution. Now, to make things worse, they wanted already distressed Detroit and the rest of the nation to pay the bill to clean up Los Angeles.

But Waxman rejected those attacks. He also dismissed the view of many conservatives and others in Washington that the aggressive era of federal regulation during the 1970s had produced a backlash against all of government. Instead, Waxman contended that the public had grown hostile because government bureaucracy did not seem to work well. He went to work to protect and strengthen the clean-air law by defining what was at stake and building coalitions inside and outside Congress. "The Reagan administration came to power with a tremendous fervor to accomplish the conservative agenda," Waxman said. "That included a gutting of the Clean Air Law. With Congressman Dingell, they tried to eviscerate the principal sections of the law."

The administration fell short for two chief reasons: Waxman's legislative stubbornness and the coalition's overreaching. "We made mistakes," said a Dingell ally. "It was not our intent to weaken the law but to make it more flexible for the struggling auto industry." But the administration failed to get its act together. First, it unveiled in August 1981 a set of clean-air "principles" that constituted a major assault on the 1970 law. Not until mid-December 1981 did administration officials issue a lukewarm endorsement of a bill submitted by Dingell and his allies. Reagan officials failed to defend adequately their provisions to weaken automobile and other pollution standards. (Reagan sympathizers, in what may be an ex post facto rationalization, said years later that the administration's half-hearted approach showed that the White House did not fully support efforts by some of its more aggressive environmental officials to weaken the law.)

The result gave Waxman an opening eventually to exploit his adversaries' weaknesses. When his Health and the Environment subcommittee met in February–March 1982, Waxman lost control of the measure to the Dingell steamroller, mostly on 12–8 votes. Then in April, the bill went to the full committee where Dingell hoped for speedy action. But Waxman skillfully turned the tide. After holding lengthy hearings in his subcommittee; Waxman used parliamentary tactics, such as forcing the committee clerk to read the bill. Although this approach can anger an adversary, the legitimate use of legislative rules also gives all sides an opportunity to discuss options with uncommitted colleagues. Meanwhile, Waxman also worked with environmental lobbyists to identify a handful of the committee's centrists who did not want to be allied with polluters. One of his tactics was to force divisions among business groups by convincing one industry that it might escape tougher restrictions if the committee approved tighter limits on another industry. When Waxman narrowly won a battle over amendments to retain air-quality protection in national parks and to prevent heavily polluting new plants, Dingell reversed tactics. He adjourned the committee for months, made one last unsuccessful bid to craft a majority and then called it quits.

Had Waxman worried that the Reagan-Dingell coalition would succeed? Absolutely, he said. Even though Reagan had barely mentioned clean-air issues during the 1980 campaign, his attempt to weaken that law had the support of the chairman and top Republicans on the House committee. In the face of mixed signals about the legislative prospects, what does an ideological advocate like Waxman do? "You fight," Waxman said. "Sometimes, you win. Sometimes, you lose." In fact, his efforts resulted in the breakdown of the Reagan administration's assault on the Clean Air Act.

Waxman gained unexpected allies. The more that Interior Secretary Watt and Environmental Protection Agency boss Gorsuch tried to reverse long-standing policies, the more they discredited the Reagan administration's case. In December 1982 the House cited Gorsuch for contempt, following her failure to provide documents on the EPA's management of the nation's hazardous-waste cleanup program. To make things worse, Rita M. Lavelle, a top Gorsuch aide at the hazardous-waste program, was charged with favoritism in awarding EPA contracts. In 1983, she was convicted and sent to jail for perjury in a conflict-of-interest case. And who was the congressional chairman who most aggressively pursued Lavelle? None other than Dingell, ever the defender of congressional prerogatives. From that point in late 1982, Dingell appeared to have decided that if he could not get his own clean-air proposal enacted, then he would hinder attempts by other lawmakers to do it their way.

Waxman was not ready to quit his fight for stronger legislation. In 1984 he thought that after months of delicate negotiations his subcommittee was close to approving a bill to limit acid-rain emissions from heavily polluting midwest utilities. But the vote went against him, 10–9, following the surprise decision by Rep. Dennis E. Eckart, an Ohio Democrat, to oppose the deal because he feared the impact on electricity rates and the economy in his home state.

Waxman and his environmental allies, who believed that their efforts to subsidize the Midwest's added costs had swung Eckart their way, blasted him for double-crossing them and caving in to Dingell and to industry groups. The failed efforts to accommodate the Midwest, they added, would represent that region's high-water mark in winning federal help to clean its power plants. They won support from an editorial in Eckart's local newspaper, *The Cleveland Plain Dealer*: "Although Eckart may well pick up support from Ohio for his proposals, he runs the risk both of delaying controls and building support for the alternatives. He should consider backing off."[3] In defending his vote on the time-honored tradition that all politics are local, Eckart later argued there were too many political obstacles in 1984 for Congress to pass an acid-rain bill. "Without [the support of] George Bush, it [was] impossible to pass a clean-air bill," he said.

As it turned out, both Waxman and Eckart were right. Waxman was steadily increasing the pressure for a strong clean-air bill. And Eckart had used his leverage as the subcommittee's swing vote to obtain concessions from Waxman. Although Eckart insisted that he backed strong environmental enforcement and that his decision was based on protecting his constituents' interests, Dingell clearly welcomed the muddying of the political waters and the delay in the time when Congress would impose new burdens on industry. The committee chairman opposed Waxman's acid-rain bill not so much because of his stated concerns about its impact on Michigan or Midwest industry as because of his fear that piecemeal enactment of the clean-air agenda would split and weaken the overall opposition. Dingell, like Waxman, knew that legislation was coming. It was just a question of whether and when Congress would pass a series of separate laws or whether, as Dingell preferred, it would become one huge bill. Dealing with the subject comprehensively gave Dingell more leverage to assure support for his views in one area—chiefly, protection of the auto industry—by making concessions elsewhere.

After the 1984 deadlock, Waxman shifted ground. A December 1984 explosion at Union Carbide's chemical plant in Bhopal, India, which killed more than 2,000 persons, awakened international concern about the hazards posed by toxic substances. Although that issue had been only at the periphery of the clean-air debate, Waxman saw an opportunity to build domestic support for new controls. To do that, his Health and the Environment Subcommittee launched an investigation, including extended hearings in which witnesses said that a Bhopal-like incident was possible in the United States. Although other members of Congress and the Reagan administration said that Waxman had overstated the risk, his 1985–86 efforts served two vital legislative functions. He helped to educate his subcommittee members and other interested players, and he began the often laborious task of drafting a legislative response.

In late 1987 clean-air legislation reached the House floor for the major showdown during the Reagan administration. The unusual scenario developed as follows: The 1977 law had set a 1982 deadline for local areas to comply with its revised local clean-air standards, but it permitted the EPA to grant a five-year extension for the chief pollutants, ground-level ozone and carbon monoxide, before imposing sanctions. (Although the auto industry had largely met its separate requirements, many metropolitan areas were in noncompliance with the overall standards because of continued high pollution from "stationary" sources.) The agency could not extend the deadline beyond 1987, at least in theory. But Congress and the administration had blinked in the face of earlier deadlines to meet requirements. The EPA, for its part, was reluctant to impose sanctions for failure to meet its standards unless a local area had committed a more serious violation, such as failure to submit a clean-up plan.

By 1987 House members decided to make a fight over this largely symbolic issue. Clean-air proponents, led by the late Silvio O. Conte, a Massachusetts Republican, tried to extend the deadline only until September 1988. On the other side, Pennsylvania Democrat John P. Murtha, who was an advocate of home-state steel and coal companies, among others, wanted to delay sanctions until August 1989. Waxman and the environmentalists supported Conte. Dingell, strongly supported by industry groups, lobbied actively on behalf of Murtha. Murtha's proposal lost on Dec. 3 by an unexpectedly large margin, 257–162, and the House adopted Conte's eight-month extension by voice vote.

Both sides agreed, in retrospect, that the largely symbolic vote carried important messages for the clean-air debate. For Dingell, the unexpected setback was a sharp lesson on the inadequacy of industry's lobbying efforts. In early 1988 he lectured many Washington corporate representatives that they would have to do a much better job when the inevitably broader clean-air bill reached the House. The vote also was a strong message to Dingell that his influence in committee was not nearly as effective in the full House, giving him incentives later to resolve disputes without floor votes. Groups such as the coal industry and mineworkers, which had steadfastly opposed tougher clean-air requirements, also began to see the handwriting on the wall. They began to consider the framework of an eventual compromise that would be most acceptable to them. As for Waxman and his allies, the vote was additional ammunition to fire at Dingell: if the committee did not act on the legislation soon, it risked subjecting its control of the clean-air law to demands from other House members to use it or lose it. To his own friends, Dingell privately cursed "goddamn Waxman." But the chairman and his cohorts got the message: in early 1988 they launched serious efforts to patch together a bill.

Waxman's ploy and Dingell's reaction to the December 1987 showdown were a reminder that committee politics could not be fought in a vacuum. Both sides knew that pro-environment was the "safe" vote for a majority of House members. Dingell's bluster and threats, which could quickly win loyalty from committee members, would have less impact on other House members less dependent on his granting or withholding of favors. Waxman's implicit threat to take their disputes to the House floor, it was now clear, would give him added leverage in their negotiations and confrontations within the Energy and Commerce Committee. Dingell did not have to acknowledge publicly the effect of this atmospheric change but he would soon show an unexpected increase of interest in finding a compromise with Waxman. Even for Waxman, the relatively uninformed judgment of members on the House floor could be a volatile factor; better to reach agreement close to his goals without a showdown than to depend on an unpredictable and, quite possibly, bitter outcome.

Meanwhile the Senate was looking very different in the Reagan years than it had in the 1970s, especially the Environment and Public Works Committee. Six months before Reagan was elected, Muskie had resigned to become President Carter's Secretary of State. Republicans then won a 12-seat gain in the November election, giving the GOP a Senate majority for the first time since 1955. The committee became, however, an even stronger champion of stringent clean-air laws. The new Republican chairman, replacing coal-state Democrat Jennings Randolph of West Virginia, was Robert Stafford of Vermont. Reflecting the views of the Green Mountain State, Stafford was a hard-liner in favor of environmental clean-up. He and his often zealous committee aides took a good-versus-evil approach to polluters, consciously deciding against industry on nearly all disputes. They were even more hostile to Interior Secretary Watt and the EPA regulators.

When administration officials complained to him that the clean-air law was not working properly, Stafford said he was willing to review it. But he became such an ardent defender of the law that he and they had little common ground and were barely on speaking terms. Although some committee Republicans took the political risk of antagonizing environmentalists by not embracing their views, the panel had enough other senators—including a disproportionate number from New England—to override them. Stafford usually got his way, at least in committee. Oddly, Stafford gave more support to environmental issues than did many of the committee's Democrats, who were badly divided and had difficulty adjusting to their minority status from 1981 to 1986. "Democrats appear to be in complete disarray, with no effort to coordinate their participation or proposals," said a lobbyist in describing Environment and Public Works Committee Democrats at the time.

Almost as a ritual, Stafford's committee drafted an ever-tougher clean-air bill biennially during the six years Republicans controlled the Senate. But, in an unusual rebuke to the panel, Senate Republican leaders never scheduled the bill for floor action. According to leaders and Reagan administration officials, the committee had become a captive of the environmental lobby and it had lost touch with other legitimate viewpoints, especially those in the Midwest. Another key factor was the strong-willed opposition to acid-rain and other environmental controls by Byrd, who was Democratic leader throughout the Reagan era. As the debate became more polarized, Senators grew less willing to choose sides. "It was a very unpleasant time," said a veteran aide to the committee.

The 1986 election, which returned Democrats to the Senate majority, created a big change in the Senate's willingness to strike a compromise. Replacing Stafford as Environment committee chairman was North Dakota's Quentin Burdick. The aging Senator was far less interested in environmental issues than in the panel's everyday menu of economic-development and other pork-barrel projects. That left control of clean-air legislation with Maine's George Mitchell, who took Muskie's old Environmental Protection Subcommittee chairmanship. In the tradition of Muskie and Stafford, Mitchell postured himself as an avid environmentalist. In his legislative politics, however, he was much closer to the pragmatic Muskie, his former boss and political patron, than to Stafford. The committee, as usual, gave a strong environmental cast to a new clean-air bill, which it sent to the Senate in October 1987. But Mitchell then turned his attention toward Byrd and his coal-industry allies.

The 1988 Byrd-Mitchell discussions, both direct and indirect, involved only a few people. The negotiations sometimes were so secretive that one side did not know the other was using the same set of outside experts as a source of information and ideas. Most other players on Washington's clean-air stage were completely unaware of how far the negotiations had progressed. In the end, the decision to limit the number of players was an important reason why the talks failed (and Mitchell learned a vital lesson for passing a bill in 1990, when he would adopt a much more inclusive approach). The outcome was important for two other reasons as well: Mitchell, who would succeed Byrd as majority leader in 1989, had good reason to feel let down by his predecessor. And the result offered a window into the virtual breakdown of the Senate's deliberative process. Formal committee or floor negotiations were doomed, so key players were forced to go behind closed doors.

At issue between Byrd and Mitchell was how the nation should control acid rain, which results when sulfur and nitrogen oxides are emitted into the air and eventually fall to earth as sulfuric and nitric acids. This results, according to federal studies, in significant damage to lakes and streams and high-elevation forests in the northeastern United States and southern Canada as well as potentially serious health consequences. Of the 23 million tons of sulfur dioxide (SO_2) that were emitted in 1985, more than two-thirds of the total was released by electric utilities, chiefly those in the Midwest using the high-sulfur coal that is mined in the Appalachian region of the eastern United States. To Mitchell, the threat was beyond dispute, both to his beloved state of Maine and to the nation. He later made his case in a book about the environmental catastrophes he believes are threatening the earth. "These acids and their heavy metal allies are killing life. They are killing fish in the water and trees on the land. The army of metals set in motion by the acids are leaching into the soil, eating at the delicate root systems that supply water to trees and plants, and drifting into lakes and rivers."[4]

Byrd had been the chief barrier to Senate action on acid-rain legislation during the Reagan era. But in 1987 he began to understand that the political tide was turning against him and his West Virginia constituents who mined high-sulfur coal. Byrd's decision that he had to deal with Mitchell came slowly, reluctantly, but ultimately with conviction. "We clearly have our work cut out for us," he said in December 1986 to a meeting of the Edison Electric Institute, the trade association representing the nation's largest utility plants. "We need to refine our message. We need to do a much better job of educating consumers, voters and members of Congress on these issues." Less than three months later, Byrd took his case to the lair of the enemy. "For a decade we have been warned that without immediate and drastic control measures, our lakes and forests would be faced with impending doom" because of the spread of acid rain, Byrd lectured Mitchell's subcommittee in March 1987. "We are not facing Armageddon. . . . Not only would these bills be expensive, socially disruptive and injurious to our competitive position, but they could also harm the environment in the long run." The reaction to Byrd was mostly stony silence, except for some quiet snickers from subcommittee members and aides.

Mitchell and his staff deliberately kept Byrd informed of how they planned to pursue all-out efforts to enact significant acid-rain cuts. As majority leader, Byrd had wide discretion for setting the Senate schedule and deciding when the clean-air bill would reach the Senate floor. The aides most involved in the talks between the two sides were Kate Kimball, who had been a Mitchell aide on environmental issues since 1984, and Rusty Mathews, who joined Byrd's staff in 1986 after serving seven years as a policy expert at the Energy Department. Kimball is something of an anomaly in the buttoned-down, pin-striped world of Capitol Hill. Not only is she a woman in an important committee staff position, but she also has an unassuming manner that belies her deep knowledge and commitment on environmental issues. She also had the advantage of a boss who studied the issues in detail and, once he made a decision, showed a single-minded determination to achieve his goal.

Mathews faced a more difficult task. In helping Byrd through one of the most difficult passages of his legislative career, Mathews had to deal with a senator whose strength and interests were more in Senate procedures and internecine politics than in the substance of a complex scientific issue like acid rain. In Mitchell, Byrd confronted a shrewd opponent, one who had gained high political marks as successful chairman of the Democratic Senatorial Campaign Committee in 1985–86. With Democrats headed toward a presidential election in which they wanted their party lined up behind an enlightened political agenda, Byrd was viewed by many senators and many other Democrats as an anachronism. His position on important environmental issues and his old-fashioned style, which showed little sensitivity to the public-relations demands of the television era, made him somewhat embarrassing to many younger Democrats who viewed Mitchell as their leader. The two senators shared a reason to handle the acid-rain issue in the best interests of their home states: Each faced a re-election campaign in 1988, although neither expected serious opposition.

Even before the Environment Committee completed its bill, Mitchell made several efforts to win Byrd's support. His proposal required utilities to make widespread use of expensive industrial scrubbers, which were designed to permit more use of high-sulfur coal by reducing the amount of sulfur emissions after coal-burning. Another inducement to Byrd and West Virginia's miners was a restriction on the number of utilities switching from coal to other fuels. But the committee's bill proved to be only a starting point for Mitchell and Byrd. Mathews for months had been sending memos to Byrd, outlining possible legislative scenarios and strategies for making a deal to minimize damage to the coal industry. It was crucial for Byrd to solicit and win the support of United Mine Workers of America president Richard L. Trumka. Byrd, who knew he lacked the votes on the Senate floor to stop Mitchell, believed that working with the UMW would reduce the risk of home-state political fallout. "Byrd decided that his best position was to be joined at the hip with Trumka," said a close observer. While

Byrd, Trumka and other members of the West Virginia congressional delegation met regularly in Byrd's Capitol office to prepare their political strategy, Mathews worked with UMW legislative director Bill Samuel on a specific acid-rain proposal.

Byrd gave Trumka and his UMW staff the green light to meet separately with Mitchell during the spring to discuss a possible compromise. Ironically, their first session came on April 12, 1988—at the very hour that Byrd announced he would not seek another term as Senate majority leader, opening the door for Mitchell to succeed him. Ever the pragmatist, Mitchell told Trumka that he was not wedded to specific dates or forms of technology. Trumka subsequently held a series of meetings with Byrd to discuss options in the plan being drafted by Mathews and Samuel. Their plan, with its emphasis on mandated technology, finally reached Kimball in July 1988 through a group of expert bill drafters and policy analysts at the EPA, the Congressional Research Service at the Library of Congress and ICF, a private consulting firm in the Washington suburbs. At the same time, Byrd called in chief executives from several of the nation's largest utility and coal companies to gauge their reaction and urge their support of the proposal. But those discussions proved less fruitful. Utility executives lectured Byrd that their prime responsibility was to give their customers the lowest possible rate, and they angrily told Trumka that it was not for them to protect coal miners' jobs.

Mitchell, meanwhile, was pushing relentlessly to bring the clean-air bill to the Senate floor. On July 13, he and 27 other senators—mostly from the Northeast and Western, low-sulfur coal states—agreed to compromises in the bill reported by the Environment Committee. They set a goal of an annual 10-million ton, instead of 12-million ton, reduction in the amount of sulfur-dioxide emissions and agreed to steps that would spread the cost to utility customers across the nation, reducing the burden on the Midwest. "We are committed to move the legislation this year," the group announced. Although the changes were not sufficient to win the support of the chief opponents, Byrd told his team to keep alive the search for a compromise. The result was a set of negotiations between Mitchell and Trumka, which began at the Bangor, Maine, airport in mid-August. Although Byrd later publicly denied that Trumka was negotiating on his behalf, the players at the time had no doubts that Trumka was representing Byrd, at Byrd's suggestion, in seeking a deal with Mitchell. "I had the impression that if we were going to satisfy Byrd, we had to get an agreement with the UMW," Mitchell said later.

Further meetings during the next month prompted the exchange of several proposals between Mitchell, Trumka and their staffs. On Sept. 22, they finally agreed to what was termed the UMW's fifth proposal. In addition to reducing sulfur-dioxide emissions by 10 million tons, it allowed a three-year delay, until 2003, in achieving that goal. The plan also endorsed the Byrd-UMW demand for a national fee on the use of electricity, which would help Midwest utilities pay the cost of cleaning high-sulfur coal. Mitchell and Byrd, in effect, had crafted a heavy-handed "command and control" scheme that a top Bush administration official later called "an unholy alliance between environmentalists and high-sulfur coal interests, leading to more costly solutions than were needed."

But the deal would not hold. When Mitchell confidently sought to take the agreement to the Senate floor, several unexpected complications arose. As environmental activists learned of the details, many bitterly complained about the results of Mitchell's free-lancing; they correctly determined that they could get a better deal after the election. "This proposal does not achieve adequate emission reductions," environmental lobbyist David Hawkins told *The Boston Globe*, the major newspaper serving New England. "It is not an adequate program to deal with acid rain."[5] Sen. Stafford, after a tense meeting with Mitchell in the Vermonter's private office in the Capitol, urged him to postpone action until 1989. Mitchell reacted angrily, accusing critics of being "rigid and unyielding, wholly unwilling to compromise." Although the *Globe* reported that his criticism was directed at Stafford and other senators, Mitchell insisted that he was referring to outside interest groups. Byrd, too, became the target of strong criticism from his erstwhile allies and got cold feet. Some of the opposition was expected— Southern and Midwestern utilities worried about the costs. Western coal interests separately feared they would be disadvantaged in dealing with those from the East.

But Byrd received his strongest criticism from Dingell. During his months-long indirect talks with Mitchell, Byrd also had met privately with Dingell to inform him of developments. Reinforcing the advice of Mathews, Dingell had encouraged Byrd to strike a deal, partly because of their mutual concern that whoever was elected president in November 1988 would be a stronger supporter of clean-air legislation than Reagan had been. Plus, they knew Byrd's departure as majority leader would weaken their leverage in the Senate. In effect, their assessment of the congressional politics led Dingell and Byrd to agree that it was time to get the best possible deal—Dingell for the auto industry, Byrd for coal.

But when the ever-skeptical Dingell gained information, some of it apparently inaccurate, about details of the emerging Mitchell-Trumka deal, he reportedly went "ballistic" about the fruits of those unusual private talks. He demanded that auto-industry lobbyists marshal their forces to kill the deal, according to one target of Dingell's verbal assaults. The House chairman's opposition was fueled by his concern that when the bill reached the Senate and House floors in the closing days of the 100th Congress, he and Byrd would be unable to control Waxman, Mitchell and others who would want to strengthen the clean-air package. Dingell's fears were compounded when Mitchell told Byrd that he planned to merge their acid-rain deal into a broad-based Senate package. "We had a lot of discussions," Dingell said later. "But very few people would sign off on any part until they were aware of other parts." A stunned Byrd concluded that he and Mitchell may have been proceeding for months with a fundamental misunderstanding about the scope of the bill. Likewise, Kimball and Mathews apparently had failed to address this vital point.

In simultaneous negotiations whose details were largely unknown to their Senate counterparts, a small group of House Energy and Commerce Committee members led by Dingell and Waxman had held private meetings that summer. They were seeking a deal to strengthen the centerpiece of the clean-air law to force local areas to reduce their pollution. Those talks were convened in the wake of the December 1987 House setback to Dingell and his allies. Participants later said that they believed they were 24 hours from an agreement on the House side that could have been married to the Senate acid-rain deal. But when the Senate deal collapsed, House negotiators called it quits.

Byrd and Dingell, despite their earlier warnings to industry, may have ill served themselves and their allies by their late-1988 caution. "The whole scheme was to reach a last-minute proposal and then slam-dunk it to get ahead of the curve with the new administration," said a leading coal-industry lobbyist. "But it failed for several reasons. Utilities mistakenly thought they could continue to hold off a bill. . . . Byrd's fear of the unknown also kept him from trying to understand other issues." And Dingell's fear of losing control of the legislative and political debates—to other lawmakers, let alone to the United Mine Workers president—caused him to overlook the prospect that his situation would worsen in the next two years. Although Mitchell was not yet a sure bet to win the contest to succeed Byrd as the Senate Democratic leader, he was bound to have a stronger hand on clean-air legislation no matter who replaced Byrd. And Mitchell, having made a good-faith effort to accommodate the coal industry's concerns, would feel less pressured to make another special effort to help it.

Although Mitchell later laughed about the collapse of his compromise efforts, observing that the legislative process demands risk taking, the result at the time was a bitter disappointment. "I tried my best, but we didn't quite make it this year," Mitchell said in a 1988 post mortem.[6] His decision to challenge Byrd on acid rain was an unusual personal gamble for Mitchell, who was in the midst of his campaign to become majority leader. But he warned the Senate at the same time that he was not ready to give up on an issue where public health was so jeopardized. Indeed, Mitchell told Democrats that if he won he would use the power of his leadership post to press for the legislation. He learned important lessons about clean-air politics that would prove useful when the Senate finally passed the bill in 1990.

In countless cases, political leverage depends upon timing. In this one, the pro–Clean Air forces led by Mitchell and Waxman held all the cards. The country was so strongly in their favor, as were the Democratic-controlled floors of the House and Senate, that they only needed a change in the presidential administration to gain the upper hand. Dingell and Byrd certainly knew that, but they failed to take it seriously enough to capitulate in time. The "four horsemen," with their varied regional backgrounds and views of how Congress should work, had made their initial stands and would return to fight again.

As it turned out, the high-sulfur coal industry suffered a double hit in the Senate after the 1988 election. Mitchell's victory in the majority leader contest also led him to relinquish his post as chairman of the Environmental Protection Subcommittee to Max Baucus. The Montana Democrat's allegiance was with low-sulfur coal interests in Western states; he showed little sympathy for the Eastern-based UMW. The lesson of the 1988 effort, Baucus later said, was, "Any clean-air bill with an acid-rain title must be regionally balanced." In the House, Dingell retained his influence as Energy and Commerce chairman and did what he could to protect Detroit. But, as we shall see, he was forced to accept a broad set of new environmental rules that imposed tough conditions on the automobile and related industries and on other manufacturing sectors.

The end of the Reagan era meant that lawmakers could no longer posture on clean-air legislation with political tactics or use their concerns about local impact to avoid facing national problems. The key change between the 1970s and the 1980s happened at the White House: Nixon and Carter supported clean-air laws and legislation went through. Reagan opposed it so nothing happened. With the election in November 1988 of George Bush, the self-proclaimed "environmental president," the gridlock of divided government would no longer be an excuse for inaction.

Endnotes

1. Rochelle L. Stanfield, "Plotting Every Move," *National Journal*, March 26, 1988: 793.
2. David Maraniss, "Powerful Energy Panel Turns on Big John's Axis," *The Washington Post*, May 15, 1983: A-1.
3. "Eckart's acid-rain risk," *The Cleveland Plain Dealer*, May 20, 1984: 4-AA.
4. George J. Mitchell, *World on Fire: Saving an Endangered Earth* (New York: Scribner's, 1991), 30.
5. Michael Kranish, "Maine Senator backs down on acid rain," *The Boston Globe*, Sept. 29, 1988: 11.
6. Rochelle L. Stanfield, "For Acid Rain, 'Wait Till Next Year,'" *National Journal*, Oct. 15, 1988: 2606.

4

Bush Breaks the Logjam

White House aides Roger Porter and Boyden Gray led countless meetings around this table in 1989 to shape President George Bush's clean-air proposal. Those decisions gave new direction to clean-air efforts.

Presidential inaugurations typically are associated with private hoopla and a public sense of renewal. Bands march, revelers party and politicians pledge to renew the nation.

What is often overlooked is that the following months provide the best opportunity to move legislation during any chief executive's term. Reagan, for example, accomplished more legislatively during his first six months than he did in the remainder of his eight years in office. A new president, in most cases, has a public mandate and the desire to exploit it. Congress is more willing than usual to listen. Because the bureaucracy and interest groups have not yet figured out how to deal with the new team, they stand by powerlessly as new laws sail through. Even though Bush was the first vice president since Martin Van Buren in 1836 who was elected to succeed the president whom he had served, the sense of change and regeneration was palpable in Washington following Reagan's relatively quiet second term.

The relationship between the president and Congess always is a fragile and shifting balance, based on a range of political factors. But the policy-making initiative at most times lies with the White House. Only the president can mount the national bully pulpit and claim that he represents and speaks for all parts of the diverse nation. When the president wants something, Congress cannot ignore him.

Within days of Bush's sweeping victory over Gov. Michael Dukakis of Massachusetts, several of the president-elect's senior aides began to prepare their plan for the first 100 days. They wasted no time starting to work on a clean-air package. Even though Congress had made progress on some parts of the conflict during the previous year, the White House had wide discretion to re-examine all of the issues in the clean-air debate and to prepare its own recommendations. Capitol Hill would welcome a quick jump from the starting gate. The ups and downs of the past eight years had created growing pressure to resolve the impasse. Adding to the momentum was a growing public consciousness of the environmental hazards facing the nation; not long after what was in many urban areas an unusually hot and smog-filled summer of 1988, the disastrous March 1989 oil-tanker spill near Valdez, Alaska, presented pictures of oil-coated water, shores and animals.

Bush sent strong messages that he was serious about addressing environmental problems. In his inaugural address, he referred to the need for a "kinder and gentler" nation. Three weeks later, he told Congress in his first formal message, "I will send to you shortly legislation for a new, more effective Clean Air Act." His only specific description was endorsement of acid-rain reduction by a "date certain." He also pleased the environmental community by selecting William Reilly, who had been president of both the Conservation Foundation and the World Wildlife Fund, to head the Environmental Protection Agency. But it took an unexpectedly long time—six months—to translate those good intentions into specific legislative proposals.

Actually, the Bush team had begun work on cleaning the air long before Inauguration Day. Even before the campaign, Bush had privately told several of his top political advisers that the environment would be the first area where he would show differences with Reagan. As early as 1986, when confidants such as Nicholas F. Brady (who later became Bush's Treasury Secretary) and pollster Robert M. Teeter asked what issues he cared most about, Bush responded that the nation needed to do more to combat pollution. Although he had previously done little to identify himself publicly with the issue, he had organized and chaired a Republican task force dealing with the environment when he served in the House from 1967 to 1971. That group did not play much of a legislative role, but Bush's effort placed him in the vanguard of the anti-pollution forces on Capitol Hill.

Russell E. Train, who served presidents Nixon and Ford as EPA administrator and later chaired the World Wildlife Fund, had been acquainted with Bush when he served in the House and held several posts with those two GOP presidents. As United Nations Ambassador in the mid-1970s, Bush gave a reception for Train; as ambassador to China, Bush hosted Train's family during a visit to Beijing. When Bush was planning his 1988 presidential bid, Train agreed to volunteer advice to the Bush campaign. "He did not know many environmentalists," Train said. "I was worried about how the then-Vice President would be postured on environmental matters." Train joined at least two discussions in early 1988—one at the vice-presidential mansion, the other at Bush's White House office—with other Bush advisers and Republicans who had held top environmental posts. Participants, mindful of the political benefits of environmentalism, agreed that Bush should take the lead on those issues during his fall campaign. Also present at the second session were campaign strategist Teeter, Bush's longtime lawyer C. Boyden Gray, New Jersey Gov. Thomas H. Kean, and William D. Ruckleshaus, another former EPA administrator. "There was a general discussion," said another participant. "Clean air was one of the issues on the plate. We also talked about, for example, the problems of hazardous waste and global warming."

One result of those talks was a campaign speech in which Bush presented his environmental vision. Train wrote the first draft in longhand. "Of the many environmental issues facing us today, some have long been with us and some are just emerging," Bush told a Seattle business luncheon on May 16, 1988. "Some seem almost intractable. Most are much more complex than they were a decade ago." After those words carefully distancing himself from his predecessor, Bush noted the progress that had been made since 1970 to clean the air, but said that "nearly 80 metropolitan areas are flunking federal clean-air standards." He also made a seemingly innocuous call for looking "to the marketplace for innovative solutions." With that new wrinkle, a coal-industry lobbyist later said, "the die was cast" in the acid-rain debate.

Despite its intentional lack of specifics, the Seattle speech and others were designed to make the point that the time for study had ended. As president, Bush would demand action on a host of environmental problems. His initiative served another important campaign purpose by innoculating him against liberals' attacks that he lacked substance. "We chose issues where George Bush had something to say and where the public had concerns," said Robert E. Grady, Bush's campaign speechwriter who later became one of his chief advisers on environmental issues. "We never just attacked Dukakis. We laid out specific policy proposals."

As in any campaign, however, the political element was front and center. Teeter and his team determined that six states were critical to Bush's Electoral College victory—California, Illinois, Michigan, Missouri, New Jersey and Ohio. Of those six, environmental problems were acute in California and New Jersey. "The issue appealed to the suburban, independent, more moderate voters" who were vital to the Bush coalition, said Grady, who had been a top aide to Gov. Kean during his 1985 re-election in New Jersey. As with Kean, Bush's embrace of the environment showed a major contrast with Reagan, whose electoral appeal was directed more toward blue-collar voters concerned about earning a decent salary and protecting their neighborhoods' security.

One of the defining moments of the 1988 election came in an Aug. 31 speech on the Michigan shore of Lake Erie, in the midst of Bush's week-long emphasis on the environment, which was designed to broaden his political coalition. "I am an environmentalist," he told the crowd. "Always have been, from my earliest days as a congressman, when I first chaired a House task force on earth resources and population. And I always will be, to my last days as president of this great and beautiful country. That's not inconsistent with being a businessman. Nor is it with being a conservative. In fact, it is an essential part of the thinking that should guide either one." Adding new emphasis but few specifics to his Seattle speech three months earlier, Bush said that "the time for study alone has passed" on the acid-rain issue. He announced that he would ask for a program to cut "millions of tons" in sulfur-dioxide and nitrogen-oxide emissions from industrial smokestacks. And he endorsed international action to cut back the production of ozone-depleting CFCs.

Dukakis, whose earlier 19-percentage point lead in national polls had started to fade, responded with a curt dismissal. "Talk about an election-year conversion," Dukakis said. But he failed to follow up with attacks on what even Bush's advisers feared were vulnerabilities in his environmental record, notably his chairmanship of Reagan's regulatory-relief task force. Environmentalists had harshly criticized that White House-led operation for reducing important federal controls on the auto industry and other businesses and for encouraging efforts by Dingell and others to weaken the Clean Air Act.

On the next day Bush delivered his most devastating political blow on the environment. Speaking from a boat in the middle of Boston Harbor, Bush attacked the Massachusetts governor for his failure, during 10 years at the helm, to clean that filthy, sewage-filled basin. "Two hundred years ago, tea was spilled into this harbor in the name of liberty," said Bush. "Now, it's something else. We've got to do better." Dukakis, traveling in California, tried to ignore the attack. Then Bush turned up the heat, turning the rhetorical attack into a widely viewed political advertisement. "The [Dukakis] campaign had still made no effective response when Bush aired his deadly Boston Harbor television ad at the beginning of September," wrote the authors of *All by Myself*, a chronicle of the Dukakis campaign. "The paid media were now reinforcing the messsage carried so powerfully for Bush in the press."[1]

Dukakis and his close advisers continued largely to ignore the attack, despite mounting evidence that Bush was scoring points with crucial swing voters across the nation. Democrats blamed the Reagan administration for the Boston Harbor mess because Washington had substantially reduced federal funding to states for the clean-water program during the past eight years. But that distinction was lost in the public debate, especially in the face of records showing repeated fail-

ures by Dukakis and his aides to keep promises and to meet federal-
court deadlines for cleaning the Harbor. Despite his good-government
image, Dukakis had not dwelled on environmental issues as governor,
preferring to emphasize the economic development associated with
what he labeled the "Massachusetts miracle." "We screwed up the environmental issue," said Leslie Dach, who had been director of environmental issues for the Audubon Society in Washington before joining
the Dukakis campaign as communications director and a campaign
spokesman. "Any campaign has limited space and time. We didn't
think that we could use the environmental issue to get new votes. So
we decided to focus on the economy. It was probably a mistake that we
did not first occupy the turf on the environment."

Although the controversy was an important factor in the unravel-
ing of the Dukakis campaign, it did not win Bush many points with
ardent environmentalists. "Dukakis was inept in failing to respond,"
Train said. "But I thought the Boston Harbor speech was too poli-
ticized. I was invited to attend but I did not want to be publicly identified with political actions." Frank Blake, a former aide to Vice President Bush and EPA general counsel, who was a Republican campaign
adviser on environmental issues, said that it remained a mystery to him
"why Dukakis gave us the issue." Whatever the cause, Dukakis' reti-
cence allowed Bush to claim the title of "environmental president."

With the election victory in hand, Bush's team felt an obligation
to deliver on his campaign promises. Whatever the limitations of his
ideology or vision, Bush believed that these pledges should have some
meaning. This was especially true with the environment, given Bush's
limited attention to other domestic issues. Even close advisers could
only guess at why he pushed for strong legislation, but he clearly
decided that it was time to break the clean-air stalemate. Aside from
the public-policy obligation, presidential advisers also believed that
passage of a revitalized Clean Air Act would be an important step
toward locking up the even more crucial 1992 vote in California. That
state's gain of seven House seats and Electoral College votes following
the 1990 Census meant that the presidential winner in California would
lock up 20 percent of the electoral votes needed for victory.

The Bush administration's main players in the clean-air debate
comprised a medley of political and policy specialists. Two of them
had an almost messianic belief in the need to increase the use of alter-

native fuels in automobiles. None had extensive experience in the federal clean-air debate. But during literally hundreds of meetings in the White House and around tables in the adjacent Old Executive Office Building, they struggled to prepare the framework and to fill in the details of one of the most important initiatives of Bush's presidency.

Any major effort by a president involves a complex team of advisers. Some, like his chief of staff or secretary of state, get lots of press coverage and become household names. Most presidential aides, however, operate with wide latitude but under little public scrutiny. White House staffers, in particular, have become the focal point for most important presidential actions. They ride herd on other agencies for information and options papers, settle many of the disputes that arise among agencies and represent the president's best interests, both on policy and politics. In the case of the clean-air bill, four such key players immediately surfaced.

Leading the group was Roger Porter, Bush's chief domestic-policy adviser. In organizing the intricate review of the clean-air issues, Porter took advantage of his expertise in executive branch operations. The author of a widely read text on the subject, Porter believed that effective presidential leadership required that White House advisers conduct a thorough examination of the major issues in the subject under review. In his book, he seemed to describe prospectively his own role in preparing Bush's clean-air proposal. "The honest broker ... views his principal role as that of mobilizing resources, identifying various alternatives, defining and clarifying differences between competing viewpoints and insuring that all perspectives are adequately represented," he wrote.[2] His "honest broker" role sometimes required him to move from a neutral arbiter to a more activist role in settling disputes, he said later.

Those who have worked with Porter at the White House and on Capitol Hill praise his fair and indefatigable approach to the decision-making process. But some add that he suffered, at least initially, because he had limited experience in working on complex environmental issues. As a White House aide during the Reagan years, he worked on acid-rain issues but he was not deeply involved in the congressional debate. "He is not the most creative person in coming up with new solutions," said a close observer. "He is brilliant without being creative." Although he chaired the group preparing the clean-air plan, Porter often allowed other White House aides to take the lead on specific issues. When the proposal reached the Senate in early 1990, however, his role took on new dimensions.

Working at Porter's side was Grady, the Bush campaign speech-writer who had gained broad experience on environmental issues during his New Jersey tenure with Gov. Kean. After the election, Grady joined the Office of Management and Budget in the strategic position of associate director for natural resources, energy and science. In that post, he gained responsibility for budget and policy development in federal agencies dealing with the environment. Like Porter, the younger Grady brought a keen intellect and seemingly boundless energy to his work. But he had a greater understanding of some of the technical issues than did Porter and was helped by a few OMB aides with lengthy experience in overseeing the work of the EPA. "Grady was the most reasonable and politically attuned person on the White House's clean-air team," said an EPA aide who worked on the bill. Another official who worked on the bill said, "More than anyone else, Grady was the critical person in the administration who made things happen."

Although he reported to OMB director Richard G. Darman, who was distinctly unenthusiastic about expanding federal clean-air enforcement, Grady had a broad mandate to shape the proposal. He benefited from his previous close associations with Bush and members of the Bush team, including Teeter. Like Darman, Grady is smart and brash. With his modishly long hair and efforts to shoot some basketball after a long day at the office, Grady has sought to avoid the pretentious airs that can come with a White House job. Asked whether Grady might be his successor in the next political generation, Darman quipped, "He's better." Despite their differences on environmental issues, Grady appeared firmly ensconced in Darman's inner circle. Grady and Darman both were well aware that whatever their private views, as expressed in top-level White House meetings, new clean-air legislation was a top personal priority for Bush.

A third key player on Bush's clean-air team was C. Boyden Gray, the president's chief in-house lawyer. As Bush's longest-serving senior aide, Gray played an important role for two reasons. With an aristocratic breeding and a manner that struck some observers as eccentric, he had gained Bush's trust to a point that allowed him to pursue pet interests not normally within the purview of the White House counsel. And his strong interest in promoting greater efficiency in government regulation, plus his support for the development of alternative fuels, piqued Gray's interest in the clean-air law while Bush was vice president. "The Clean Air Act is an enormously difficult law crafted by lawyers," Gray said. "It takes a lawyer to translate it." He also had developed friendships with several respected environmentalists, which would prove helpful as the White House prepared its proposal.

One of Gray's most important moves was to encourage Bush's selection of the fourth "hidden" team member, William G. Rosenberg, as the EPA's assistant administrator in charge of clean-air issues. A lawyer who supervised federal development of energy resources during the Ford administration, Rosenberg in 1977 had returned to Michigan where he became a wealthy real-estate developer and investor. During those years, he also took a special interest in stimulating economic development in his home state through greater use of agricultural products in alternative fuels. That shared expertise had led Rosenberg to Gray in 1987. Although Rosenberg had not known Reilly prior to Reilly's selection as EPA top boss, they developed a good working relationship. Reilly, who brought credibility for the EPA with environmentalists, usually deferred to Rosenberg in the crafting of clean-air details, both in the White House and with Congress.

Rosenberg's determination to become a player in the clean-air debate was good news for the EPA employees who worked on those issues. By allowing the agency's experts a front-row seat in the White House negotiations from an early point, Rosenberg revived their morale and influence, which had sagged during the Reagan years. Because many EPA aides were the federal government's long-term repository of knowledge on clean-air issues and had more detailed information than did the White House experts, that created a dilemma for the White House team: How could the administration utilize the bureaucrats' expertise without becoming too dependent on their advice, which was viewed in some quarters as too sympathetic to the environmental activists? Because they had begun to draft working papers in 1987, when Bush and his political advisers were still thinking in broad conceptual terms, the EPA staff gained a head start in setting the framework for the president's review. "Some people may have felt that we were too dependent on EPA," Grady said. "There was a tremendous learning curve. But we immersed ourselves and learned quite a lot. The creative tension between EPA and the OMB staff resulted in a full formation of the debate, making sure that all of the questions were asked."

The importance of EPA officials and career staff in preparing Bush's clean-air bill demonstrated the major impact of Washington's often-maligned bureaucrats. Without them, even a well-informed and energetic president would lack the resources and expertise to change federal policy or to rally public support. At the same time, the complex relationship between the White House and various agencies also demanded a retinue of capable presidential aides. They must ensure that other officials, who often have their own constituencies in Congress and the private sector, march first to the president's tune. And they often must impose discipline on warring agencies, which may have competing or overlapping spheres of influence.

The Energy Department, in this case, was much slower than the EPA to join the White House discussion. Although Bush later praised the department's role in helping to prepare his clean-air proposal, the energy policy-makers, most of whom traditionally have had a pro-production mindset, had a hard time getting into the act. Partly because his department's ranks had been decimated during the Reagan years, it took several months for Energy Secretary James D. Watkins and his top lieutenants to find in-house experts on air-quality aspects of issues such as coal-burning and alternative fuels. That task ultimately fell to Linda Stuntz, a former House Republican aide whose background was chiefly on energy, not environmental, issues. But she did not take the post of deputy undersecretary for policy, planning and analysis until mid-May. By that time, the White House clean-air group had made many of its critical decisions.

The Energy Department's slow start enhanced the quick-moving EPA's influence in providing crucial resources for the complex decision-making process. As often is the case in government, the control of information became a vital source of power. "EPA called the shots," said an administration official. When the Energy Department, for example, challenged the EPA's computer model for analyzing the economic impact of various proposals, Porter and his team supported the EPA.

Despite its own suspicions of EPA's leanings, the White House team feared challenging the EPA staff's credibility on Capitol Hill and with sympathetic reporters. These environmental specialists, in many cases, have held their jobs under several presidents and expect to serve under several more from both parties. In contrast to presidential appointees, their interests and their loyalty lie chiefly with issues, not with individuals. "EPA bureaucrats, many of whom are environmentalists themselves, and environmental lobbies are quite experienced at the Washington game," Robert W. Hahn, a former Bush administration economist, wrote in 1990. "They know how to manipulate the press, EPA political appointees, and Congress, and it is in the interest of these players to oblige in most cases. . . . Sensational stories get good press, and environmental issues are easily sensationalized."[3]

In defending their political impartiality and their stature within the administration, EPA staffers responded that they were careful not to take actions to undercut that influence. "If we tried to deceive anyone at the White House, our credibility would have gone down the tubes," said a veteran EPA official. The leader of the EPA's non-partisan professionals was Rob Brenner, who was director of policy analysis and review for issues related to air quality. Brenner, who was almost always at Rosenberg's side during meetings at the White House and later during intensive negotiations with the Senate, had received a master's degree in public policy from Princeton University and then joined the EPA staff in 1980. Probably more than any other single participant in the clean-air debate, he possessed a unique influence in the best sense of government civil service. He combined a meticulous and wide-ranging understanding of the clean-air law and proposals to amend it, with the respect and working relationships that he had built over the years inside the executive branch, as well as with congressional experts and interest groups. Although he sometimes frustrated players from both the White House and Congress with his professed impartiality and left them complaining that he was in fact taking sides, Brenner insisted that he always served as an evenhanded expert.

Others who contributed to the Bush proposal included White House Chief of Staff John H. Sununu, a relatively hidden but, no doubt, influential player on some issues. Although news reports said that he tried to weaken parts of the proposal, he backed strict controls of acid rain based on his experience during six years as New Hampshire governor. Also working behind the scenes to urge enactment throughout the clean-air debate was Teeter, Bush's long-time confidant and chief political adviser and one of the nation's foremost polling analysts. What proved most important, however, was the willingness of Bush and his team to reverse the Reagan mindset and to make positive use of the policy experts at the EPA. Despite the inevitable tensions and suspicions, the combined force presented Congress with credibility and a package that, whatever its shortcomings on some parts, would be difficult to ignore.

Although the clean-air policy-makers failed to meet their original goal of unveiling a proposal by April, they moved quickly and quietly enough to keep their operations largely under wraps. Even visits by the Bush team with key members of Congress and their aides were relatively perfunctory in substance, although the atmosphere was positive. "Because it was the administration's early days and few people were involved," said a disgruntled official, "a lot of things got by that should not have gotten by and would not have, if this had happened later." The proposal they finally produced thus packed a wallop. Over time, with secrecy, expertise and wide latitude, the Porter-Grady-Gray-Rosenberg forces came to write the first draft of the far-reaching and ambitious overhaul of the nation's Clean Air Act.

Bush and Congress took their first joint steps on clean-air legislation when top officials from the new Bush administration traveled to Capitol Hill to seek the views of key senators. Even though months would pass before Bush unveiled his proposal and lawmakers began drafting their own alternative, the participants at a March 1989 meeting moved toward a significant agreement, which would prove to be vital to the final bill.

Even though the session came, Porter said, on March 10, the day following the Senate's unprecedented rejection of the new President's choice of a Cabinet officer—John Tower as Secretary of Defense—both sides termed it a cordial meeting. As they sat in Room S-224 of Senate Majority Leader Mitchell's Capitol office suite, where a year later they would spend dozens of grueling hours, Porter carefully noted that on the once-contentious acid rain problem, Mitchell voiced strong support for reducing the current allowable annual total of sulfur-dioxide emissions from utility plants by 10 million tons. Although Porter did not explicitly signal agreement at that time, the participants made more progress in agreeing to clean the nation's air during that unannounced, closed-door session than did the president and Congress during the previous eight years.

Within the White House, the Bush team spent the largest share of its time working on the acid-rain details, which proved to be the most innovative part of the president's proposal. Not surprisingly, that recommendation proved to have the biggest impact on the congressional debate and outcome. Although Bush aides devoted extensive time to other parts of his package, these sections lacked the creative features of the acid-rain plan and did not fare as well in Congress.

Several factors explain why the White House advisers made control of acid rain the engine that drove their internal deliberations and, ultimately, their proposal: (1) The subject had received the most political attention during the national clean-air debate and for years had been widely discussed on Capitol Hill, even though consensus had proved elusive. (2) Resolution of the issue was especially important to

Canadian prime minister Brian Mulroney, who had become a confidant of Bush. (3) The solution to the acid-rain conflict offered a market-oriented mechanism that appealed to the administration's free-market ideological principles. (4) In the end, the debate over acid-rain control became a numbers game that the Bush team knew could be settled with old-fashioned horse trading, at which members of Congress are especially adept.

"The most important intellectual contribution that we in the Administration made was to forge a new coalition on acid rain," Grady said. The potent new axis included the Western states, which had relatively clean coal-burning and did not want to pay the cost for Eastern states to meet their standards; both Eastern and Western producers of low-sulfur coal, who would benefit when coal users were free to choose which fuel they preferred; advocates of less intrusive government interference in the marketplace; and the Northeastern states, which were the original proponents of control. The big losers were the United Mine Workers, which had its greatest presence in high-sulfur coal mines, and the Midwest states, whose utilities have relied on high-sulfur coal.

The innovation that cemented the new acid-rain coalition was a new system of "allowances"-trading among utilities across the nation, combined with a nationwide cap on total acid-rain emissions. Although this plan initially seemed complex to most laymen, including members of Congress, it was based on a relatively simple premise: companies would receive economic incentives from the federal government to clean the heaviest polluting utilities across the nation at the cheapest cost. Of the annual total of more than 20 million tons of sulfur-dioxide emissions, the chief component of acid rain, roughly two-thirds results from the burning of coal by electric utilities. The incentive-based solution gave a new kind of governmental solution: utilities would be issued "allowances," equal to one ton of emissions. Those companies that did the most to reduce their emissions would sell unneeded allowances to utilities elsewhere in the nation, helping to offset some of their own costs of control. Utilities that failed to reduce emissions sufficiently would have to buy allowances from other utilities or pay big fines to the government.

Under the proposal, for example, if one utility was able to reduce emissions by an amount greater than required, it could sell its extra allowances to another utility that was not able to achieve its needed reductions. As long as a given utility's allowances covered its total emissions at the end of each year, it avoided strict fines. Supporters of this approach contended that upgrading costly and inefficient facilities creates an economic drag. Their proposal represented a merging of economic and environmental techniques. It sharply reversed the heavily regulated "command and control" approach on which Sens. Mitchell and Byrd failed to reach an accord in 1988.

The concept of market-trading to meet environmental goals was not entirely new among economists. Bush and his advisers might well have developed on their own some version of the system that they actually proposed. But a Republican president's endorsement of a free-market approach to clean-air policy might not have generated much excitement in the Democratic-controlled Congress. What made his proposal click was that its intellectual rationale and the political support came from an important member of the environmental community, the Environmental Defense Fund.

Daniel J. Dudek, an EDF economist with a special interest in environmental policy, first presented his plan for an acid-rain emissions-trading system at a late-1987 Columbia University conference on new directions in environmental policy. Recognizing that he needed a lawyer to serve as a partner, Dudek also encouraged the EDF to hire Joseph Goffman, who had previously worked with the Ralph Nader network in Washington. Their proposal gained added currency when Dudek and Goffman sought support from the sponsors of Project 88, a bipartisan set of environmental initiatives, for whoever would be the new president. The chief sponsors—Sens. Timothy E. Wirth, a Colorado Democrat, and the late John Heinz, a Pennsylvania Republican—endorsed Dudek's idea.

Aides to then-Vice President Bush first became aware of the idea in the summer of 1988 and liked it. "Boyden Gray learned about our idea from Project 88 and he contacted EDF," Dudek said. "He was looking for ideas but he was constrained by civil-service rules from getting ideas from federal agencies." But the EDF faced the challenge of moving the discussion from abstract concepts to specific proposals; in other words, it was time to put up or shut up. When he later learned about the specifics of Dudek's plan, Gray said, "I was stunned that an environmental group had given someone like him so much leeway" to work out the details of a radically new acid-rain proposal.

Many obstacles remained in the way of final approval of the emissions-trading program. Not the least was that some in the EPA objected to the idea. "The EPA staff was not especially sympathetic," Dudek said. "They saw our trading approach as untried, risky and a burden for EPA to enforce. They preferred the more conventional approach," he added, of "scrubbing" a specified and relatively small number of large Midwest utility plants fueled by high-sulfur coal; that had been a fundamental tenet of the plan that Mitchell and Byrd had developed. Even though it was far more costly, some EPA veterans had helped to draft that earlier approach and were initially reluctant to abandon its obvious political cachet in the Senate in favor of the free-market EDF version. "It was primarily a bureaucratic impulse," presidential counsel Gray said. "If it works, the [EDF] proposal allows the marketplace to make decisions, instead of the planners at EPA. It is human nature for any regulatory agency to resist that. . . . But, in the end, it was encouraging that EPA embraced the idea." Gray said that EPA Administrator Reilly "never had any hesitations." Rosenberg, for his part, agreed that some EPA aides initially were skeptical that the idea would work. After the internal differences were resolved, the top-level cooperation within the administration assured endorsement of the new acid-rain approach.

The extensive research and analysis, both within the White House and at the EPA, necessary to prepare Bush's overall proposal, took more time than had been expected. And the more time that Bush aides spent debating the acid-rain plan, the less time that they could devote to other issues. But Gray and Rosenberg, the alternative-fuel enthusiasts, made sure that Bush's plan included a significant proposal to reduce automobile-tailpipe pollution, which remained the source of nearly half of nitrogen-oxide emissions. Like the EDF acid-rain proposal, the alternative-fuel plan became an important new part of the clean-air debate in Congress. But because the details of the latter proposal, which mandated the annual production starting in 1997 of a million new automobiles operated by clean fuels, had not been as fully aired during the internal White House review, it became the subject of far more legislative refinement. "The final proposal [as enacted] was different than what we proposed," Rosenberg said. "But the administration captured the high ground with our initiative. . . . And we challenged the automobile and fuel companies to come forth and work with Congress on a strong alternative."

Despite Bush's support for the alternative-fuels program, there were strong pockets of opposition within the administration, chiefly at the Energy Department. Secretary Watkins and his top aides voiced strong doubts that consumers would voluntarily purchase the new cars and fuel and worried about the economic impact. In one humorous exchange during a White House meeting, Gray touted the benefits of methanol, one of the leading alternative fuels. When a dubious Deputy

Secretary of Energy W. Henson Moore, who had been a Republican Representative from Louisiana, trumpeted the advantages of more conventional fuels, Gray responded that he would drink a glass of methanol if Moore would consume an equal amount of gasoline. As we shall see in chapter nine, the congressional bartering that resulted on the alternative-fuels section of the new law produced elaborate dealings by both lawmakers and lobbyists.

The Gray-Moore exchange took place during one of six sessions of the White House Domestic Policy Council devoted to a review of options for the clean-air proposal. In a strong signal of his interest, Bush attended four of those meetings, which typically lasted 60 to 90 minutes and included many federal agencies. Although the council did not make actual decisions, its discussions aired the thoughts of a more diverse cast of characters. At one session, Secretary of State James Baker made an important pitch for the acid-rain plan by saying that its approval was vital to Mulroney of Canada.

After Porter's group resolved most of the issues, a few uncertainties remained. Those were condensed into three presidential decision-making memos that, in effect, allowed Bush to mark his choices on several questions. The president reviewed the papers at Camp David on the weekend of June 10–11 and, in the presence of Sununu, made his decisions. Sununu then telephoned a group of senior aides sitting in the White House office of James W. Cicconi, a Sununu deputy, and communicated the final details of Bush's clean-air plan.

Bush unveiled the outlines of his clean-air proposal on June 12 before a large audience in the ceremonial East Room of the White House. "We've seen enough of this stalemate," he said. "It's time to clear the air. . . . This legislation will be comprehensive. It will be cost-effective. But above all, it will work." He listed as the first goal of his package a 10 million-ton cut in sulfur-dioxide emissions by the year 2000 to be achieved by "allowing utilities to trade credits among themselves for reductions they make." Bush said that his package embraced five main principles: harnessing the power of the marketplace, encouraging local initiative, emphasizing prevention instead of merely clean-up, fostering international cooperation and ensuring strict enforcement.

In addition to the acid-rain and alternative-fuel proposals, which grabbed the most public attention, Bush called for improved enforcement of local smog-control efforts and changes in the program to control auto emissions. He also included, with little fanfare, an overhaul of the EPA's much-criticized regulation of toxic chemicals, with a goal of a 75 percent cut of the poisons in the next decade. Because of weak enforcement and its complex risk-based standard, that program had resulted in controls of only seven of more than 280 known air toxins since the original 1970 law. Bush's team adapted their toxic-control plan from a plan assembled in 1988 by an EPA staff group headed by Brenner and under the direction of then-EPA Administrator Lee Thomas—one of the few positive environmental legacies of the Reagan administration. Without Thomas's initiative, many clean-air experts believe, Bush and congressional leaders, consumed by their plateful of other problems, would have lacked the wherewithal to find common ground on the growing risk posed by cancer-causing toxins.

After the generally enthusiastic reception for their clean-air program, administration aides thought that they had mostly finished the initial phase of their work. Their optimism proved premature. Drafting the actual legislative proposal, which had been expected to take a few days, required six weeks and a new series of intensive discussions on a wide range of issues. White House and EPA drafters held countless meetings in an intensive line-by-line review of the more than 300 pages of their actual legislative proposal. EPA lawyers had been working on the language for months but could not submit it for formal review until Bush and Porter's group made their final policy decisions. The acid-rain proposal, for example, triggered a new internal conflict. EDF proponents of emissions trading believed that the only way to force companies to participate in the system would be to set an annual ceiling on new power-plant emissions. At the White House, Sununu and others initially opposed such an approach on the ground that it would retard economic growth. But Dudek and Goffman, who had been joined by the experts at EPA and had the continued strong support of Gray, eventually carried the day with their response that the proposed cap simply would force more shutdowns of older power plants in favor of newer, cleaner versions. "There would not have been a cap without the efforts of EDF," Grady said.

The six-week interval allowed major industries an opportunity to influence the vital details and various shades of meaning in the legislative language. The auto industry used the time to win a provision that the required cut in tailpipe emissions for new vehicles would be on an average, fleetwide basis rather than for each new car. And the number of cities entitled to a longer delay in meeting smog-control rules was increased. Administration officials, who were miffed at the public disclosure of earlier documents with an "OMB Draft" stamp on them, said that the resulting modifications were consistent with the letter and spirit of Bush's June 12 announcement. But the public conflicts, though not widely publicized, gave a hint of the fights that would result when it came time for Congress to act.

Bush took advantage of the additional internal review to gain an unusual political benefit. When his staff finished writing the actual bill for him to send to Capitol Hill, he held on July 21 yet another public ceremony full of ruffles and flourishes—this time in the White House rose garden—to trumpet its goals and to declare, "It's time to break the gridlock on this issue."

Once the specifics arrived in Congress, however, some of the praise dissipated. Senate Majority Leader Mitchell criticized Bush for weakening his previous month's promises. "The president's words are bold but his deeds are timid," he said. Following a busy weekend in which his subcommittee staff made a detailed analysis of the Bush plan and its shortcomings, Waxman held a Monday morning hearing on July 24 in which he attacked the proposal as "riddled with exemptions and relaxations that were never mentioned in the president's statement and are wholly inconsistent with many of his stated objectives." Although the session received relatively sparse national press coverage, in contrast to the page-one coverage for each Bush announcement, Waxman staked a claim for himself, and for many of his colleagues: with the six-month administration review over, it was time for Congress to act.

Many good intentions, including Waxman's goal to bring a clean-air bill to the House floor in three months, would be sacrificed as members of Congress began to confront the kinds of practical and political problems with which the White House had wrestled. Whatever the result of the coming debate, however, the Bush team was pleased with its impact on setting the direction for congressional action on new clean-air protections. Without Bush's efforts, Porter and other White House aides said, there would have been no new law. Lawmakers agreed. "The fact that President Bush sent us a bill was the pre-eminent change," said chairman Dingell. "We had a document that gave us a view of the entirety." Democratic Rep. Gerry Sikorski of Minnesota, hardly a Bush enthusiast, agreed. The details of the Bush plan, Sikorski said, were less important than its principles and the fact that the President "had removed the camouflage for many opponents in both parties."

Endnotes

1. Christine M. Black and Thomas Oliphant, *All by Myself, The Unmaking of a Presidential Campaign* (Chester, CT: The Globe Pequot Press, 1989), 194.
2. Roger B. Porter, *Presidential Decision Making* (Cambridge: Cambridge University Press, 1980), 248.
3. Robert W. Hahn, "The Politics and Religion of Clean Air," *Regulation* (published by the CATO Institute), Winter 1990: 26.

5

Crumbling Committees

Rep. Henry Waxman and his aides were the driving force in the House for strict environmental restrictions. After years of frustration, they began to make progress in late 1989.

Initiating legislation is one thing. Enacting it is a far more challenging task in the modern Congress, as the Bush White House would soon learn.

No president can dictate to Congress the terms of major legislation. But when he took control following his inauguration in January 1989, Bush faced unusually severe obstacles—even with his electoral mandate. In contrast to most newly elected presidents, he entered the White House as virtually a lone rider: Republicans had lost seats in the 1988 election. As a result, he took office with his party holding the fewest House seats for any 20th century president starting his term— 175 of 435. And the Republican-controlled Senate that President Reagan swept into office in 1980 was a dim memory.

But not only were the numbers stacked against the president; congressional Democrats and their leaders were less than awed by Bush and his political skills. As vice president, he had left the impression that he was a Reagan lapdog who during eight years had made little measurable impact. Many Democrats viewed his overwhelming Electoral College victory over Dukakis as a fluke. They blamed Dukakis's abysmal campaign and Bush campaign operatives' disreputable use of rhetorical and advertising techniques. "Our view is that Bush defeated Dukakis, who is not one of us," a senior Democratic congressional aide said after the election. Moreover, Bush appeared to have only a modest agenda of his own, eschewing what he cavalierly dismissed as "the vision thing."

If Bush had a limited set of domestic-policy initiatives, the Democrats running Congress had a much more aggressive view of their own role. They exuded confidence and their own sense of mission following the 100th Congress in 1987–88. During the final two years of Reagan's tenure, they had reversed his momentum and used their power base as a platform to undermine the credibility and influence of the Republican administration. They had produced several important pieces of legislation, some of which Reagan had reluctantly signed and others that had become partisan footballs. Democrats also had gained extensive publicity with their investigation of the Iran-Contra affair, in which they attempted to show that top Reagan officials had sent weapons to Iran in an elaborate scheme to aid the rebels seeking to overthrow the Communist regime in Nicaragua. Some Democrats saw a similar opportunity after the 1988 election to investigate the mushrooming losses in the savings and loan industry as a way to spotlight the shortcomings of the Reagan-Bush team.

The start of the two-year congressional cycle has taken on growing importance as an opportunity for agenda setting. In part, this historical shift mirrors the increased prominence of party leaders at the expense of committee chairmen. Before the 1970s, the elected leaders of Congress operated largely at the mercy of committee chairmen. If and when the chairmen produced a bill, the leaders could schedule it for floor action. With many conservative Southern Democrats serving as committee chairmen, legislation favored by a large share of the majority party—such as civil rights or federally financed medical care for senior citizens—often would remain bottled up.

The 1974 congressional reforms, by forcing committee chairmen to be selected by and thus accountable to their party caucus, revolutionized the exercise of power. The culmination and most dramatic evidence of those changes came with the 1975 replacement of three House chairmen, two from Texas and one from Louisiana, by new chairmen from the states of Illinois, Wisconsin and Washington. In the zero-sum world of legislative power, this overthrow of autocratic barons was a victory for party leaders, chiefly the House speaker. Under the new system, for example, Speaker Thomas P. O'Neill Jr. of Massachusetts created a temporary, leadership-controlled panel in 1977 to steer President Carter's energy legislation around the rocky shoals of the committees, which might otherwise have forced more changes and delay. Like clean air, energy legislation was a major event that required cooperation by several committees. With the 1974 reforms, such proposals could be accomplished in ad hoc fashion.

Like committee chairmen, however, party leaders cannot simply command allegiance. They must reflect the wishes or secure the support of their rank and file. The biennial setting of the legislative agenda is a prime example of this changing leadership role. After surveying the views of members, including committee chairmen, the leaders decide which issues are ripe for action, from both legislative and political perspectives. Then, they typically unveil roughly a half-dozen top priorities for the new Congress. Such a list gains special importance as a statement to the general public, and as a prod within Congress, where the setting of deadlines often is a vital action-forcing tool.

So it was that clean-air legislation moved to the top of the agenda for the 101st Congress. In the Senate this was no surprise after Senate Democrats chose Mitchell to succeed Byrd as majority leader in a first-ballot victory over Daniel K. Inouye of Hawaii and J. Bennett Johnston of Louisiana. The picture in the House, however, was murkier. Though Speaker Jim Wright, a Texas Democrat, stated his support for clean-air legislation, it was not clear how strongly he would push the reluctant Dingell, who had become his ally in internal House politics. More important, Wright was increasingly preoccupied in early 1989 by the House Ethics Committee's investigation of his personal finances, including charges that he and his wife Betty had received income in violation of House rules on outside income.

Like the president, congressional leaders cannot guarantee the passage of their agenda. The experience during the Reagan years with clean-air legislation had shown that it is far easier to play defense than offense. Congress provides more leverage for opponents to stop controversial bills than for supporters to pass something. "Moving legislation can be stomach-turning, deliberative and very slow," said Rep. Sikorski, who played an important role in Energy and Commerce Committee clean-air legislation. "Like a dinosaur, once it moves, that is a statement in itself."

Critics, especially those outside Congress, have blamed delay on the influence of special interests, which bestow campaign money and other favors on lawmakers to stymie public-spirited legislation. But most members reject such attacks on their integrity as superficial. The criticism, they respond, overlooks the difficulty of achieving consensus in a nation of diverse interests, where all sides have the right to advocate their views on frequently complex issues.

The crumbling of the power of committee chairmen has been a mixed blessing for party leaders in the House and Senate chambers. In recent years, the internal changes resulting from the erosion of the committee process have produced a growing trend toward informal, ad hoc arrangements on important legislation that place greater demands on the party leaders. Consider how Congress, especially the Senate, handled several important bills in 1989–90: A comprehensive anticrime bill came to the Senate floor in the spring of 1990 after virtually no action in the Judiciary Committee, forcing Mitchell to schedule more than a month of debate and to broker decisions on several major disputes to assure passage. Campaign-finance bills were crafted by leadership-controlled task forces, as Senate and House committees were largely bypassed. The same was true of a pay raise–ethics reform package in 1989. And the most pervasive issue of the 101st Congress, the struggle to reduce the federal deficit, was negotiated for several months in a so-called summit. In that case, congressional leaders circumvented routine budget procedures as a few committee chairmen and top White House officials met at locations ranging from small rooms in the Capitol to Andrews Air Force Base outside Washington, D.C.

Well-placed legislators have said that, in each of these cases, there has been no conscious or concerted effort to bypass committees, if only because the result makes it more difficult to manage legislation. The temporary devices have been used chiefly because many committees and their chairmen have lost the ability to develop a consensus that can be enforced through Senate and House passage. In part, that has been the case with panels that have become "constituent committees"—captives of the interest groups most affected by their work. Seats on the agriculture committees tend to be filled by lawmakers representing farmers; members from states with large urban centers flock toward committees dealing with labor issues; and Western and Southern senators gravitate toward the Energy and Natural Resources Committee.

These legislative changes have had important ramifications that have received little public discussion. "The committee process is designed to weed out problems," said a veteran Senate aide. "When bills are put together on an ad hoc basis, the trouble can be that there are no hearings and more staff control, which increases the risk of unintended consequences." A prime example came in 1989, when the outrage of senior-citizen groups over the 1988 law providing insurance to cover the costs of catastrophic illnesses forced Congress to repeal the measure, in part because of the lack of public understanding of the new law. The few senior members and aides to the House and Senate committees that drafted the health-care law were convinced that it was good policy. But their failure to engage and educate many lawmakers fueled public and private-sector opposition that contributed to its downfall. "The problems we face are becoming more complex, and the solutions don't fit neatly into the baskets represented by the committee system," said a former top aide to Sen. Mitchell. "[In the past], there was more respect for seniority and learning your committee assignments. Now, it seems that there is more of an entrepreneurial spirit in the Senate and in politics, generally."[1]

The Senate and House committees responsible for clean-air legislation have exemplified these problems, each in its own way. Reflecting their names and separate jurisdictions, the two committees have taken very different approaches to clean-air legislation. The Senate Environment and Public Works Committee since the 1970s has largely come under the control of members and staff with ardently pro-environment views. The panel has been criticized, even by some of its own members, for not paying enough attention to the impact of its actions on national economic and energy policy. The House Energy and Commerce Committee, by contrast, has sometimes seemed unduly concerned with the effects of environmental legislation on both national and home-state economies. The House committee, in contrast to its

Senate counterpart, reflects the "deal-making" approach of most House members, who tend to focus more on parochial and local concerns. As a result, the House panel generally has attempted to soften the impact of environmental controls. Another prime contrast is that the House panel, with its ability to initiate legislation in virtually any aspect of domestic commerce, ranging from health-care to communications policy, is a prized committee assignment for House members. The Senate panel, in contrast, has largely become a second or third choice for most of its members, who consequently have given less attention to its legislation and rely more on their staff to do much of the work.

When the committees began to work on clean-air legislation, their actions reflected both these institutional problems and their members' predilections. The Senate committee in 1989 granted most of the environmentalists' wishes, while its House counterpart became bogged down in internal disagreements. But the consequence, not so oddly, is that the House committee was in a much stronger position to carry the day a year later.

The rivalry between Dingell and Waxman had become the overriding factor at the House Energy and Commerce Committee. "They hate each other," said a committee aide who has watched them closely for many years. Although that is a slight overstatement, there was no question that their personal clashes and competition had come to overshadow most aspects of the committee's operations. Another aide said that their dealings had created a breakdown of trust and confidence between Dingell and Waxman, which was even more deep seated among their respective aides on environmental issues. The fight was not simply a result of their philosophical splits and their personal styles. It also was a struggle for political control of the committee.

This complex and often bitter relationship, which produced public displays of outright hostility, left many committee Democrats increasingly restless and in search of alternatives to break the deadlock on clean-air legislation. They worried that the continuing conflict, if not resolved, would soon threaten the influence of one of the House's most powerful committees. On a more personal level, members said, Dingell needed to show that he could pass an important bill in the House, especially a clean-air measure that most Democrats wanted and on which he had been defeated during the 1970s; otherwise, his standing as chairman could be jeopardized. And Waxman, although he had displayed success in winning enactment of important changes in federal health policy (the other half of his Environment and Health Subcommittee), was perceived as losing influence in the late 1980s to other House Democrats from California—chiefly Majority Whip Tony Coelho and inside operator Vic Fazio. "The pressure on Henry was to produce a bill after 10 years of work, to put up or shut up," said Rep. Eckart of Ohio. "The pressure on John was to respond to his Democratic Caucus."

In a demonstration of the maxim that "power abhors a vacuum," the Dingell-Waxman tensions led nine Energy and Commerce Committee Democrats to enter the fray by creating their own legislative mechanism in 1988. They became known as the Group of Nine. They would play, both as a group and as individuals, vital roles in breaking the deadlock and in helping to pave the way toward the 1990 Clean Air Act. Their activities created considerable unhappiness and suspicions within the committee, not least from Dingell and Waxman. Perhaps as a result of selective memory, both at the time of their efforts and in retrospect, participants and observers have differed slightly in explaining how and why the Group of Nine was created, how it operated and the nature of its impact. Whatever the case, their story offers important insights into both clean-air politics and the modern Congress.

The nine Democrats were all self-styled moderates who said that they had grown weary of the impasse between Dingell and Waxman and wanted to find a satisfactory middle ground. "We shared a belief that, for the good of the committee and the good of John Dingell, we should do something to break the deadlock," said Rep. Al Swift, a Washington Democrat who became the group's informal leader. "We sent a signal to John that stonewalling was no longer in the committee's interest." Swift, who was widely known to be a friend of Dingell's, dismissed Waxman's view that the group was a stalking horse for Dingell. Both Dingell and Waxman eventually viewed the group as "an annoyance," Swift added. Another member of the Group of Nine said that it may have been "spawned by John Dingell, but it quickly went awry and became independent of him." Rep. Mike Synar of Oklahoma, the Group of Nine member who was probably the closest personally to Waxman, agreed. "Anytime [House members] get together as a force, others get fearful," Synar said. "Most sides were suspicious of our group. But I told Waxman and Dennis Eckart told Dingell, 'Cool your jets.' I don't know if they believed us."

Waxman's suspicion was fueled when Sikorski, a Waxman ally, complained that he was excluded from the group. "It was very clear that I was not invited," Sikorski said. "I think that I was objectionable to Dingell." But Synar and Eckart both denied that Sikorski or any other committee Democrat was excluded, suggesting that he simply did not make the effort to join. On the other hand, some participants later said that Swift and Synar informally recruited members. In addition to Eckart, Swift and Synar, the other Group of Nine members were Reps. Rick Boucher of Virginia, Terry Bruce of Illinois, Jim Cooper of Tennessee, Phil Sharp of Indiana, Jim Slattery of Kansas and Billy Tauzin of Louisiana; its Midwest industrial-state tilt increased Waxman's suspicion that it was a Dingell front. (Another view of the Group of Nine, voiced separately by friends of Dingell and Waxman, was that its organizers were less interested in being middlemen for the two chief combatants than in giving themselves cover so that the nine did not have to choose one side or the other.) The organizers confined their membership to Democrats because they believed that the committee's clean-air deadlock was largely an internal party problem.

After the Group of Nine was organized in late 1987 (with a name that its members modified slightly from the "Gang of Nine" label supplied by industry lobbyists), they decided to tackle the non-attainment controversy, the failure of many areas of the nation to meet the local clean-air standards in the 1977 law. Operating without a formal structure, they initially instructed their aides to prepare a report on their legislative options. That five-page report, issued on Dec. 16, 1987, briefly reviewed the legal and regulatory background of the problem and concluded that the staff would further examine legislative options during the year-end recess.

Aides to Group of Nine members subsequently held nearly two dozen meetings on Capitol Hill with aides to the dispute's major players, including Dingell, Waxman, the EPA, industry groups, environmentalists, and other experts. In each case, participants discussed the problems and proposed solutions. That resulted in a Feb. 3, 1988 staff report of 44 pages outlining a proposed recommendation, which gave EPA broader legal authority and scientific capability to enforce local air-quality standards. The Group of Nine members then launched their own series of meetings during the following month, making refinements in the staff report. On March 17 they held a press conference and released their 77-page proposal, saying that it was time to "complete the job" of reducing urban smog. "We need to go after emission reductions just about everywhere we can find them," they said in a statement. "The fact that a particular industry might contribute only one or two percent of the problem is not a reason to let them off the hook." Their timetable, which would have extended to the year 2005, fell between earlier Dingell and Waxman proposals.

What was the Group of Nine's impact? In the short term, its members spurred the sporadic efforts by Dingell and Waxman to reach agreement in 1988 on the non-attainment section. Swift and Synar met informally that summer with Dingell and Waxman in secret discussions later limited to their aides. "The talks were amiable but we did not get far," said a staff participant. But he and others said that if in late 1988 Mitchell and Byrd had managed to lead the Senate to an acid-rain agreement, the private talks could have laid the groundwork for a virtually instant agreement in the House. Whether that would have been the case proved to be moot. But the Group of Nine's work provided encouragement to Bush administration officials as they prepared their proposal in 1989. Lawmakers also later helped to bring together Dingell and Waxman by providing the basis for an eventual deal on some key issues.

"Dingell and Waxman are very busy people and they do not have the necessary time to get together and discuss details," Cooper said. "In effect, we acted as their staff to formulate alternatives." As often is the case in a legislative body, leadership worked on a two-way basis; the Group of Nine became a prod in its own right, showing that consensus was possible and spurring Dingell and Waxman to make their own moves. Dingell, who denied suggestions that the Group of Nine was a challenge to his leadership of the panel, called their proposal "a meaningful contribution, both to the politics and to the substance of the debate." Waxman, after his initial dismissal of the Group of Nine, later said that its efforts eventually helped him to forge a compromise with Dingell. "At a time when no one else was working on the issue, we demonstrated that there was a way to bring together the concerns of business and environmentalists," Swift said.

The Group of Nine's efforts also proved useful to the participants themselves. Their informal approach helped them to learn the complex array of issues that are difficult, if not impossible, to digest in the more formal committee hearings. "Hearings are too time-consuming," Synar said. They are structured in such a way that members find it difficult, or awkward, to ask questions about technical disputes they do not fully understand. "I see what we have done as the committee structure of the future," Cooper said. "The learning curve for members needs to be private. . . . You need a sustained focus that you can't get in the formal hearings. The learning process here is subtle because most members have a limited attention span."

But the Group's failure to move the debate forward on two other important issues, auto-emissions standards and acid rain, also was politically instructive. Although the Group of Nine staff developed an acid-rain proposal, none of the members would put his name on it. In part, they were stymied by their Midwest tilt against strict acid-rain controls. Three of the nine members also had auto plants in their districts. By contrast, their proposal for combating urban smog had more of a national focus and did not strike so directly at a particular region or industry. And the fact that none of the Group of Nine members served districts that included the nation's largest cities or had especially dirty air meant that they had less reason to fear adverse local reaction.

Despite the progress made on some issues by the Democrats' Group of Nine, the House Energy and Commerce Committee was badly fractured when it received Bush's clean-air plan in mid-1989. In addition to the overriding Dingell-Waxman feud, the 43-member committee was also divided by geography.

Numbers are often vital to understanding legislative politics. The Midwest belt in 1990 had nine seats on the House Energy and Commerce Committee; the Appalachian coal states had another seven seats on the panel. As chairman, Dingell had worked closely with Wright and other Democratic leaders to recruit sympathetic members to his committee. On the Senate Environment panel, by contrast, those 12 Appalachian and Midwest states—from Pennsylvania west to Iowa and south to North Carolina and Tennessee—were represented only by the relatively inactive John Warner, a Virginia Republican. The bottom line: the region had 37 percent of the seats on the House panel writing the clean-air bill, compared with only 7 percent of those in its Senate counterpart. Those "industrial heartland" states were at the center of the two most politically intractable issues in the clean-air debate: the acid rain that results from the region's coal-burning power plants, and the tailpipe exhausts from automobiles, most of which also are manufactured in the region.

Dingell's deft use of his parliamentary power to set the committee's schedule also enhanced the Midwest's influence. During all of the maneuvers since 1981—in Waxman's subcommittee, in private negotiations between Dingell and Waxman, in the Group of Nine—Dingell controlled the full committee's ability to send a bill to the House floor by wielding the gavel. Since becoming chairman in 1981 he had with-stood the pressure to act, chiefly to protect the interests of the auto industry. Following Bush's initiative, however, Dingell accepted the advice by allies inside the House (including Majority Whip Coelho) and outside (notably, his wife Debbie, the General Motors executive) that delay and defensive tactics would no longer succeed and that he must avoid blame for inaction. Otherwise, he was warned from several quarters, he risked erosion of his influence. But deciding to support legislation was only preliminary to taking the steps needed to gain enactment. "Dingell always knew that he could delay action for a time, but that he then would have to fight for the best deal he could get," said an aide to the House Democratic leadership.

To control that outcome, Dingell had to control his committee. After his extended battles with Waxman during the 1980s, that was no easy task. And he faced an even tougher challenge to produce a bill that would avoid a politically dangerous fight on the House floor. After his late-1987 setback on the Murtha amendment, Dingell could no longer be sure that he had those votes. If he were serious, the best way to break the logjam, he resolved, would be to take the bull by the horns and strike an early deal with his chief adversary on what was the most vital issue for Dingell and his constituents—tailpipe emissions.

Some members of the automobile industry were unhappy that they would be the first target in the debate, partly because they feared that Waxman would not honor an agreement. With shrewd timing and a willingness to set aside their antagonisms, however, Dingell made several vital calculations: He decided that his own hand would be strongest early in the debate, that he could trust Waxman once they cut a. deal and that the two of them working together would pre-empt the middle and prevent a legislative brawl in the House. He also correctly concluded that a deal reached in the House would have a big impact on the Senate debate and on public perceptions of his reasonableness. "John Dingell determined that he would have more influence if the decisions were made in a small group," said a senior Democrat on the House committee. "The auto-industry lobbyists were naive to think that they could win on the House floor."

The scenario began in a subdued fashion soon after Congress returned from its Labor Day recess, when Waxman convened his Health and the Environment Subcommittee to rewrite Bush's bill. The first big vote came on Sept. 19, and Waxman suffered a narrow defeat on his proposal to toughen requirements for local air-quality standards. The proposal was similar in many respects to the plan from the Group of Nine, but only two of those nine Democrats served on Waxman's 23-member subcommittee. Waxman then switched to automobile pollution and began working with members of both parties to find a majority.

His first target proved to be an easy one. He unexpectedly won the subcommittee's unanimous approval of his amendment to remove from Bush's plan a provision that would have weakened current law by allowing the auto manufacturers to average the tailpipe emissions from all of their new cars to meet the federal standards. Dingell had earlier favored the proposed elimination of "averaging," but when he saw how the vote was going, he joined Waxman to make the vote unanimous. Then, Waxman gained a second victory on Sept. 28, when conservative Republican Thomas J. Bliley Jr. of Virginia gave critical support to an amendment requiring a large canister and other controls in new cars to trap fumes that escape when cars are refueled at a service station.

While he picked up this public momentum, Waxman continued private negotiations on a broad-based plan to strengthen Bush's proposal for auto emissions. His first opportunity came when Thomas J. Tauke, an Iowa Republican, said he would be interested in a deal if Waxman could resolve a potential problem for farm and other off road vehicles, many of which were manufactured in his district. Tauke wanted to force uniform standards for these vehicles across the nation so that the manufacturers would not have to contend with separate rules. Waxman then began discussions with the subcommittee's two most conservative Democrats, Ralph M. Hall of Texas and Roy Rowland of Georgia, and found that his new proposal satsified many of their objections as well. One important concession made by Waxman was to extend enforcement deadlines for new cars, in accordance with a recently announced decision by California regulators to delay similar rules. The Southerners then informed Dingell of these intriguing developments and he joined the back-room discussion with Waxman. The committee chairman raised some of the same objections and likewise learned that some of his fears were no longer valid. Dingell, surely mindful of Waxman's two recent victories on other amendments, then reportedly leaned back in his chair and said, "Henry, you may have something there." His understatement meant that a deal was at hand. As a Dingell confidant later described it, "John put the family jewels in trust with Henry."

Subcommittee members and staff spent several more days, including a hectic weekend, completing the details. On Oct. 2, Dingell and

Waxman jubilantly announced the deal and the subcommittee then voted its unanimous approval in front of disgruntled lobbyists. Politically, it was a win-win package for both principals, who agreed to stick with its provisions for the duration of congressional handling of the new clean-air law. Dingell could tell the auto industry that the package, especially its new standards for tailpipe emissions, might not be entirely pleasing, but that it had gained some time and regulatory flexibility for the industry; more important, this was the best deal Congress would offer. Dingell also felt that avoiding an extended fight with Waxman on what had been perhaps the most controversial clean-air issue would benefit both the committee and himself and would expedite the package on the House floor. He also won Waxman's oral agreement not to press in the clean-air bill for higher fuel-efficiency standards for autos, which many environmentalists had demanded. Waxman could tell his environmental allies that he had taken an important step to passing the first legislative reduction in auto emissions since 1977, that the language was much tougher than restrictions that he had proposed— and environmentalists had backed a year earlier—on tailpipe emissions and that, as a sweetener, his arch-nemesis Dingell was on board.

Advocates on both sides were less than enthusiastic. "Dingell and [his aide] Finnegan pushed us to the edge and when they felt that we were tottering, they stopped," said a lobbyist for one of the Big Three auto companies. "The deal initially shook us up, but we feel that we can live with it even though our people in Detroit say that compliance will be a tremendous engineering task." *The Detroit News* criticized the local members of Congress, notably Dingell, for having "buried their heads in the sand in the face of environmental extremism."[2] On the other side, chief clean-air lobbyist Richard Ayres called the agreement "a genuine step forward," but he said that deficiencies remained, including deadlines extended for 13 years. Another environmental lobbyist said that the compromise sacrificed public-health standards at the altar of the auto industry. *The Los Angeles Times* ran articles questioning the wisdom of Waxman's deal and its delay of cleaner automobile emissions. On the other side of the Capitol building, Senate Environment and Public Works Committee insiders and other environmentalists soon moaned that Waxman had caved too much and too quickly to Dingell.

Much more work on a new clean-air law remained for Waxman's subcommittee. It would be months later before the full committee finished writing the bill. But the Dingell-Waxman tailpipe deal showed the progress that they and the committee had made from a year or two earlier when, according to a committee Democrat, "each side thought that it would be a fight to the finish and that only one would win." The result was a vital step in the shaping of the 1990 Clean Air Act, according to another committee Democrat. "It allowed the process to go forward dramatically," said Rep. Sharp of Indiana. "And it made it clear that we were going to move forward on a bill. . . . This would not have happened without the preliminary decision by President Bush and the leaders of Congress" to support new legislation.

So much for the House. In the Senate, as Mitchell learned in 1988, the resistance would come from outside the committee handling the bill. The chief problem that the Senate Environment and Public Works Committee faced on clean-air legislation in 1989–90 was not its internal dealings. On many issues, it was largely unified. The problem, especially on clean-air legislation, was that it was out of sync with the full Senate. This was a familiar problem for several Senate committees. But probably none of the others so starkly faced the pressure to move a top-priority measure for both President Bush and congressional leaders. To compound the problem, in the dozen years since the committee had last taken a clean-air bill to the Senate floor, the panel had suffered virtually a complete turnover in membership. And Baucus, unlike the experienced Dingell and Waxman, was brand new to many of these issues and less skilled in the use of power than either of them when he succeeded Mitchell in 1989 as the panel's Environment Protection Subcommittee chairman. As often happens in Congress, personnel changes can affect legislative dealings and outcomes.

The most significant problem facing the committee was the regional imbalance of its membership. Of its 16 members, five were from New England, the region most politically sensitive to the acid-rain dispute, and two others were from New York and New Jersey. Only Warner, a junior Republican on the panel, was from the Appalachian region or Great Lakes states that produced and burned most of the high-sulfur coal that causes acid rain. Four other committee members were from Rocky Mountain states that are the chief source of less polluting low-sulfur coal. Congressional committee assignments are largely controlled by party leaders. But because Midwest senators anticipated little besides aggravation if they joined the committee, the leaders were unwilling to force the issue to assure more balance. During the 1980s, in fact, relatively conservative senators such as

Lloyd Bentsen, a Texas Democrat, and Pete Domenici, a New Mexico Republican, quit the panel to take other assignments. The resulting discussion, not surprisingly, was one sided. "Unless Members come from a state without a lot of heavy industry, they do not want to be on this committee," said one of its senior aides.

Committee members and staff viewed environmentalism as "a secular religion," and they were its Senate spokesmen, according to committee insiders. Although Mitchell and Baucus were often reminded of the problem, they found that it was virtually impossible to craft a middle ground within the committee. The view inside the panel was that it should set the high-water mark and that it would address complaints from industry groups and make concessions, as necessary, on the Senate floor or in the House. "It's clear that the committee is not representative of the Senate," Mitchell said later. "But criticism of the committee is not justified. Without the committee, we would have had a much weaker bill."

Other problems limited the Environment and Public Works Committee's influence. John Chafee of Rhode Island had replaced Stafford, who had retired in 1989, as its senior Republican. Despite the fact that his environmental views and style were more accommodating than those of Stafford, Chafee had relatively little influence with other Senate Republicans or with the White House on clean-air issues. He was an integral part of the committee's bipartisan coalition that claimed credit for several major environmental bills during the Reagan era. "Environment and Public Works was a committee without a party," said an industry lobbyist. "It had become an advocacy group for the environment."

The committee also suffered because its 82-year-old chairman, Quentin Burdick of North Dakota, had little interest in the clean-air legislation except for the impact on his home state. Although he rarely interfered with the legislation, neither did he give Baucus or Mitchell much help. David Strauss, Burdick's staff director, understood some of the problems resulting from the committee's weak standing inside the Senate and sought to be an honest broker. But it is difficult for an aide to play that role when other senators are clashing. "Staff derive their power from their senators," said a lobbyist who has watched the committee closely. "Strauss could not do much because Burdick was so out of it."

Even the most active committee members were ignorant on most details of major legislation and relied heavily on their staff to do the work. "Because the senators don't act, we do," said a committee aide.

The staff could do most of the work required to stage hearings and prepare the often highly technical legislation. But a committee whose staff is stronger than its senators risks creating a lot of activity but accomplishing little. And this was no ordinary staff. Many of its aides had worked on the committee for several years, in anticipation of a new clean-air bill. They had adopted a collective mindset that was closely attuned to that of environmentalists and they conveyed an arrogance that dismissed most viewpoints of other special-interest groups. Therefore, they were often dangerously divorced from the real world of politics. A former Senate Democratic aide with broad experience and sympathy for clean-air legislation said that many of the committee aides engaged in "self-delusion" and practiced a form of polarization that discouraged opinions different from their own.

Baucus, as the new chairman, faced this precarious institutional role. Prior to 1989 he had largely supported Stafford and Mitchell on clean-air issues, partly because Montana's scenic beauty and the dangers posed by mining interests gave his state a strong pro-environment tilt. But he had not been active on the panel. Another vital factor was that, in contrast to those of Mitchell, Stafford and Chafee, his home state had sizable low-sulfur coal deposits; he therefore had little incentive to help the high-sulfur coal interests in the East.

Like other senators, however, Baucus was busy with other responsibilities. He was a senior member of the powerful Finance Committee, where he chaired its International Trade Subcommittee. And he also was keeping a close eye on the home front, where he faced what he feared could be a difficult re-election challenge in 1990. Sen. John Melcher, another Montana Democrat, unexpectedly lost a re-election bid in 1988 because of over confidence, and Baucus did not intend to fall into that trap. (Baucus eventually demolished his Republican opponent, Lt. Gov. Allen Kolstad, winning 70 percent of the vote.) Despite his best efforts to become comfortable with the complexities of clean-air legislation, therefore, Baucus met serious obstacles in trying to move onto the same legislative track with the more skillful Dingell and Waxman.

Baucus was sympathetic to parts of the Bush administration's clean-air plan, chiefly the attempt to reduce acid rain without stiff requirements for new technology to clean high-sulfur Appalachian coal. The reason was obvious: Baucus and other westerners wanted to increase the use of Montana's low-sulfur coal. Apart from that issue, however, Baucus generally deferred to the staff in his early months as subcommittee chairman in 1989. Other senators on the panel also took nominal responsibility for parts of the bill in which they were most interested: Dave Durenberger, a Minnesota Republican, and Frank Lautenberg, a New Jersey Democrat, on toxic chemicals; Chafee on CFCs; and Mitchell on acid rain. With no Midwesterners on the committee, it mandated further reductions of as much as 80 percent in nitrogen-oxide, carbon-monoxide and hydrocarbon emissions from new automobiles. As has long been the case on the committee, partisan labels played virtually no role.

After four days of debate in Baucus's subcommittee, the committee formally "marked up" (agreed on amendments to) the entire bill in one day on Nov. 16. He emphasized that the panel had to finish its work that day because Mitchell had scheduled the bill as the first item on the agenda after the Senate returned on Jan. 23 from the recess about to begin. "Keep going," Baucus urged committee members inclined toward delay. "Keep going." Although few senators on the committee had a clear idea of what was in the measure, they approved it, 15–1. "I wanted the strongest possible bill," Baucus later said. "I always knew that the committee-reported bill was only one part of the process. It was the start down the road."

But the committee did not anticipate how much trouble lay ahead. "We knew that a lot of things in the bill would require compromise on the Senate floor," said a committee aide who worked on the bill. "But we felt that we eventually would pass it without jeopardizing major parts of the bill." But Mitchell, whose leadership post gave him a broader view and understanding of the institution, knew the Senate better than did the committee insiders.

In contrast to the strife-ridden House Energy and Commerce Committee, its Senate counterpart outwardly seemed like a model of efficiency. But the Environment and Public Works Committee had ignored a cardinal rule of legislating: Conflicts cannot be wished away. The decision by Dingell and Waxman to make their peace at an early point would bear fruit much later. For the Senate panel, the pain and ineffectiveness would surface soon enough.

Endnotes

1. I have written at great length in *National Journal* about changes in Congress. See, for example, "Crumbling Committees," August 4, 1990: 1876–1881, from which part of this discussion is condensed.
2. "War on the Automobile (Cont'd)," *The Detroit News*, Oct. 4, 1989: A-14.

6

The Senate Leader
Takes Over

During month-long meetings in his Capitol office, Senate Majority Leader George Mitchell cajoled other senators and Bush aides to agree on a compromise package. Empty pizza boxes piled up outside the room.

When Majority Leader Mitchell scheduled the clean-air bill as the Senate's initial business in 1990, his comments about its immediate prospects were justifiably cautious. "It is not my intention to force the pace on this bill in a manner that would deprive any senator of the fullest possible opportunities to consider, deliberate on, debate on, ask questions about, and offer amendments to this bill," he told the Senate on Jan. 23, the first day of debate. Not even Mitchell, however, could have foreseen that the Senate would work continuously on the bill, to the virtual exclusion of all other business, until April 3. Although it is common for senators to spend two or three weeks debating a bill, the time required for the clean-air bill has few parallels in recent history. Other examples—notably, the three-month debate on the 1964 Civil Rights Act—usually resulted from the Senate's inability to gain the votes needed to stop other senators from talking a bill to death in a filibuster.

The 10 weeks needed to pass the clean-air legislation were unusual in several respects. There was no extended talk and procedural delay on the Senate floor, as is traditional in a filibuster. Instead, most of the debate was conducted behind closed doors a few feet away from the Senate chamber in the back room of Mitchell's spacious leadership suite. From all reports, that discussion among senators was exceptionally spirited as lawmakers abandoned their aides and speeches to engage in real exchanges of views. Another feature, perhaps unprecedented, was that a delegation of high-ranking White House officials participated as equals, both in the debate and in subsequent agreement on a consensus package. Nor was the conflict resolved when the negotiators unveiled their deal on March 1. Instead, in one of the most dramatic clashes of power in Senate annals, Mitchell engaged Byrd, his predecessor as majority leader, in a pitched battle over a relatively extraneous amendment.

The Senate's consideration of the bill began inauspiciously. First, Mitchell invoked his power as majority leader to call up the bill for debate. Leaders of the Environment Committee—Burdick, Baucus and senior Republican Chafee—followed with perfunctory introductory statements. There followed a strange phenomenon. Despite many senators' objections to the bill, no one stepped forward to propose amendments making changes in the measure. Having written a stringent bill in committee, its members were prepared eventually to make some concessions. But, as a senior aide to the committee said, "Nothing happened. We were being ignored. And the opponents were such a disparate group that there was no one to whom we could go to address their problems." To complicate that humiliating dilemma, the proponents did not dare push for passage of the bill because they knew that they lacked the 60 votes required to stop the certain filibuster that would result. A setback on such a cloture vote would not only continue the talkathon, they feared, but also undercut momentum for the bill and embolden opponents to attack it openly.

The result was a nightmare scenario for the committee members and staff, who were often criticized as intractable and out of the Senate's mainstream: their delicately crafted product, which had taken nearly a decade to prepare, faced a painful death by a thousand cuts—one amendment at a time on the countless issues in the bill. "I forgot, and probably Sen. Mitchell forgot, just how complicated it all is, substantively and politically," Baucus said at the time. "It takes longer for senators to understand the legislation than we thought." Baucus later added, "Senators not on the committee . . . have other interests. They tend not to focus on a bill until it's on the floor. Then they react, 'My God, this is complicated'."

Imagine that you are George Mitchell and you must find a way out of this deadlock. After working on the subject for nearly a decade, you badly want a big clean-air bill. You are the Democratic leader and your party controls the Senate. And your president, though a Republican, has taken the public lead on the issue and supports passage of a bill. But your Senate committee has produced a bill that inspires no debate and widespread opposition by senators preparing to file their amendments. What do you do?

In today's Senate, you prepare to convene a series of closed-door meetings among interested players, whether or not they serve on the committee. Mitchell met privately with Minority Leader Robert Dole of Kansas and, at Dole's suggestion, he held preliminary discussions with White House aides and EPA boss Reilly in search of an accommodation with the Bush administration. Despite his frequently partisan approach, Mitchell realized that he could not employ such tactics to push the bill through the Senate. Many Democrats had told him of their strong opposition to the measure. Although he would gain their support in the end, Mitchell also could not look to Senate Republicans for immediate help. Dole, who considered parts of the bill bad for businesses in Kansas and across the nation, told Mitchell that he would not vote to cut off debate until major changes were made to the bill. Given the lingering pain from his bruising 1988 battle with Bush for the Republican presidential nomination, the brooding Dole could not be counted on to carry the burden for one of the White House's top priorities. But Dole helped Mitchell to get the talks started by calling White House Chief of Staff Sununu to urge that the administration participate.

The Bush administration, in effect, was Mitchell's only potential source for helping to find a secure and sizable bloc of votes. It also was the source of most of the technical information about the legislation, which had been flooding Capitol Hill. Bush designated Roger Porter his chief domestic-policy aide who had supervised the preparation of his proposal a year earlier, to take the lead in response to the Mitchell-Dole invitation. The Senators had requested that one official speak on behalf of the administration delegation during the talks in Mitchell's office. Despite some preliminary doubts by White House officials, it made sense for them to negotiate directly with Mitchell. Any deal ultimately would require presidential approval before it could pass the Senate or be enacted into law.

At that time, no one expected that the talks would last more than a few days. When Mitchell told the Senate on Thursday, Feb. 1, "We began, earlier today, a series of meetings in an effort to resolve differences over some aspects of the clean-air bill," he predicted that the bill would return to the Senate floor by the following Tuesday. Dole echoed Mitchell's forecast, adding that senators should expect late-night votes in the chamber during that following week.

But the bill did not reach the floor during the next week, nor during all of February. Instead, the Senate and White House teams spent the entire month consumed by private negotiations in Mitchell's office across a small corridor from the Senate chamber. They met around a long table that filled most of the Capitol's Room S-224, with its view looking directly up at the dome. In the next room was Mitchell's own office, with its view of the Washington Monument. For much of that time, the participants conducted a relatively unstructured discussion of dozens of details of the bill, making many important changes to the Environment Committee version. The meetings, which sometimes ran late into the night, were essentially three sided. Mitchell sat at one end flanked by Baucus, Chafee and other Environment Committee members. At the other end was Porter, flanked by Grady of the OMB, White House counsel Gray, the EPA's Rosenberg and Stuntz of the Energy Department. Along the sides of the table, which in normal times would comfortably seat about a dozen people, were other senators who filtered in and out of the negotiations to raise issues of personal interest. Behind all of the negotiators in a room of approximately 300 square feet were crammed a phalanx of aides, often numbering in the dozens. During the seemingly endless meetings, the air quality in Mitchell's office ironically would become so poor that the site was known as the "locker room." But Mitchell kept the talks in his room rather than move them to a larger area so that he could participate personally and keep closer control; in effect, he challenged the bill's opponents to an endurance test.

Mitchell's extraordinary leadership in handling the clean-air bill became a personal tour de force rarely matched in Senate history. "In my [12] years in Congress, I have never seen a member dedicate the attention and devotion to an issue as George Mitchell has done on clean air," said Sen. Tom Daschle, a South Dakota Democrat. "He has used every ounce of his energy to cajole senators and come up with imaginative solutions."

There were several keys to Mitchell's success in handling the clean-air bill. Most important was the knowledge of and commitment to the goals and details of the legislation that he had gained during two years as Environment Protection Subcommittee chairman. When he won the post of majority leader, he pledged that the legislation was a top personal priority. Mitchell also benefited from a stern discipline and mastery of timing that allowed him to push 99 often unruly and idiosyncratic senators and the White House toward a compromise. The meticulous Mitchell, who prefers not to deal in ambiguities, had strikingly manifested his personal control. He did not allow the many competing forces to deter him from his ultimate goal of reaching an agreement during the many long hours of negotiations. "I have the best-developed patience muscle in America," he told a few reporters in an environmentally sanitized S-224 following the bill's enactment. "It has been remarkably strengthened in the past two years."

At least as important to Mitchell's success on both the clean-air bill and other issues was his hands-on control of Senate operations. Although he was elected as majority leader after less than a decade of seniority, he quickly asserted himself in determining what the Senate would and would not do. During the same two-year period in which he was instrumental in helping Bush to score his biggest legislative win, for example, Mitchell also infuriated Bush and his aides by single-handedly preventing enactment of the president's chief economic initiative, a cut in the tax rate on capital gains.

Despite his great influence and public presence, Mitchell does not easily reveal himself to outsiders. He rarely engages in public displays of anger or joy. More often, he expresses emotion with a wry grin, a glaring frown or a nervous shake in his leg. With a reserved, sometimes severe, manner that is a caricature of his home state's laconic style, the Maine Democrat displays a judicial mien and caution that often mask his partisan effectiveness. Some observers have caustically labeled him "the judge." In informal conversation, Mitchell playfully welcomes the reference because, he says, it reminds him of a time when he had real power and did not have to accommodate 99 other individuals. He served as a federal district court judge for less than one year before he was appointed by Maine's governor to fill the Senate seat vacated when President Carter named Muskie as Secretary of State in 1980. Except for a surprising defeat in a 1974 bid for governor, he usually has been underestimated in his political career, including his come-from-behind victory in 1982, when he ran for his first full Senate term. His lawyerly demeanor served him well and gained him national attention in 1987 when Mitchell was a member of the Senate committee investigating the Iran-Contra affair. In those televised hearings, he invoked commonsense values during his aggressive questioning of former White House aide Oliver North.

Senators, aides and lobbyists who have worked closely with Mitchell have termed him single-minded, purposeful, self-contained and independent. More critical sources use descriptions such as aloof, calculating and passionless to describe his leadership, especially on the clean-air bill. "George is basically a judicious type of person," said Sen. William S. Cohen, the Maine Republican who has worked closely with his colleague. "But he would not be majority leader if he were not a partisan. . . . I say that in a positive way." Mitchell sometimes wields his partisanship so subtly that a novice would not know that his pockets had been picked. Although he does not wear his ideology on his sleeve, his views on most economic and foreign-policy issues have placed him in his party's liberal wing.

His intellectual skills have been evident in both his private and public activities. In interviews, Mitchell is articulate and polished, often speaking in whole paragraphs that make incisive points. He anticipates questions or responses by others, including fellow senators, and sometimes seems as though he is on a track 10 steps ahead of everyone else. He relies less on staff for advice than do most other senators, a reflection of both his analytical skills and his self-confidence. His independence occasionally has caused him problems; for example, other Democrats have complained that he has made mistakes or has failed to check with them or to understand their own political needs.

That assertiveness is not what his party expected when he was selected as majority leader. But Mitchell allies respond by pointing to the results, a record that produced very few political or legislative miscues during 1989–90. Some Democrats have been so impressed by his performance and by his skillful television appearances that they say he should run for president. But Mitchell has often said that he is not interested, at least not until 1996.

Probably the most important aspect in his handling of the clean-air negotiations was Mitchell's decision to cast his lot with the Bush administration, instead of with his erstwhile environmental allies. "He stood up and was counted on a lot of difficult issues because he wanted a bill," said Gray, the White House counsel. "It's not possible to do something in this area without taking on the environmentalists." Even when some Democrats said that Mitchell already had negotiated enough and that he should allow the remaining conflicts to be settled on the Senate floor, Mitchell insisted that he wanted to reach an agreement with the White House on the entire bill. The chief lobbyist for the environmentalists, Richard Ayres, differed not so much with Mitchell's view of the issues as with his undue eagerness to craft a compromise. "Mitchell just was not willing to roll the dice and take on the administration," said Ayres. "He could have presented it as a case of Democrats versus the administration and allowed the public to see that the Republicans were filibustering. . . . But our frustration was more with George Bush than with George Mitchell."

In his largely pragmatic approach to the clean-air debate, Mitchell said that his liberal critics had to decide whether they wanted to make a speech or to pass a law. After a decade of toiling on the issue and facing the reality that he had no choice but to deal with a Republican president, he applauded what was good in Bush's proposal, chiefly the acid-rain section, and he sought middle ground on other parts. The environmentalists wanted him to be their ally. But, as Mitchell often said, he wanted to get things done, instead of just making a statement. Mitchell reportedly told Sen. Alan Simpson of Wyoming, the number-two Republican leader and a close friend of Bush, that many of the details in the legislation were less important than passing a bill. Mitchell recalled, with obvious anger, that if environmentalists had not helped to scuttle his tentative deal with Byrd in 1988, the intensified national clean-up would have begun earlier.

Mitchell later rejected leading environmentalists' assessment that the negotiations resulted in too many concessions, contending that the Senate "got as strong a bill as was possible under the circumstances."

Ayres and his allies were "very much misinformed," Mitchell added, about the prospect that they could win Senate passage of a bill without the administration's support. "I told them that they had become too accustomed to glorious defeat and that they ought to try to become accustomed to winning," he said, with a bitterness that festered months after the enactment of the bill. Their opposition to his efforts produced for Mitchell what he called "the most difficult aspect" of the debate. Despite his praise for Bush's original support for a new clean-air law as essential to the eventual enactment, Mitchell also had some harsh comments for the president's role. "There was an enormous gap between his rhetoric on the subject and the position of his staff in the negotiations," Mitchell said. "Their whole thrust was opposition."

Like Muskie, his predecessor and one-time mentor, Mitchell took and returned flak from both sides of the clean-air debate. Despite their common experiences, however, Mitchell rarely called on Muskie for advice nor did Muskie impose himself. Mitchell later explained that the issues had grown "more complicated" since Congress last dealt with the clean-air law. From his own perspective, Muskie added, "I did not want him viewed as my instrument."

Mitchell, in effect, was the ringmaster of the clean-air negotiations in his office during February 1990. Although he often did not participate during the actual discussions, he set the daily agenda and he cracked the whip on all sides, urging them to reach a deal. Mitchell designated Baucus and Chafee as his chief lieutenants in charge of finding the delicate balance between defending the Environment Committee bill and gaining the votes required for Senate passage of a bill. The talks operated with a three-sided consensus: agreement could not be reached without approval from the Mitchell team, the White House and other senators advocating their own views. Once participants reached an understanding on the concepts, often after lengthy discussion, they ordered their aides to put the deal on paper and to draft legislative language. Those additional details sometimes would prompt further disagreement and compromise.

The month-long discussions in S–224 substituted for the deliberative bill-drafting that the Environment Committee failed to pursue in its day-long drafting of the clean-air bill in November 1989. It featured real bargaining and debate. Among the important differences was that the Mitchell-sponsored talks were conducted behind closed doors and they spurned roll-call votes that would have revealed the legislative divisions. Mitchell believed, probably correctly, that senators would not get down to hard negotiating on environmental issues so long as they were in the public spotlight, where they might make statements that a political opponent could use against them. The closed-door meetings also allowed senators to ask questions and to educate themselves about the often complex issues in a way that might have proved embarrassing in front of a television camera. "To resolve the differences required an explanation of the problem," Mitchell said. The informal talks could not have occurred, participants said, under the far more structured rules for Senate debate. At the very least, White House officials obviously could not have participated as equals on the Senate floor.

Aside from the political difficulties in gaining the votes to pass a bill, the complexities of clean-air legislation forced additional delay. Even when tentative agreement was reached on one section of the bill, nothing was final until the entire package was settled. In part, that was because requirements in one area of the bill could affect another section. Senators also wanted to hedge their support until they were certain that they would vote for the whole bill. The negotiations usually focused on one section at a time (automobile emissions or acid rain, for example), with the White House officials or other senators challenging the Environment Committee's proposal. One or all of the three negotiating groups often would meet separately for internal discussions and planning. "It was a very exhausting process," Gray said. "But we broke a political logjam."

The Bush administration's participation was especially noteworthy, not simply because of its unusual negotiating role. Aware of Bush's desire to be the "environmental president," his advisers shared with Mitchell a mutual interest in identifying positions that would build a Senate consensus. "Although it was a tough, protracted negotiation, there was never any rancor or ill will," Mitchell said. Despite their disagreement on some issues, Mitchell said that Porter was "a very good person to deal with in skillfully and honorably representing the administration." As happened earlier in the preparation of the initial White House proposal, the OMB's Grady played a critical role at Porter's side in identifying problems and finding a middle ground.

Bush had formally conveyed his concerns with the Environment Committee package in a Jan. 19 letter to Dole. He outlined his five "minimum tests for balance and reasonableness" in the clean-air package, which were similar to his earlier statements on the bill. The White House letter was prepared as leverage to "get us into the game," Grady said, and to offer suggestions to avoid a presidential veto. The letter emphasized that the $40 billion cost of industry compliance with the Senate committee version, compared with the administration's estimate of $19 billion for Bush's original plan, was unacceptable and would result in "a less competitive American economy with fewer jobs for American workers." He would not sign a bill that increased costs by more than $21 billion, Bush wrote. White House officials later voiced satisfaction that the negotiations achieved each of Bush's major goals.

But that satisfaction ultimately was not fully shared, either by environmentalists or business groups. Environmentalists objected to the back-room dealing, where they had little influence, as opposed to an open fight on the Senate floor, where they were confident that they could muster votes. In his obsession to pass a bill, they said, Mitchell was too willing to spare senators tough votes and to cave in on important details. Business lobbyists, on the other hand, complained that the Porter-Grady team was too eager to modify Bush's bill because of the administration's obvious desire for an agreement. The business critics also said that the White House relied too heavily on the EPA staff for its technical expertise and credibility on Capitol Hill. And they complained that because presidential aides were more interested in scoring a political success for their boss, they failed to understand the burden that they were imposing on corporate America. Sununu implicitly acknowledged this tradeoff when he reportedly told an angry group of business lobbyists at a White House meeting soon after the deal was reached, "Sometimes, you just have to punt."[1]

Details of the negotiations were tightly held by the participants. Very few news stories reported on the conflicts and agreements. Lobbyists stood in the ornate hallways and reception rooms outside Mitchell's office to catch glimpses and details from their allies in the room. On occasion, they would try to influence the outcome by quickly giving a message to a senator or an aide entering the room. The month-long negotiation was as much a marathon for the lobbyists as for the senators. When the talks continued into the night and the pizza delivery man arrived with stacks of boxes, the lobbyists would groan because they knew that they faced many more hours of hanging around to get a few valuable morsels of information. Meanwhile, empty pizza boxes piled up outside the normally majestic Room S-224.

Important parts of the bill were handled as negotiations within the negotiations. Probably the best example concerned acid rain. Despite some objections from the chief environmental lobbying groups, Mitchell and Baucus had mostly embraced the emissions-trading system that the Bush team had crafted with the Environmental Defense Fund. Democratic senators went along with Bush's acid-rain plan in large part because they recognized that their support was essential for convincing the White House to accept other parts of the bill. In other words, an old-fashioned horse trade had occurred. As happened at the White House, most of the participants made acid rain the engine that drove the clean-air bill. But the Appalachian and Midwest senators, led by Byrd, were not ready to give up their fight for national sharing of the region's costs for the acid-rain cleanup.

Although insiders knew that a consumer fee was not in the political cards, they sought alternatives that would spread the burden imposed on the users of high-sulfur coal. Their challenge was to find an acceptable form of indirect cost-sharing. Several senators and their aides offered a range of proposals: Howard M. Metzenbaum, an Ohio Democrat, outlined an expanded tax credit for utility plants using expensive scrubbers to clean the dirty coal. Others split on how many utility plants should undergo the required cleaning. It was left to Byrd, with extensive help from his aide Rusty Mathews, to craft and sponsor the formula that ultimately gained approval from the coal-state senators. Exploiting the novel system of allowances in the White House plan, they proposed to increase incentives to Midwest power plants by giving them more of the cashlike credits as a bonus to encourage their use of cleaner fuel.

Byrd coordinated the region's strategy during frequent meetings of senators at his Capitol office one floor directly below Mitchell's suite. These meetings amounted to preparatory negotiations among Midwest allies, prior to a summons upstairs to sit at one-third of Mitchell's table. In other words, in what has become typical Senate fare, they negotiated to prepare for negotiations to prepare for the bill's return to Senate debate. Although he was no longer the majority leader, Byrd's new post as chairman of the Appropriations Committee, which doles out federal money, gave him considerable political leverage within the Senate. After an informal head count, however, Byrd learned that the Senate would not pass his fee for reducing acid rain. Most senators outside his region were unwilling to support Byrd on a cost-sharing plan that would increase utility rates for consumers across the nation. In addition, White House officials pressured Midwest Republican senators not to join Byrd. Politically, this GOP group saw little benefit in siding with the heavily unionized high-sulfur coal companies against nonunionized low-sulfur interests in many of their own states.

With these factors in mind, Byrd's lieutenant and aide, Mathews—a shrewd back-room dealer whom one business lobbyist called a "genius"—prepared a plan that proved vital in allowing Byrd's group to salvage something from the acid-rain debate. His innovative plan doubled the credits available to many Midwest utilities. The scheme was based on an idea from Environmental Protection Agency experts that Mathews had seen in an early draft of the administration's emissions-trading system. In effect, Byrd's proposal would give the heaviest violators extra credits to help them buy their way out of their pollution.

Mathews initially won an unenthusiastic response. In large part, the senators and their aides failed to understand that local companies could use these allowances to trade with other utilities across the nation for the right to pollute. Like most lawmakers, they placed greater value on cash transactions. They had a hard time grasping the significance of paper documents having no fixed value and of economic theories for environmental cleanup. The administration's earlier agreement to a nationwide cap on acid-rain emissions, however, made the scheme for trading allowances far more attractive to heavily polluting power plants because the market system would increase the exchange value of the federal credits to the utilities that acquired them.

Mathews finally won a tentative go-ahead from Byrd and other coal-state senators by showing them a private study that concluded that his proposed changes in the allowances program would reduce job losses by half for local miners. With unpaid help from Charles Curtis, a private Washington attorney who had chaired the Federal Energy Regulatory Commission during the Carter administration, Mathews drafted his complex plan. Mathews unveiled the proposal at an informal Saturday-morning breakfast in the Virginia suburbs attended by many clean-air players. Mitchell adviser Kate Kimball gave him an unexpectedly positive response. Soon, the proposal would become known as the Byrd-Bond amendment; in addition to Byrd, the other chief co-sponsor was Sen. Christopher Bond, a Missouri Republican. The EPA's Brenner and other public and private experts provided the technical help to the drafters that they were also giving to other interested players.

While negotiations on other sections of the clean-air bill continued in Mitchell's office, Mathews refined his proposal and responded to comments from other Senate aides. Perhaps the most difficult job that Mathews faced was convincing the United Mine Workers to support any version of Bush's acid-rain plan. UMW officials feared that the allowance-trading system, which encouraged greater use of low-sulfur coal, could be the death knell for their already depleted union ranks. Following the setback of the 1988 Mitchell-Trumka talks and the elections of Bush and Mitchell, however, the miners had lost much of their political influence on acid-rain legislation. Despite heavy-handed threats and other pressure on Mathews from miners to pull back from his plan, Byrd faced little choice if he wanted to affect the Senate's acid-rain agreement.

Finally, in early February, Mitchell summoned the negotiators to discuss acid rain. When he asked at an evening session if Byrd or other Midwesterners were ready to negotiate, Mathews found himself in the embarrassing position of requesting a delay from the negotiators because his group had gone home for the day. But, in effect, the deal already had been informally accepted by the leading players. After preliminary discussions, the participants postponed discussion until the next day. Then, Byrd and his group agreed to present their plan formally in S-224. Porter and Grady went along, despite their reservations about regional benefits. Western senators, representing low-sulfur coal interests, said that they would make no further concessions to their Eastern brethren. Mitchell asked questions about how the plan for extra acid-rain trading credits would work. Brenner, as the official voice of the EPA, responded that the numbers in the Byrd-Bond plan appeared valid.

After committee aides spent several more days exchanging legislative language, the negotiators expressed their tentative agreement. In effect, they had cooperated to help Byrd and his region in a face-saving exercise that provided some artificial currency to salve their economic wounds. It was "crass political horse trading," a disgruntled participant later said. But the harsh reality was that the agreement was much less favorable for miners and users of high-sulfur coal than was the deal that Mitchell erroneously assumed he had sold to Byrd less than two years earlier.

Similar negotiations within negotiations, and negotiations within negotiations within negotiations, accompanied other sections of the bill. To get an idea of the task that was faced, refer back to pages 22–24, where the major topics of the bill are summarized. Each of those issues spawned coalitions, schisms, battles and reconciliations on issues both large and small. In an orderly committee process, a panel might take weeks or months to decide on the issues sequentially and eventually reach judgment. But these negotiations were far different than the usual procedure. Because the Senate floor had virtually shut down pending resolution of the clean-air bill, there was intense pressure to finish. But, as Mitchell knew, the bill could not be completed until a consensus was reached on the dozens of complex issues. In and around his office, those issues provoked fights between West Virginia and Montana; Detroit and California; OMB and EPA; business lobbyist and environmentalist; and Republican and Democrat. In almost every case, Senate ego was matched against Senate ego. Managing this mess required nearly superhuman intellect, organization and patience.

One relatively small test of Mitchell's patience came when a group of state regulators held a press conference to complain that the "back-room Senate deal [had] cut the heart out of the Clean Air Act's program for achieving healthful air quality." Although he did not say so publicly, Mitchell and his aides were especially angered that two of its instigators were Thomas C. Jorling, New York State's environmental commissioner, and Leon Billings, the ex-Muskie aide turned Washington lobbyist on environmental issues. Jorling, who remained a close friend of Billings, had been the chief Republican aide with Billings on the Environment Committee when it wrote the 1970 Clean Air Act. At a time when Mitchell was carrying water for the Bush administration because of the environmentalists' failure to garner enough Senate votes to defend their original package, the majority leader reportedly was infuriated by the attack from his erstwhile allies. "Mitchell felt that Leon and Tom had personalized their criticism by saying that he was selling us short," said a Washington lobbyist for the state regulators.

In spite of many problems and pressures, the Senate and White House negotiators sealed their agreement on March 1. Part of the deal was a vital commitment to oppose all amendments that might be offered on the Senate floor.

At a press conference in the Capitol, Mitchell hailed the compromise as "sound and comprehensive legislation that dramatically expands and strengthens the clean-air law." Trying to accentuate the positive, especially for reporters who had little idea of the extent to which the measure had been weakened during the previous month, Mitchell did not mention these cutbacks. He was trying to reassure environmentalists inside and outside the Senate that the committee bill had not lost its environmentalism. He faced an even more difficult task in reassuring Byrd.

Although he attended the press conference unveiling the agreement, Byrd conspicuously failed to give his full endorsement. "I want to commend all senators involved in the many long hours and days that have gone into producing this agreement," he said. "Though the agreement does not allay all of my concerns, it is a significant improvement over the bill reported" by the Environment Committee. But Byrd closed with an ominous warning: "I remain concerned about the significant job loss and dislocation that will result from even this compromise." In the next month, senators would learn how seriously Byrd took that concern.

Before Byrd could launch his offensive, however, the environmentalists struck. Rather than accept Mitchell's apparently accurate assessment that the agreement was the best proposal that could pass the Senate, they stormed the Senate floor with strengthening amendments. Under the terms of the S-224 deal, Mitchell and his negotiating partners were obliged to oppose all proposals. As a result, he was forced into the uncomfortable spot of manning the barricades against clean-air lobbyists and some of their newfound Senate allies, many of whom were more interested in playing to the grandstands with "pro-environment" votes than in trying to craft legislation. "These were cheap environmental votes," said an Environment Committee aide. "Mitchell responded like Michael Jordan managing the end of a basketball game. He knew how many senators he needed and how many he could release."

Two strengthening amendments, both of which were heavily lobbied, came closest to passing. One, sponsored by Sens. Timothy Wirth, a Colorado Democrat, and Pete Wilson, a California Republican, would have reimposed a mandatory tighter set of automobile-tailpipe emission reductions. The amendment was defeated, 52–46. The other, backed by Sens. Wilson and John F. Kerry, a Massachusetts Democrat, tightened the local smog-control rules that were of great concern to state environmental regulators. Mitchell won that fight, 53–46. But the margin in each case was wider than it seemed. Many Democrats wanted to prove their support to the environmentalists, who were keeping score in the gallery and would distribute the results to their contributors. Some Democrats were prepared to come to Mitchell's rescue if he needed their vote. "I tried to be with him on some issues," said Environment Committee member Joseph I. Lieberman, a Connecticut

Democrat. "But it was more important to me to keep my promises to Connecticut than to be a good soldier. In the short run, he was not happy."

Though Mitchell was disappointed that many of his Senate allies, including most Democrats on the Environment Committee, were voting against him, he considered his dilemma the price of the leadership, both in title and in fact, that he was providing. And the politics of posturing could be played by all sides. Among those voting for the Wirth-Wilson amendment was conservative Republican Steven Symms of Idaho, who had fiercely opposed the bill as too stringent.

On the final major clash in the Senate's clean-air fight, however, there was no funny business. When Byrd earlier refused to endorse the S-224 deal, he had left the door open to making one final effort to show support for his coal miners. His proposal, which amounted to an admission of failure to protect the miners in the acid-rain fight, was to guarantee for three years, to miners who could show that they had lost their job because of the new law, more than half of their salary and fringe benefits. The virtually open-ended commitment to an expected total of several thousand miners would cost as much as a half-billion dollars. Although Mitchell had been willing to consider some program to assist newly unemployed miners, that sum was far beyond what was acceptable to the Bush administration, which was promising a veto of the bill if the Byrd amendment was included.

Byrd had not pushed the issue during the earlier negotiations because he knew he lacked the votes behind Mitchell's closed doors. Once the bill reached the Senate floor, however, he engaged in an intensive and highly personal lobbying campaign, calling on more than two dozen senators in their offices to urge their support. Byrd's persistent pleas for support and his efforts to show his state's downtrodden coal miners that he was still their champion was at least as much a plea for his own continued influence in a Senate where he was no longer the formal Democratic leader.

Byrd, who was first elected to the Senate in 1958 and had become one of its most senior members, is a complex personality. In a chamber increasingly filled with wealthy senators who spend millions of their own dollars to win a seat but lack background or interest in parliamentary procedure, his acknowledged mastery of Senate rules and precedents made him a formidable adversary. During his 12 years, from 1977 to 1989, as the Senate's Democratic leader, he constantly curried the allegiance of many colleagues with favors big and small. On the other side of Byrd's legislative and political skills, however, was a hard-edged, sometimes prickly, personality that was difficult for many colleagues to penetrate. After his mother died, he was raised in the poverty of small West Virginia towns. He is a self-educated man with no undergraduate college degree, but who earned a law degree at the American University in Washington by studying at night while serving as senator. He prides himself on reading literary classics and on memorizing long passages of poetry or quotations from history.

To Mitchell, the stakes were just as high. He determined that he could not allow a relatively extraneous amendment to cause the collapse of a clean-air package over which he had labored for months and years. Despite the alarms, the budget cost and policy implications of Byrd's amendment were relatively small. The symbolic and political significance, however, amounted to a test of epic proportions. It was a showdown at the O.K. corral. The old majority leader faced the new in the dusty main street of the Senate floor. Although each of them struggled to keep the personalities out of the public story and to minimize the political implications, everyone sensed that Byrd was in effect challenging Mitchell over the leadership position that Byrd had formally relinquished a year earlier.

After more than a week of intensive maneuvering and a failed search for a compromise, a vote was called on March 29. Nearly all senators were seated in the hushed chamber. "This is a very important vote to the president of the United States," Dole said, concluding the debate. As the Senate clerk solemnly read the alphabetical roll call of senators, the tally was deadlocked. The final margin would be no more than a vote or two. Joseph R. Biden Jr., a Delaware Democrat, did not respond when his name was called. Suddenly, he disappeared into the Democratic cloakroom to take a phone call. Byrd had developed a close relationship with him during personal meetings in Delaware when Biden's wife and one of their children were killed in an automobile accident shortly after Biden was first elected to the Senate in 1972. On the telephone was Chief of Staff Sununu, who told Biden point blank that passage of Byrd's amendment would guarantee a Bush veto of the clean-air bill.

Biden returned to the chamber with minutes left and voted against the amendment. Then, during literally the last minute of voting, Symms of Idaho switched from support of Byrd to opposition. With reporters watching from the gallery, Dole had sternly lectured him on the floor that he should not allow his opposition to the bill to overshadow his loyalty to the president. The final tally was in: Byrd's amendment lost, 50–49.

Byrd, in pulling out all the stops to seek his victory, had secured the votes of more than two-thirds of the Senate Democrats. One sign of the highly personal nature of his effort was that he won the support of all but two of the 16 Democrats on the Appropriations Committee. The lone rebels on Appropriations were Patrick J. Leahy of Vermont, who is a Mitchell ally and neighbor, and Wyche Fowler of Georgia, whom Mitchell had made part of his leadership team in 1989. Even Burdick, the nominal leader of the clean-air bill as chairman of the Environment Committee, bucked Mitchell because the North Dakotan felt a higher loyalty to his other capacity as chairman of the Appropriations sub-committee on Agriculture. Of the 11 Republicans supporting him, six served on Byrd's committee and the other five were from Appalachian or Midwest coal states. But Mitchell, with the strong help of Dole and the White House, carried the day on the only count that mattered. In doing so, he assured the enactment of his greatest legislative victory and entrenched himself as the Senate's new leader. Byrd made it clear that he was greatly disappointed by the treatment he received from his successor. But the result, Baucus told an aide, was "a new day in the Senate."

When the Senate finally passed the clean-air bill, 89–11, on April 3, all sides issued statements of congratulations. But the wounds from the bitter battle clearly remained. "From the outset, I have made clear that I support the goals of this legislation," said Byrd, who voted against the bill. "Yet, I believe we also have a responsibility to pass legislation that is balanced. Legislation that pits one region of our country against another is unwise." For his part, Mitchell told reporters in his office the next day that "each Senator has a perfect right to vote as he or she wishes." But he added the unmistakable message that, without his own effort, the negotiators would not have accepted the Byrd-Bond amendment increasing the acid-rain allowances for utilities using high-sulfur coal. In effect, Mitchell clearly implied, he had worked hard to achieve Byrd's support but, as also happened in 1988, the two leading Democrats had been talking past each other.

Mitchell and Byrd would work together again on other legislation. But the rift between them would be a difficult one to heal.

Endnote

1. Paul Gigot, "Clean Air Game: Green Machine Routs Bush Team," *The Wall Street Journal*, April 6, 1990: A-18.

7

Special Interests
and Influence

★ ★ ★

Richard Ayres (*left*) led groups lobbying for tougher clean-air legislation, and Bill Fay (*right*) spearheaded a coalition of business
groups on the other side. By the end of the debate, they mostly were
observers.

Mitchell and Byrd staged their showdown in full view on the Senate floor and in front of cameras that beamed the vote to the public via C-SPAN. The corps of lobbyists, however, had little opportunity to savor the moment. Many were on double duty that day, also monitoring the clean-air discussions of the House Energy and Commerce Committee, which was meeting in the Rayburn office building.

The lobbyists probably would not have shared much credit for the Byrd vote or the broader bill, in any case. In the back corridors of Capitol Hill, most lobbyists are scorned as overpaid big talkers. For the self-confident lawmakers and their aides, they provide little useful information and more often are a nuisance. The lobbyists surely have become a larger and more polished group in the two decades since the first clean-air law. But their influence is more difficult to grasp or decipher.

Senate passage of the clean-air bill should have been a banner day for the nation's leading environmentalists. As lobbyists, however, they were bedeviled by their own political problems, both internally and with their congressional allies. On the opposite side of the lobbying fence, there was disarray among the business groups, which had fought for the past decade to prevent tougher clean-air requirements. In both camps, the tensions and ambivalence regarding the legislation demonstrated the perils posed by the growing sophistication in Washington's lobbying community and by the complexity of the policy issues that they faced. As interest groups made more use of diverse coalitions to strengthen their influence, they found themselves the victims of a dilemma similar to that for which they were criticizing the members of Congress. With their increased numbers, these lobbyists were caught between choosing the lowest common denominator or offending their would-be allies.

The lobbying over the Byrd amendment illustrated the problems faced by modern lobbyists. The amendment had split the environmentalists' movement as painfully as it had split the Democrats. In general, they supported Byrd. But in a one-page letter sent to Baucus and Chafee, one of the nation's largest environmental groups opposed the proposal. "The National Wildlife Federation does not support the Byrd amendment," wrote Jay D. Hair, the group's president. "We do not believe that environmental protection comes at the cost of jobs over the long term. While there may be short-term dislocations, we must be careful how we fashion worker protection in these instances." What seemed like a benign statement masked vigorous and loud disagreements both within the federation and within the broader camp of Washington's environmentalists.

Bill Klinefeltner was dumbfounded when he learned about Hair's letter opposing the Byrd amendment. As the wildlife federation's senior lobbyist on the clean-air bill, Klinefeltner had worked vigorously to protect miners. Not only had his boss openly undercut him, but Hair had failed to inform him of the move. Within days after Congress finished the bill, he vented his anger by quitting the federation's staff to become a lobbyist for the Teamsters union. Equally as surprised as Klinefeltner were the leaders of the National Clean Air Coalition, which was the umbrella group representing the array of private-sector environmentalists and including the Wildlife Federation as a leading member. The coalition, with the active participation of Klinefeltner, had earlier written its own letter in support of the Byrd amendment. "It is generally recognized that control programs designed to minimize the cost to consumer in high-sulfur coal states could have an impact on high-sulfur coal mine jobs," said Richard E. Ayres, the coalition's chairman. "Adjustment assistance and job retraining programs such as those established by the Byrd amendment can build a bridge between yesterday's job and tomorrow's opportunity." This view was consistent with the coalition's earlier support for an acid-rain plan that would continue to rely on major use of high-sulfur coal through an expensive program of coal scrubbing by power plants.

Even though the White House had said that passage of the coal-miners amendment would jeopardize the entire bill, the leading environmentalists dismissed that concern by saying that the jobs issue would not affect the outcome of the clean-air debate. But Mitchell, struggling to preserve support by Democrats for the non-Byrd package, was angered by what he considered the environmental lobby's cavalier attitude toward the Byrd amendment. "They were not helpful in this process," he told reporters on the day after the Senate passed the bill. "They spent most of their time attacking their friends."

A little-known reason for the coalition's dissension was that its membership included an important part of the organized labor movement. Some union leaders were distinctly unenthusiastic about the environmentalists, complaining that they placed a higher priority on "green" principles than on jobs. But the United Steelworkers of America, in particular, believed that both goals could be met. Its leaders felt a special kinship for their brethren in the coal mines and also felt pressure from other parts of the AFL-CIO. So, the steelworkers' legislative director Jack Sheehan, based on his past support, demanded the environmental coalition's loyalty on what he considered an issue of fundamental fairness. That Klinefeltner strongly agreed with him was not surprising. He had worked for the steelworkers for 13 years, as a field organizer and then as Sheehan's deputy, before he joined the Wildlife Federation.

What seemed a matter of fairness to the unions, however, seemed like a very bad idea to other parts of the clean-air coalition. Leaders of the Sierra Club, which joined the Wildlife Federation as the two largest national-membership groups within the environmental movement, strongly opposed the coalition's planned letter on behalf of the Byrd amendment. After lengthy review, however, they decided not to rock the boat.

On the other side of the fence, as the White House struggled to assure defeat of the Byrd amendment, an aide sought what seemed like the logical cooperation of the leading business coalition working on the bill. Even though some coal companies might informally welcome federal money for their employees, corporate lobbyists nearly always oppose legislation that they view as special-interest proposals for tax-payers to aid workers. But the administration got the stiff-arm from the leader of the Clean Air Working Group, which was the corporate front in the debate. "The White House tried to get me to oppose the amend-ment," Bill Fay said. "But I wouldn't, because I sympathize with labor when the government is putting workers out of a job." The business group, which may have seen the issue as a way to stay on good terms with Dingell, later supported a watered-down version of the jobs plan when the bill reached the House floor. The lobbying picture was thereby turned on its head: pro-environment lobbies supported its friends on an extraneous amendment that threatened to scuttle the entire clean-air bill while pro-business groups opposed it but without much conviction.

In the end, the mixed views within industry and among the envi-ronmentalists probably had little impact on the outcome of the Byrd amendment, which was fought largely inside the Senate. But the con-flicts and the positions taken by each side were instructive lessons in how lobbying has changed in Washington. When Congress passed the 1970 Clean Air Act, there were no groups such as the National Clean Air Coalition or the Clean Air Working Group. The environmental movement, which had recently organized Earth Day, barely had a Washington presence at all. Corporations represented their own inter-ests in a straightforward fashion, with little pretense that they were serving the public interest.

The increased use of lobby coalitions, made possible by tech-nological advances in communications and direct mail, which allow groups to stay in contact with large populations, affected how Congress handled the 1990 clean-air bill in several important aspects. Lawmakers and their aides were often deluged by information, both on paper and in visits from constituents. The coalition lobbying forced members to address not only hometown issues but also a broad array of clean-air problems. The acid-rain dispute, for example, generated nationwide lobbying even though the problem chiefly affected one region. And lobbying was waged far more widely. By 1990 grass-roots contacts of members of Congress by workers and political activists in their home districts and states, as well as by coalition representatives, often were as effective as the more traditional Capitol Hill visits by pinstriped company spokesmen. And lobbyists did more than just make visits; they also used skillful public-relations tactics, such as press conferences and advertising, to sell messages to broader audiences.

Because so much of the clean-air debate was conducted behind closed doors, lobbyists were under increased pressure to coordinate their activities with lawmakers sympathetic to their views. That gave a special advantage to the automobile industry, for example, during deliberations in the House Energy and Commerce Committee, where Chairman Dingell was virtually the chief strategist for his hometown industry. The increased lobbying also added pressure on members of Congress to decide how much time they should allocate among the interested groups. Groups that had made campaign contributions often had a better chance of eliciting sympathy inside congressional offices. Environmentalists complained that the political money from big business distorted fair consideration of the clean-air bill. If so, that may also help to explain why the steelworkers had a special influence within the Clean Air Coalition, most of whose other members were not campaign donors. The steelworkers—whose political action committee contributed $897,675 to congressional candidates in 1989–90—had better lobbying access to many congressional offices than did environmental lawyers.

In the case of the clean-air bill, unlike many other bills, the lobbying coalitions had plenty of time to prepare their arguments and techniques. The eight-year deadlock during the Reagan years allowed lobbyists both to identify approaches to their key issues and to target members of Congress who were potential supporters or opponents. The extended time also gave them an opportunity to react to claims from other participants in the clean-air debate and to offer fallback positions as needed.

Members of Congress who worked on the clean-air bill often referred to leaders of the environmental groups as "purists." They did not intend the label to be flattering. "We have lost a lot of time on this issue due to environmental purity," said Rep. Jim Cooper, the Tennessee Democrat. Another lawmaker who was usually an ally of the public-interest sector recalled former Vice President Hubert Humphrey's comment that "purists are honest but a pain in the ass." The fault of Majority Leader Mitchell was that he "was not 'religious' enough for the environmentalists," said a lobbyist who is an avid Democrat. Regardless of its members' tactics or personal skills, however, the National Clean Air Coalition was hard to ignore. It had the strength of numbers. Its leaders were smart. And they were persistent.

As the coalition's longtime chairman, Ayres was the leading organizer and spokesman for the environmental movement in Washington. His broad experience and understanding of the clean-air law made him a force to contend with throughout Washington's environmental community. Ayres also wore an important hat as the cofounder of the Natural Resources Defense Council, a Washington law firm that was created in 1970 to intervene in environmental cases and where Ayres continued to work as the senior attorney on the Clean Air Act Project. Because the federal tax law limits lobbying by NRDC and other tax-exempt organizations with a nonprofit status, Ayres and a handful of other environmentalists activated the coalition in 1975. Their initial focus was to influence what became the 1977 Clean Air Act amendments. At the time, Ayres was one of two active lobbyists representing public-interest groups on the clean-air issue. After the 1977 law, the coalition became largely moribund.

With Reagan's election and his appointment of environmental officials intent on sabotaging the federal clean-air laws, the Clean Air Coalition struggled to change its focus to the guerrilla tactics of political opposition. "We had a substantial impact in stopping the Reagan efforts," Ayres said. His group also acquired new members, such as the National Wildlife Federation and the Audubon Society, which had not been politically active during earlier fights over clean-air legislation. The staff at Audubon, in particular, proved especially adept at packaging stories and events that captured the sympathetic attention of many news organizations. These efforts created political pressures that not only stymied the Reagan administration but also laid the groundwork of national support for what became the 1990 law.

The coalition operated informally and never had a staff of more than three aides. But it provided a forum for often lengthy and heated discussions among its members, and it served as a focal point to coordinate their activities. Once the coalition agreed on a decision and on the tasks that were needed, the follow-up work was performed largely by its member organizations. The leading groups included NRDC, the Sierra Club, the steelworkers' union, the American Lung Association, plus the National Wildlife Federation and the Audubon Society. The Lung Association was especially important in giving the coalition both access to health data on pollution risks and credibility within the scientific community. Less active roles were played by Washington offices such as the National Council of Churches and the League of Women Voters. According to other environmentalists, however, the NRDC lawyers almost always were the dominant and most knowledgeable members of the coalition. That lawyerly approach may have accounted for the coalition's political shortcomings, a subject that generated much private hand wringing and many arguments at lengthy meetings among the often-warring factions.

Even among the attorneys of the environmental movement, there were marked divisions. Although the Environmental Defense Fund was a member of the National Clean Air Coalition, it had not been especially active before Dudek and Goffman began working with the Bush White House on their emissions-trading proposal for acid rain. The EDF's role created serious misgivings within the coalition and produced many tense meetings, during which Goffman reported on his negotiations. "The rest of the environmental community had deep, deep suspicion and in some cases overt hostility to what EDF was doing," Goffman said. "Some thought that we were trying to be buddy-buddy with the White House."

When Roger Porter, Bush's chief domestic policy adviser, invited leaders of the environmental groups to the White House in 1989 to urge their support of the president's proposal, many of them were pleased to be invited after their exile during the Reagan years. But they did not accept Porter's advice, which some viewed as an implied threat, that they should be more supportive. "Most environmentalists are not predisposed to support a Republican president," said Train, the Bush friend and ex-EPA boss who was president of the World Wildlife Fund. "That is probably understandable. But it is a mistake because it reduces their effectiveness in achieving their goals." One participant at the meeting defended the groups: "We did not have much influence at the White House, anyway."

Train lectured the group at the White House meeting that it was a mistake for them not to give more credit to Bush. "I warned them that they should be very careful not to paint themselves into a political corner for being so critical of the president," Train said. "I think that some very sore feelings resulted at the White House toward the environmentalists. John Sununu told me that they had lost their entree into the White House." In a 1990 Earth Day speech, Train said that his fellow environmentalists are too often "perceived as negative, antagonistic, overly demanding and unwilling to recognize the validity of other concerns." The resulting image, he added, "is surely a disservice to our environmental goals."

Even many Democrats remained unhappy with the environmentalists' operating style after the debate concluded. "They were very much misinformed," said Senate Majority Leader Mitchell. For him, he added, the most difficult aspect of the entire bill, was fighting off "pro-environment" amendments during debate on the Senate floor. "I was pissed off that the environmentalists were so suspicious of us," said Rep. Sharp of Indiana, an important Democrat on the House Energy and Commerce Committee. "In fact, some of their lobbyists played a duplicitous game, playing off one member against another. Although they were a force in the debate, they did not distinguish themselves."

Chairman Dingell was even blunter. "I hold them in very low esteem. Their lack of competence, integrity and decency was obvious for all to observe." When the bill was finally enacted, he added, the environmentalists were reluctant to lose their platform in Congress. "They were like Irishmen at a wake. They wanted to keep the party going forever."

The Clean Air Coalition undeniably played a major role in shaping the 1990 law. Its views on specific provisions were carefully considered by both friend and foe. But it may well be that its influence peaked when Bush unveiled his proposal. "Any lobbying group starts to lose power when the inevitability of passage comes into play," said a veteran Washington-based environmentalist. "At that point, the proposal becomes vulnerable to many other forces that can radically change its contents." Viewed from this perspective, the environmental lobby played its most important role during the Reagan years, first by helping to defeat weakening legislation and then by gradually building public support for a stronger law. By 1990, when the clean-air bill was at the top of the agenda for Washington power brokers, the environmentalists had been pushed toward the sidelines.

Ayres' coalition was not the only group working for strong clean-air legislation. The conflicts and jealousies among the environmentalists showed that like-minded lobbyists can come in many forms and take varied roles.

Playing a low-profile lobbying role on behalf of a major part of the clean-air bill was the Alliance for Acid Rain Control. Its leaders played much more of an insider's game and were largely ignored or dismissed by their presumed cohorts at the Clean Air Coalition. The alliance was created in 1985 by a dozen governors from Northeast and Midwest states who had grown unhappy with the failure of the National Governors' Association to break its deadlock on acid-rain control. Its board of directors is made up mostly of these bipartisan governors, whose states pay dues to keep it running. Fortuitously, one of the two governors chiefly responsible for creating the alliance in 1985 was the then-governor of New Hampshire, John Sununu. As it turned out, Sununu later intervened at crucial moments in the congressional bargaining to support the Alliance's efforts after he became White House chief of staff. In contrast to the environmentalists who backed steps that would have hiked utility costs for consumers, the Alliance supported the Bush administration's goal of keeping down the costs of the acid-rain proposal. Its leaders, for example, opposed two items to save jobs of coal miners: mandatory coal scrubbing by utilities and the Byrd amendment.

Ned Helme, the group's executive director, also worked closely with Energy and Commerce Committee members to derail efforts that would have benefited Great Lakes states whose utilities were fueled by high-sulfur coal. "My strategy was to attach myself to certain members and, in effect, to serve as their staff to provide expertise and lobbying," Helme said. "We could offer them high-level access to the governors and to Sununu." Rep. Cooper of Tennessee, who sponsored the Alliance's initial acid-rain control proposal, became its prime advocate on the committee. With Bush's proposal partly drawn from that plan, Cooper felt gratified that he eventually prevailed in the House although he won little public credit. "None of the main environmental groups endorsed our proposal because they had already backed a weaker bill by Reps. Waxman and Sikorski," Cooper said. "That made me quite cynical about them. But it would have been hard for national groups to tell their members that they were changing their minds."

Another important group favoring stronger clean-air policies was the Washington office of STAPPA/ALAPCO—acronyms for organizations representing nearly 300 state and local clean-air regulators. Many of these officials wanted a stricter federal law that would increase their leverage over their own governors and state legislators in challenging local polluters. "Our members have the primary responsibility for implementation of the Clean Air Act," said Bill Becker, the group's executive director. "We have pushed for a more prescriptive federal law. Air pollution doesn't respect state boundaries." After encountering obstacles in trying to influence Mitchell's Senate negotiations, the state officials displayed more effectiveness during the House bill drafting. Although the local groups were not a formal part of the National Clean Air Coalition, they occasionally worked together and shared goals. "Becker and the state regulators are the big, new emerging voice of expertise on the clean-air law," said a veteran environmental lobbyist. "These are the people who are working in the trenches across the nation."

During most of the Reagan years, businesses that opposed extension of the clean-air law could sit back and depend on Congress and the White House to tie themselves in knots. That confidence eroded in December 1987, when Waxman and his allies won their unexpected victory in the House over Dingell on the largely technical dispute over extending the deadline for the 1977 Clean Air Act. The outcome shocked the business groups, which had worked with Dingell to lobby House members and were confident that they would prevail. Having gained from the conflict a clear sense of the two sides' relative strength, knowledgeable members of Washington's corporate community realized that enactment of a new law had become a foregone conclusion. Now, they faced a challenge of damage control.

About a week after the House vote, a worried Dingell summoned more than a dozen leading corporate lobbyists to his Capitol Hill office. "He was very frustrated by industry's inability to influence the vote," said one of his guests. "He said that he needed better help from business interests if he was to prevail when the House had a full-fledged debate. And he said that we had not done as good a job as had the environmentalists."

The lobbyists got the message and in January 1988 incorporated the Clean Air Working Group. That organization, whose members were mostly Washington representatives of industrial firms and trade groups, had met informally each week since 1981. It had no staff or office. Its chief focus had been acid-rain proposals. Setting up this kind of industry wide coalition had become a frequent practice for the business community in the 1980s: It encouraged the sharing of information and the forming of a united front. But a big problem was that these groups often failed to assign final responsibility to anyone. "Dingell was right," said Bill Fay, who had participated in the group as a National Coal Association vice president. "Industry had done a horrible job. Unlike the environmentalists, who were speaking in harmony, industry had many voices."

Once the Clean Air Working Group members agreed to intensify their activity, they named Fay as their executive director. Like the environmentalists' coalition, CAWG's staff never exceeded three aides. Instead, it relied on the resources and membership of other business groups in Washington, including both general-interest organizations such as the Chamber of Commerce and the National Association of Manufacturers as well as industry-specific groups like the Motor Vehicles Manufacturers Association and the Chemical Manufacturers Association. Its membership reached nearly 2,000 at the peak of the legislative battle. On some issues CAWG increased its lobbying muscle by cooperating with representatives of organized labor. The United Auto Workers, for example, worked in tandem with the auto industry to emphasize concerns about job losses in Detroit. Earl Mallick, who supervised the Washington office of USX (formerly known as U.S. Steel), was CAWG's chairman.

Fay divided CAWG operations into roughly 10 separate teams handling the key clean-air issues. Each team was headed by a lobbyist whose company was directly affected by the issue. After the lead companies developed a proposed position for CAWG, other lobbyists typically offered their own suggestions. CAWG sought unanimity, according to Fay, and tried to accommodate the concerns of each of its members. Part of its goal was to discourage individual companies from cutting their own deals with the environmentalists or members of Congress who pushed a divide-and-conquer strategy. Its weekly meetings, usually attended by more than 100 corporate lobbyists, often featured freewheeling discussions between different industry groups. This format contrasted to the environmentalists' coalition, where most participants viewed the bill more as generalists.

The consensus approach by business often produced a lowest-common-denominator solution that was not very effective during the debate, especially as congressional staff tried to resolve nuances and technical differences. At other times, said a Republican aide who worked with the business groups, "some businesses went their own way." The principal case where CAWG members failed to compromise among themselves was a dispute between automobile and oil companies as to which industry should bear responsibility for more efficient service-station pumping of gasoline. In that case, Congress ultimately decided to impose some burden on each industry. The auto manufacturers were required to change to a more sophisticated on-board refueling system that captures evaporating emissions during refueling; the oil companies had to comply with rules for an improved fuel-pump delivery system.

When the legislative action was at a fever pitch, CAWG responded by creating an operations base at the Quality Inn three blocks from the Senate office buildings. With a bank of 25 telephones and with computers to coordinate information and its activities, the "boiler room" had all the trappings of a high-powered political campaign. The cinder-block room also served as headquarters for the lobbyists' daily late-afternoon meeting to map tactics.

Like their environmentalist counterparts, CAWG members actively promoted their cause with the news media and the general public. Fay and some of the group's members toured 25 cities across the nation to brief local editors and reporters about the activities in Washington that might affect them. The CAWG officials also participated frequently with spokesmen for the Clean Air Coalition in forums such as radio talk shows or community debates. And Fay hyped his efforts with reporters for national news organizations, including frequent press releases on the latest developments and assistance to reporters and editorial writers handling a piece of the overall story.

Despite criticism that he sometimes glibly oversold his case or conveniently overlooked legitimate environmental problems, Fay's work generally won praise for bringing his clients' problems to the attention of Congress. Dingell, whose top committee aide John Orlando often met with Fay as a tool to communicate with the business community on the bill, was pleased with the result. "It was important to keep the business coalition unified," he said. "Bill Fay did an extraordinarily good job." A Senate Democratic aide on the Environment Committee agreed: "The environmentalists were incapable of responding to CAWG's effectiveness in getting its constituents to talk to senators."

Individual companies welcomed the coordination provided by CAWG. But when the legislative push intensified, the more successful lobbyists understood that they could not rely on the industrywide group to defend their own, more specific interests.

Perhaps the most effective advocates were those representing the auto industry, according to several lobbyists. "They did their work and we often saw them on the Hill when no one else was there," said a lobbyist for the clean-air coalition. "They came out smelling like a rose. Although the industry will complain, the standards in the bill were already being set in California." The auto lobbyists surely benefited from the well-placed assistance of chairman Dingell; though he sometimes took steps affecting them without seeking their advice, they apparently took nothing for granted. First, the auto manufacturers worked to adopt a unified approach for the industry. By also working, for example, with the UAW and with the oil companies on various issues, they enhanced their own leverage and made sure that they did not become the chief target of legislators, as happened in the 1970s. That industrywide cooperation, however, may have had a downside later in the debate when Detroit and Dingell joined the oil industry in resisting clean-fuel requirements that auto lobbyists could have cited as a rationale to reduce the burden on their own firms.

The utilities industry probably won the booby prize for the least effective lobbying. Some of its problems, in retrospect, were inevitable, once Bush and Congress agreed on a ceiling for acid-rain emissions from power plants. That created an internal zero-sum competition among the utilities for the right to pollute. But the industry increased its vulnerability to the tough controls that were slapped on its operations by refusing to take the threat seriously until it was too late, according to congressional aides and other lobbyists. The Edison Electric Institute, which is the industry's lobbying arm, also failed to resolve internal differences between its so-called "dirty" facilities and its "clean" members who already had begun to reduce their emissions. In part, industry leaders appeared to believe that they could continue to go their own way and assume that their longtime allies, Byrd and Dingell, would protect them. But they failed to appreciate the changes created by the arrival of Bush and Mitchell on the scene.

"The utility lobbyists would not even give us information about their operations, let alone consider support for alternatives," said an aide to a House Democrat representing some of the most vulnerable dirty plants. "They felt that they could not trust us with the information. And they continued to insist that there was no acid-rain problem." Some large utilities eventually scrambled to protect themselves by hiring their own lobbyists to plead their separate cases. But, said a veteran Washington lobbyist, "the result proved the axiom that divided industries do badly on Capitol Hill."

A former Energy and Commerce Committee member concluded that many businesses took an approach to the clean-air debate that sought to avoid risks. "Most Washington representatives find it hard to explain to the CEO at their corporate headquarters why it was important to agree to limited changes now in order to avoid more sweeping changes later," said Tom Tauke. "That is short-sighted but it is the way that business deals with Washington." Tauke became a Capitol Hill lobbyist after he lost in 1990 when he sought a Senate seat from Iowa.

Although CAWG and the last-ditch lobbying operations helped industry to weaken some proposals that they found the most inflexible, they were operating mostly on the defensive during the fight on the 1990 Clean Air Act. "It took industry a long time to realize that we had nowhere else to go to reduce pollution," said Rep. Al Swift of Washington, who was among the Energy and Commerce Committee Democrats warning that the costs of cleaning the air would have to be widely shared. "All of the belching smokestacks and the dirty tailpipes are gone."

When it came time for the Energy and Commerce Committee to confront the clean-air bill, these lobbyists also would quickly learn that the game would be fought inside the panel. In the end, the lawmakers' endurance and their deal-cutting skills would prove at least as important as their lobbying connections.

8

Behind Closed Doors

Dave Finnegan (*center, in shirtsleeves*) used deep knowledge of clean-air policy, close ties to Rep. John Dingell and a hard-nosed style to craft legislative details during round-the-clock staff negotiations.

Congressional sages invoke an old adage in comparing the Capitol's two legislative bodies. The Senate is for show, they say; the House is for dough. Spine-tingling drama, though infrequent, more often appears on the Senate floor. But when you want to get down and dirty into the muck of legislation, follow the House. More often, the decisions made there draw the fine lines separating winners from losers once new laws take effect.

It was one thing for senators and White House officials to set into motion a new clean-air law. Much work remained unfinished and many conflicts unresolved, however, in writing its often obscure details, especially in light of its haphazard handling by the Senate. Trying to make sense of the stew was the challenge facing the House.

Mitchell and President Bush had prepared the policy framework for expanded clean-air enforcement. They also had provided equally vital political support for achieving that goal. For legislative aficionados, those steps would only begin the task. The heart of the process often rests in the minutiae, where such trivial matters as choosing between similar words and phrases can in fact dictate winners and losers or affect huge sums of money at the local level. Likewise, the precise crafting of the statutory language can determine whether federal regulators ultimately have the enforcement tools to achieve the law's goals a decade or two later. By that time, most of the legislative drafters will have left Capitol Hill and will no longer be accountable for their deeds.

Here is where the House often eclipses the Senate. Because most of the 435 House members and their staff have fewer committee assignments and narrower responsibilities than do their 100 Senate counterparts, they typically have more time to acquire and exercise the technical know-how. In the Senate, a single aide often becomes the preeminent expert and wields vast influence on a subject. But the House tends to have several members and aides who understand the nuances of a bill and can compete with each other for dominance. That had become the case at the Energy and Commerce Committee, where the combination of Henry Waxman and John Dingell had been for several years the irresistible force and the unmovable object on clean-air legislation. Each was among the most effective lawmakers on Capitol Hill because he understood power and how to use it. Legislative success demands a patience to play for the long haul and the relatively rare moments when the opportunity for action is ripe. It also requires a feel for the institution and the ever-shifting policy boundaries within which lawmakers operate.

During their nearly decade-long struggle over a new clean-air law, the Dingell-Waxman rivalry had produced severe tensions and near-paralysis at the Energy and Commerce Committee. Dingell had chaired the full committee since 1981. Waxman had chaired its Health and the Environment subcommittee since 1979. The two titans had made some progress in resolving their differences, notably in their October 1989 agreement on acceptable tailpipe emissions. And the Democrats' Group of Nine on the committee created a new force seeking the hard-to-find middle ground. But serious problems remained as the House prepared for the stretch-run of the clean-air bill. The big difference in early 1990 was that the insiders knew that the legislative timing was right and that they could not ignore the pressures. This time, they were playing for keeps.

Knowledge and skill are not the sole determinants of legislative success. Seniority, geography and procedural dynamics are among the other factors that can play a critical role. When a single lawmaker can marshal all of those resources, he gains an advantage that is difficult to overcome. And when that politician also has an intimidating physical manner, the combination can prove unbeatable. Meet Dingell of Detroit, the self-styled personification of legislative power, who was first elected to the House in 1955. Some of his colleagues call him "Big John" or "Dirty Dingell," tributes to his hulking presence and his protection of his constituents. Most know that it is wise to get out of the way when he has determined what he wants. Staring down from the wall of his congressional office are the imposing heads of several large animals that he has shot as a hunter.

The notion of his toughness is an arrow in his legislative quiver. Ask Rep. Jim Scheuer of New York, who ranks just below Dingell as the second-senior Democrat on Energy and Commerce. Many years ago, Scheuer allegedly broke his word to Dingell on an important bill dealing with automobile fuel-efficiency standards. Ever since, Dingell has made Scheuer an outcast on the committee, depriving him of a sub-committee chairmanship. And when junior Democrat Terry Bruce of Illinois challenged Dingell on an important part of the clean-air bill, the chairman was willing to prevent Bruce from participating in vital negotiations as a sign of his disfavor. As a close friend wryly commented, "It's not complicated what happens when someone fails to keep his word to Dingell." For that reason, the chairman has been especially effective in winning the support of junior Democrats on important committee votes. He had secured their allegiance, whenever possible, as a price for granting them a highly coveted seat on one of the most powerful House committees. "He is a skillful legislator," said a Senate aide who has watched Dingell closely for many years. "He is as devious as hell. And he demands loyalty."

Dingell is not afraid to use all of the tools at his command, even if his position is relatively weak. A *National Journal* cover story, an enlarged copy of which Dingell hung on his office wall, depicted him as a chess master who "thinks ahead a dozen moves, places each piece with exquisite precision, uses pawns and is not reluctant to offer a sacrifice if it advances his game."[1] When the Bush administration was preparing its clean-air plan in the spring of 1989, for example, Dingell's staff spread the word that the chairman would sponsor the president's bill so that he could influence some of its important details. Never mind that an important section mandating the use of alternative fuels for automobiles was totally unacceptable to Dingell. He has mastered the approach of defining victory on his own, sometimes selective, terms. He also knew, especially in light of his unexpected setback in 1987, that he could not necessarily count on winning a showdown vote on the House floor. That meant that he had to use all of his resources to resolve controversial issues in the committee, where he could wield his authority to reward or punish members.

Oddly, given the vast scope of his committee's legislative jurisdiction, Dingell's chairmanship has featured the passage of relatively few major bills. In part, that is because Republicans have held the White House since 1981, when he took the gavel at Energy and Commerce. They usually have had little interest in expanding the purview of federal regulation, which is the centerpiece of the Dingell committee's power. But the GOP presidents' skepticism of, and efforts to eliminate, government controls did not stop him from overseeing executive branch operations with hearings, at which Dingell was renowned as particularly fearsome. With his background as a former county prosecutor and with his assertion of congressional prerogatives, Dingell conducted frequent investigations to ferret out corruption and malfeasance in government. He also has held well-publicized hearings that attack wrongdoing in the private sector, ranging from excessive billing by defense contractors to phony research by university professors.

Even with his posturing and occasional bully tactics, Dingell was shrewd enough to avoid locking himself into a corner where other

Democrats could accuse him of killing the clean-air bill. In the free-wheeling world of internal Democratic politics, Dingell realized that he dared not jeopardize his chairmanship because of either his conflicts with Waxman or his need to protect the auto industry.

A vital element of the Dingell persona on the clean-air bill was David Finnegan, his longtime aide on environmental issues, who worked so closely and developed such a trust with the chairman that he became something of an alter ego. During more than a decade of work on the clean-air law, he had gained an intimate knowledge of clean-air issues and a dogged determination to protect Dingell's interests, especially with the law's impact on the automobile industry. Finnegan's desk in the committee's office was covered by stacks of official studies and data from lobbyists. He could locate a sheet of paper that seemed to have been buried for months and could cite details in these reports virtually from memory. By many accounts, he was the best-informed congressional aide working on the clean-air bill.

But Finnegan did not get along well with aides to several committee Democrats, especially those working for Waxman. Like the relationship between the two principals, their staff's antagonisms were so deep seated that other House aides—and, occasionally, other lawmakers—were forced to intervene to enforce proper behavior. Finnegan, who, like his boss, could use his hefty physique to intimidate, occasionally had angry clashes with his adversaries, especially those who were as feisty as he. "It helped to improve decorum when I and other members were there to temper and focus the debate," said Rep. Eckart of Ohio, who was often a Dingell ally. The staffer with whom Finnegan developed the closest relationship on the clean-air bill was Chuck Knauss, who was the Energy and Commerce Committee's chief Republican aide on the bill. Finnegan and Knauss often worked in tandem, becoming virtually inseparable during the final critical months of congressional debate.

Finnegan's power occasionally caused jealousies among other aides. But Dingell gave him wide discretion to advocate his views, with instructions to "do no harm" for the chairman or his interests. Because of his long experience, his knowledge and his sometimes devious manner, Finnegan took on a larger-than-life role that made him a central player throughout the drama.

"In the early days of the clean-air fight, he obfuscated and delayed with long questions to witnesses, which we called Finnegrams," said a Democratic member on Energy and Commerce who occasionally clashed with him. "Dave was the omniscient staff person. He did what

Dingell wanted. . . . Dingell seldom trusted any staff other than Dave Finnegan on the clean-air bill." As Dingell's surrogate, he became a one-man show; through him circulated all ideas and reactions from committee members and other aides. By the end of the debate, the zealous Finnegan had become so exhausted and overworked that Dingell feared he might have a heart attack and ordered him to share some of his duties with other aides to the chairman. He worshipped at the altar of John Dingell, not any outside group. In return, Dingell treated him as a close friend and confidant.

Finnegan started on Capitol Hill in 1969, working for several House committees until he joined Dingell's staff in 1976. He had earlier served as an Interior Department attorney, where he had dealt with Dingell for several years on fish and wildlife legislation. Finnegan considers it a badge of honor that he was forced to leave the department in 1969 by a young GOP aide named James Watt, who returned in 1981 as Secretary of the Interior and the arch-enemy of environmentalists.

As Dingell's aide, Finnegan worked more closely with business lobbyists than with environmentalists. Although he developed bitter antagonisms with some committee members with whom he clashed, he also had solid friendships and respect on both sides of the political aisle. "Finnegan could be difficult to deal with," said a Senate Environment Committee aide. "He had to make a difficult transition from a position of helping Dingell stand in the doorway to one of responding to pressure to pass a bill. I often empathized with him because he had to hold together so many different parts of a coalition."

Dingell also received important strategic advice from an unusual corps of high-powered political advisers, which he created solely for the 1990 conflict. A group of about 10 veteran congressional insiders met informally with the chairman at his office approximately twice a month to assess his legislative options. Half were from his own committee and personal staff and the other half were lobbyists, some with longtime connections to Dingell. They acted like a presidential "kitchen cabinet," said a Dingell aide who was part of the group, which had no working name. Among them were high-powered Washington lobbyists whose separate clients included the "Big Three" auto companies. Ken Duberstein, who had been President Reagan's final chief of staff, lobbied for General Motors. Howard Paster, who had been a Senate Democratic aide, represented Chrysler. And Tom Ryan, the former chief aide to Dingell's committee, advocated the interests of Ford. Although there was nothing improper about the arrangement, its sessions gave the auto companies an unusually close view of an influential lawmaker's opinions and options.

When they met to discuss Dingell's plans, "they were not acting as representatives of the auto industry, at that time," the chairman said. Instead, they tried to help Dingell protect his own political and legislative interests, mostly by helping him to find a way to keep control of the debate and to pass a clean-air bill. "They were immensely helpful and had some of the best legislative skills available," Dingell added. Their advice also helped Dingell direct Finnegan on the technical details of the bill. Separately, his wife Debbie told Dingell that it was important that he pass a bill. Dingell emphasized that she gave this private counsel apart from her work at the Washington office of General Motors. But she echoed his advisers' view that "if we did not begin to get a bill, we may end up with a vastly worse bill for the Midwest and its industries," he said.

Dingell and his team knew that effective use of the clock could be as essential to a successful legislative strategy as it is to a football quarterback in a two-minute drill. After Waxman's subcommittee voted its approval of the clean-air bill in early October 1989, Dingell waited until the following March to begin serious work in the full committee. By that time he was aware that the Mitchell–White House deal had all but eliminated the possiblity of deadlock in 1990. Factors accounting for the delay in the House included a two-month congressional recess, Dingell's decision to give himself and his allies time to get their plans in order, and some failed attempts at deal making on acid rain. But there also was a psychological tactic at play. The chairman, by scheduling and then canceling meetings to debate the bill, left the clear impression that he was using the reins of power to assert control of the committee. Later in 1990, he and his staff would again exploit a deliberative pace to increase fears that House and Senate conferees would run out of time to resolve their differences.

When Dingell and Finnegan finally decided to move ahead in committee, they used a variation of Mitchell's closed-door approach to force a resolution of the conflicts. Initially, aides to committee members did most of the negotiating over intricate issues. House staff played a much greater role in crafting the details than they did in 1977, Waxman said, because the discussion had become "too technical and time-consuming" for members with many other responsibilities. In addition, the growth in the House payroll had increased the number of aides. Their lengthy sessions often ran late into the night in Room 2123 of the Rayburn House Office Building, the committee's large hearing room. Like a college dorm in the week before final exams, the room had all the ambience that (seemingly obligatory) pizza boxes and Chinese-food containers can bestow.

In what became a more inclusive and rambunctious version of Mitchell's "locker room," the dozens of aides who met around the long table first tried to settle differences that the 43 committee members lacked the patience or expertise to address. They operated under conditions that often drove them to exhaustion. After meeting in smaller groups during the days and performing their other chores, the aides typically would assemble at 6 p.m. "By midnight, those who remained were the ones who had to be there," said Rep. Mike Synar, an Oklahoma Democrat. Like Reps. Eckart and Swift, Synar delighted in his experiences as a "baby-sitter" to the staff negotiations. "Our role was to prevent name-calling," Synar said. "It was like when I was a parliamentarian for a model United Nations, making sure that no one would be smashed." They were trying to assure fairness by "preventing people from saying that they had a 'take it or leave it' position or from trying to reopen old issues," Eckart added. These facilitators also encouraged compromise by serving as brokers who shuttled from one side of the room to the other carrying ideas scribbled on the back of an envelope. "We were trying to maneuver them to the middle," Eckart explained.

First on the agenda in the staff negotiations was the all-encompassing section of the bill setting schedules to enforce local air-quality standards. In discussing what rules to apply to areas that were in non-attainment, the staff focused on a hybrid proposal. It combined features of the plan initially prepared by the "Group of Nine" Energy and Commerce Committee Democrats plus the plan of Waxman and Lewis, his Republican clean-air ally from California. That plan, which had become more complex with each new version, set a schedule of dates and a sliding scale of five classifications for the dirtiest metropolitan areas to reduce local pollution emissions. At the most extreme, for example, the committee's bill gave smog-ridden Los Angeles 20 years to meet the new standards. The 41 areas in the "marginal" classification had three years to clean their air. One of the most difficult tasks that the drafters faced in this section was how to accommodate pollution from new industries that were critical to the nation's economic growth.

Although this title comprised the guts of the clean-air bill's enforcement power, it attracted less public attention than issues such as acid rain or alternative fuels. Many of these rules for local compliance were filled with highly technical language. But the new law, once enacted, would generate much controversy because it would affect a greater number of industries than did the 1970 law, which chiefly hit automobiles and large smokestack companies. The Office of Technology Assessment, an arm of Congress, had helped to convince key players in the clean-air debate that small businesses such as bakers, printers, paint shops and furniture makers must share the clean-up cost. "About 45 percent of all [pollutants] originate in small stationary sources producing less than 50 tons [of emissions] per year," the OTA concluded in a 1989 report. The use of currently available control methods would cut those emissions by one-third in five years, according to the study. That reduction would meet roughly two-thirds of the anti-pollution steps required in the dirtiest metropolitan areas.

Informing congressional aides and their bosses of the perils of pollution and the clean-up options was an important task facing the proponents of a new law. Although the outside lobbyists provided some assistance, their often conflicting claims were difficult to sort out. The Waxman team's ability to disseminate the data was one of the many ways in which they proved indispensable to passage of the Clean Air Act. Among their innovative tools was a thick series of "Clean Air Facts," more than a dozen primers on the major issues in the legislation. By sending these fact sheets to all 435 House offices during 1989–90, the Waxman team helped lawmakers cut to the heart of the controversies. They also were attempting to counter the problems resulting from frequent turnover of Capitol Hill staff advisers, many of whom have recently graduated from college and receive relatively low pay. "Most members have only a very general knowledge of this very technical stuff," a Waxman aide said.

Waxman, like Dingell, has wielded power through a combination of knowledge, patience and parliamentary skill. Unlike Dingell, he operates with relatively little bombast or intimidation. "Waxman—who stands five-feet-five and speaks in a quiet, unpretentious way—has managed to thrive even in the shadow of Big John—the six-foot-three [Dingell]," according to a profile of the Californian.[2] "Much of Waxman's success has come from combining long-range vision with persistence and a willingness to progress one small step at a time." And, unlike Dingell, who won the House seat held by his father, Waxman used more modern political techniques to build his political career.

Apart from their clashes on clean-air legislation, some of which reflected contrasts between their Detroit and Los Angeles constituencies,

Dingell and Waxman sometimes made a point of identifying issues where they agreed. Although they are from different political generations, both are activist New Deal Democrats who believe that government has a role to play in helping people. Dingell, for example, has regularly filed a national health-insurance bill when a new Congress convenes every two years. Waxman has adroitly used his Health and the Environment Subcommittee to expand federal health programs, especially those that aid the poor. "Waxman has blended strongly liberal views with an insider's appreciation of how the game is played on Capitol Hill," according to a profile.[3] His ability to increase funding for many health programs during the tightfisted Reagan and Bush presidencies has been a mark of Waxman's legislative skill. But the two Democrats have disagreed on issues other than clean-air policy. Dingell, as an avid hunter and National Rifle Association member, has strongly opposed federal gun control. Waxman, for his part, generally takes the side of southern California's television and motion-picture industries, which are also an important source of his campaign contributions.

As the son of politically liberal, Jewish parents who owned and lived above their grocery store in a poor Los Angeles neighborhood, Waxman became active in Young Democrats when he attended UCLA in the late 1950s. Contacts and friendships gained there eventually helped him to win a seat in the California Assembly in 1968, at the age of 29. During six years as an assemblyman, the young lawmaker quickly gained influence as chairmen of committees handling redistricting and health issues. Working with Howard Berman, who later joined him in both the Assembly and the U.S. House, Waxman also created a powerful political alliance in West Los Angeles that has served him well in both Sacramento and Los Angeles. With effective use of money, computers and campaign mailings, Waxman and Berman made innovative advances in identifying local supporters and building a multiracial network of liberal allies. The result allowed Waxman to win a House seat in 1974, where he quickly became a leader of the Watergate class intent on injecting new energy into the Democratic Party and on invigorating the House's archaic rules and seniority system.

Having used those alliances to secure his 1979 victory over old-guard Rep. Preyer of North Carolina to win the chairmanship of the Health and the Environment Subcommittee, Waxman moved quickly to establish his credentials on clean-air legislation. During the 1980s he introduced several bills and pressed his subcommittee for action. Although his unending struggle with Dingell produced little real success during the Reagan years, Waxman kept his nose to the grindstone. "In Congress, we have taken over 10 years to deal with problems that have only gotten worse," he said. "The need has long been abundantly clear but the political realities did not make it possible."

Although Waxman and his friends have suggested that he could become House speaker, his demanding work on the Energy and Commerce Committee limited his ability to develop a broader focus of issues and contacts. Compounding that problem was that his relentless push for environmental legislation earned him political enemies within the House, not the least of whom was Dingell. Those shortcomings contributed to what was an unexpected disappointment in June 1989, when Waxman made his first bid for a House leadership position. In a brief and late-starting campaign for the majority whip post that had been vacated when Rep. Tony Coelho of California resigned in the wake of controversy surrounding his personal finances, Waxman won little support and withdrew from what had been a four-candidate race. The message to Waxman was clear: he needed to stop operating chiefly as an advocate and to start demonstrating that he could be an effective legislator and consensus builder on clean air.

Waxman's eventual success in cutting deals on the clean-air bill, however, left some of his environmental allies unhappy. "He was driven more by the politics of succession to the chairman at the Energy Committee than by the issues," said a long-time lobbyist who has worked with Waxman. "He was concerned about showing that he could work with all factions at the committee, sometimes to the detriment of California." Although he benefited from a reservoir of goodwill among environmentalists, Waxman, like Sen. Mitchell, learned that compromise can anger erstwhile allies, even when he was convinced he was getting the best deal possible. "We should have criticized him more than we did," said another environmental lobbyist, referring to Waxman's compromises with Dingell on automobile emissions.

Although Waxman worked closely in crafting the policies and details of the clean-air bill, he shared with Dingell the need for creative and tireless aides who helped him maneuver through the legislative minefields. To take on Finnegan, Waxman had a team whose first-name initials led to the acronym PP&G. Phil Schiliro, Phil Barnett and Greg Wetstone were all young lawyers who became clean-air experts during the 1980s. Schiliro, the leader of the group and the top aide in Waxman's office, joined him in 1982. Barnett and Wetstone, lawyers on his subcommittee, both had worked with environmental interest groups.

Without the experience of a David Finnegan, the trio compensated by applying deep knowledge of the clean-air issues and deft forging of coalitions. "They understood the nuances and where changes could be made," Waxman said. "They had a large delegation of authority from me because I had confidence in their work." When the committee was deadlocked on the acid rain issue, for example, PP&G showed an unusual ability to work both sides of the issue: Wetstone met with one side and Barnett with the other in an effort to help the panel find a middle ground. Like Finnegan, they also attracted enemies. "Phil Schiliro is extremely political," said a House aide who has frequently battled him. "He is the evil genius behind Waxman. And he is very media-conscious." Although Schiliro and his two partners worked to develop favorable press coverage, their efforts focused on solving environmental problems and on federal-policy shortcomings more than they did on enhancing Waxman's personal role.

The Dingell-Waxman dealings caused continuing turmoil. As the House committee completed its bill drafting in March–April 1990, both players agreed to a tactical decision that would have a major impact on the House outcome. In the Senate, Mitchell believed that the divisions among Democrats had left him little choice but to allow Bush administration officials to participate as an equal partner in private negotiations on the bill. But his House counterparts strongly objected to granting such an outside voice in the handling of their legislation. To the surprise and dismay of some White House officials, the negotiating door was slammed in their face.

Several reasons have been offered for this decision. Perhaps the overriding factor was that House Democrats were unhappy with the role played by the administration during the Senate negotiations in February. "Chairman Dingell was worried about what EPA was doing" to push a relatively strong bill, said White House counsel Boyden Gray. Although he and his wife Debbie maintained cordial social relations with the Bushes, as shown by the five separate photographs of the foursome on the wall of his reception room, Dingell did not want to go so far as Mitchell in sharing control of the bill. And Waxman wanted to keep the administration out altogether because he feared that help from administration officials outside the EPA would strengthen Dingell's bargaining position. With Dingell cooperating closely with the committee's Republicans on many issues, the last thing that

Waxman wanted was to give him another partner to exploit the Democrats' splits. Waxman also was aware that White House domestic-policy chief Roger Porter had recently added Theresa Gorman to his staff to handle environmental issues. Previously, she had worked closely with Finnegan as the Energy and Commerce Committee's chief Republican aide on the clean-air bill.

What House Democratic leaders, led by Speaker Tom Foley of Washington, wanted was at least the appearance that their own party was unified. The contrast between Senate and House rules made it easier to attain that goal and less important that House Democrats satisfy their GOP colleagues. In the Senate, where there were only 55 Democrats, 60 votes were required to stop a filibuster. But in the House, the rules permit a one-vote majority to do practically anything it wants. The views of Dingell and Waxman covered such a broad sweep of the House that their agreement on a clean-air issue usually meant that enough of the 258 Democrats would go along to garner the needed 218 votes.

Additional factors made the 17 Energy and Commerce Committee Republicans far less influential on the bill than were Senate Republicans. Led by senior Republican Norman F. Lent of New York, who usually sided with Dingell on clean-air issues and did not seek an independent voice on the committee, they rarely acted as a separate bloc on the bill. Although many of them feared that the acid rain proposal and other parts of Bush's bill tilted too far toward the environmentalists, the Republicans were reluctant to challenge the popular president of their own party. They also wanted to lend some political support to his proposal. "Once Bush opened the door, many Republicans were concerned that Congress would go overboard," said Republican Tom Tauke. In other cases, such as rules affecting local areas, GOP members copied the Democrats in splitting along regional lines.

The Republican ineffectiveness also was a striking result of Dingell's ability to keep the minority party in line. On many other House committees, Democrats have largely ignored Republicans. But Dingell cultivated every vote on his committee wherever he could find it. In a highly unusual move for Congress, Dingell often attended and participated actively in strategy meetings of the committee's Republicans; many times, he was the only Democrat present. The information that he gained at those sessions undoubtedly proved useful to Dingell in counting votes on the committee and protecting his special concerns. The chairman has frequently praised Lent's cooperation and contribution. But given the sparse evidence that Lent independently sought to influence the clean-air bill, Dingell's plaudits have a self-serving tenor.

Ed Madigan of Illinois was probably the Republican on Energy and Commerce who best understood clean-air issues; he had the potential to be its most effective coalition builder. But because the coal-fired power plants in his district made it difficult for Madigan to support tough acid-rain controls, he was handicapped in creating an independent stance from which to deal with Waxman and Democrats hostile to Dingell. As the senior Republican on the House Agriculture Committee (Bush named him Agriculture Secretary in early 1991), Madigan also was busy in 1990 handling a major farm bill.

Chuck Knauss, whom Lent named in early 1990 as the senior GOP aide handling the clean-air bill, was probably the most influential Republican on the legislation. Because of his high energy and his close working relationship with Finnegan, he became the person to whom many business lobbyists turned to argue the merits of their case. Waxman and his aides also viewed Knauss as a capable negotiator. When negotiations bogged down among the Energy and Commerce Committee aides over control of toxic chemicals, for example, Finnegan, Knauss and PP&G moved to a smaller room. As a result, they worked out a middle-ground position that removed some of the complexities that had seeped into the proposal during Senate and House back-room deliberations. During the final weeks of debate on the bill, when Finnegan had become exhausted and overworked, Dingell relied increasingly on Knauss to hammer out deals.

Once the staff negotiations resolved most of the issues dealing with both toxins and non-attainment of the local clean-air standards, the House turned to two remaining areas of controversy: the Bush-driven proposals for acid rain and alternative fuels. In each case, the committee members themselves became actively involved in settling these disputes. In the debate over new fuels for vehicles, as described in the next chapter, Dingell and Waxman resumed their conflict. On acid rain, however, other members of the House committee took an active role in seeking a legislative deal. The result was a chaotic, often bitter struggle.

Energy and Commerce Committee members joined the staff negotiators in seeking a new acid-rain package. Their goal was to protect their constituents in what became a regional clash over economic power. The result was, in some respects, more bitter than the Byrd-led challenge in the Senate. Where Byrd's big fight was a relatively symbolic effort to compensate a few thousand miners who would lose their jobs because of the new acid-rain program, the House opponents of the plan cast the issue in larger terms.

"I was determined to help the Midwest," said Philip Sharp, the Indiana Democrat who fought to weaken the administration's proposal. But Sharp faced many obstacles. Although the Midwest was better represented on the House panel than it was at the Senate Environment Committee, its members were still a minority; they would need to cobble together a coalition with other lawmakers fighting just as aggressively to defend what they perceived as their local interests. The Midwest itself was split between the nay-saying utilities and those who wanted to protect the miners of high-sulfur coal. And the utility companies were divided into different groups, depending in part on a power plant's energy source and on its amount of pollution. In the end, Sharp failed to achieve his goal of a national plan to share the cost of reducing acid rain. But he and his allies did tinker with the Bush proposal at its edges.

Rep. Cooper, the Tennessee Democrat, became Sharp's chief nemesis within the committee. Cooper, who had drafted in 1988 an acid-rain proposal with some features similar to Bush's plan, fancied himself as the centrist in the committee who was trying to bridge the chasm between the environmentalists and the polluting industries. "My bill was designed to find the slender middle ground," he said. Once Bush proposed his more stringent version, including the novel system for the trading of allowances, Cooper became its ardent advocate. Meeting in Dingell's office, he faced off with Sharp in several heated discussions about the proposal.

When those talks proved unsuccessful, Sharp and Cooper moved to the back-room talks of the full committee. In the hectic negotiations on acid rain, which ran for three intensive days in early April, the opposing groups took on monikers. Sharp, Madigan and other Midwesterners from states with heavily polluting power plants, who wanted to trim Bush's plan, were known as the "dirties"; they had behind-the-scenes support from Dingell and Finnegan. On the other side, the environmentally minded members plus the lawmakers from the Northeast states most affected by the pollution became the "cleans." Each team was organized and had its own small meeting room adjacent to the main chamber of Energy and Commerce, the dirties in the Democrats' room and the cleans in the GOP lounge.

Sharp insisted that his plan for national cost sharing was designed to ensure that Midwest ratepayers did not get socked with a huge increase in their utility bills. With the staff of the Energy and Power Subcommittee, which he chaired, Sharp prepared several alternatives, including a plan to place a fee on sulfur-dioxide emissions from industries across the nation. But his search for a magic formula would prove fruitless. Advocates of the tighter restrictions adamantly objected that the Midwest had rejected offers for the earlier version during the mid-1980s.

Other committee members, most of whom were eager to avoid a direct showdown and votes, kept pressing for a solution that would include concessions by each side. With the help of Waxman's staff, Sharp tentatively made a new proposal with an indirect method to give additional valuable allowances to Midwest utilities. The Cooper-led "cleans" unexpectedly expressed interest in the option. After bargaining long past midnight, they responded that they would accept the Sharp proposal if he agreed to some new technical wrinkles. After some additional wrangling, Sharp and his allies unexpectedly backed away. "The whole proposal was a figleaf," Sharp later said. "It was fake cost-sharing. We felt that we would look stupid because the idea was a throwaway that meant nothing."

The Sharp-Cooper dealings collapsed sometime before daylight, but their search for a compromise produced an ironic result. When Sununu, who was unaware that the talks had failed, heard a radio report early the next morning about a possible deal, he made an angry phone call to Lent demanding that Republicans reject any form of cost sharing. The compliant Lent, who supported acid-rain controls because his home state of New York was a principal victim of the pollution, agreed not to support a deal. Although it probably was already dead by that point, the White House's opposition placed a stake through its heart. If, on the other hand, Sharp and Cooper had already struck an agreement, Sununu might have been too late to unglue it.

In retrospect, Sharp may have miscalculated by devoting too much of his time and staff resources to cost sharing, which was doomed. Under the pressure to reach a deal and with the difficulty of determining the precise impact of the various offers, however, it was often difficult in the heat of negotiations to determine the best course of action. "There were so many deals on the table that it was hard to keep track of details, even by members who were sponsoring them," said Eckart, the Ohio Democrat who worked with Sharp. "It was like a bazaar." In effect, said an aide who was an active participant, no one was in control. "It was a group grope. In the end, we did bean-counting on the allowances." Like members fighting over pork-barrel spending projects so that they could take something home to their constituents, their dickering over how to allocate relatively small sums seemed distant from the big picture of improving the nation's air quality.

Complicating the negotiations further was the unexpected assertiveness by the Texans on the Energy and Commerce Committee. Led by Democrat Ralph Hall, they wanted additional allowances for proposed home-state power plants that were not yet under construction. "I did not go along, nor would Waxman," Sharp said. "The Texas utilities misled their members about what they had. But Ralph blamed us. It angered me because he was so obnoxious." Sharp and the elderly Hall were "so angry and tired that they nearly came to blows over who had said what," Cooper said. Hall's demands may have been encouraged by a vague promise to meet his concerns from his friend Dingell, who wanted to make sure that he kept the Texans on his side but did not want to risk offending Sharp and his Midwest allies.

When they finally completed their drafting of the clean-air bill on April 5, 1990, the exhausted Energy and Commerce Committee members were pleased and relieved. After nine years of fits and starts, they finally could see the light at the end of the tunnel. But if that light was growing brighter, another one had remained remarkably dim during the committee's work: the light of public sunshine over the legislative process had all but disappeared.

Among the most significant institutional changes during the 1970s, when the House and Senate overhauled many internal procedures, were decisions to open most committee meetings to the public. Only in unusual circumstances did members vote to shut the doors. The "sunshine" movement had flourished in response to pressures from junior members to force more accountability by powerful committee and subcommittee chairmen. It also mirrored the public demand for openness in government, which was in part inspired by groups such as Common Cause. In the wake of the Watergate scandal of 1972–74 and the election of President Jimmy Carter in 1976, secrecy and backroom deals had gained a bad public image.

Why, then, were nearly all of the House committee's meetings and decisions on the clean-air bill conducted behind closed doors and often in the middle of the night? Why, for that matter, were the

Senate's negotiations likewise in back rooms? (The legendary "smoke-filled rooms" of Congress are a virtual relic because so few lawmakers or their aides smoke cigarettes at work. The surviving traditionalists often are the target of social pressure from unhappy colleagues who are non-smokers.) Participants in each chamber agreed that, despite some personal doubts about the process, there was no other way to build the consensus and gain the votes required for such a controversial bill.

"All of us were surprised that the meetings were so closed," said Sharp, a political science professor before he was first elected with the 1974 Watergate class. But, he continued, the public commitment to open government had diminished during the 1980s. "In the 1970s, we junior members argued strongly for openness, as did the media. But we discovered that people posture and abandon the responsibility of legislating. So, the public ethic in the 1980s shifted from openness to the 'can you decide' question." He justified the switch on the basis that "there is a big difference between closed meetings and secrecy." With the clean-air bill, he claimed, most sides of the public debate were represented in the negotiations and interested citizens could learn what had happened from their elected officials or from interest groups on all sides of the debate.

Defenders of the closed-door meetings said that the framers of the U.S. Constitution would not necessarily be surprised or disconcerted by this shift. After all, the founding fathers conducted most of their work behind closed doors in Philadelphia more than two centuries earlier. Nor would they necessarily be troubled by the lack of votes, a pattern that continued when the clean-air bill reached the House floor. Lawmakers have the responsibility not simply to choose up sides but also to educate and convince each other of the merits of their arguments. From these exchanges, it is argued, can flow a more complete understanding and coalescing of the nation's diverse views. "We had had 10 years of public meetings and posturing on clean-air that led nowhere," said Rep. Cooper. "Sometimes, the normal process can impede results. . . . Our real work is not in the votes but in our meetings in the side rooms. This was the most intensive work I have been involved with." Participants made a similar defense of the Senate's closed-door negotiations. "The alternative probably would have been no bill," Baucus said. Handling the bill and the innumerable amendments on the Senate floor would have been "a chaos," he added.

Even an informed observer who raised questions about the recent decline in congressional openness said that he could not offer a better alternative. Ex-Rep. Tauke said that the public "should be concerned" about the movement toward closed meetings in Congress. "But I know of no other way for Congress to conduct its business," he said. "An interest group with a specific issue will be very motivated to make its views known and learn what happened. The general public is not so motivated. . . . But behind closed doors, lobbyists don't know everything that is going on."

On the clean-air bill, the political complexities in moving controversial legislation were compounded by the technical complexities facing often inexperienced lawmakers and their aides, who were trying to explain and understand what was happening. Important nuances could be easily overridden in public debate with disastrous policy results, a clean-air expert said. It is more important, according to this view, for the technical experts to retain some control over the debate so that such mistakes are not made.

Many members of Congress undoubtedly welcomed the political cover that they received by having to cast so few public votes on the clean-air bill. "Many Members were not anxious to vote," Dingell said. "They were under enormous pressure from both sides. In their view, it was politically dangerous." It was far easier, and preferable, for them to tell their constituents that they had approved the landmark legislation without being forced to make the type of difficult choices that delayed approval of the bill for nearly a decade. Therefore, when Dingell and Waxman in October 1989 cut their private deal on new rules to limit automobile emissions, they not only settled a long-standing sore point between the two of them, they also saved many Democrats from a likely no-win vote in which they would have been lobbied by the United Auto Workers and others from organized labor on the one hand, and by the environmentalists on the other.

The larger trend, which has been virtually ignored by most Washington news reporters and other observers, raises important questions about how Congress operates. Representative government rests on the principle of the accountability of elected officials. But a legislative system that was designed by the framers of the U.S. Constitution to be a forum for the nation's competing factions to find common ground has virtually collapsed from countervailing pressures. If these lawmakers make all of their decisions in closed rooms or defer to a few expert colleagues and their aides, how can the voters judge the effectiveness and wisdom of their representatives? If the issues and the choices have become so difficult to comprehend that these leaders are not well equipped to decide, then the premise of self-government has become diluted. And, as was the case with most of the 1990 Clean Air Act, when press coverage of the legislating is so sparse that few citizens can receive more than superficial information, the opportunity for informed consent is curtailed.

When government makes decisions that inescapably will have a wide-ranging impact for many years, the smooth functioning of the democratic process makes it desirable that its citizens understand the changes. Many of those who are governed are likely to gripe, for example, about clean-air decisions that raise the cost of dry cleaning or limit the use of barbecue grills. But they might be more inclined to support those actions if they knew that the alternatives are more expensive automobiles or air that is more difficult to breathe.

As the House prepared to debate the clean-air bill, these dilemmas undoubtedly became apparent to many members. But in the helter-skelter world in which they often operate, it was easier to brush aside these problems and leave them in the care of the "experts."

Endnotes

1. Rochelle L. Stanfield, "Plotting Every Move," *National Journal*, March 26, 1988: 792–97.
2. Julie Kosterlitz, "Watch Out for Waxman," *National Journal*, March 11, 1989: 577–81.
3. Josh Getlin, "What Makes Henry Tick?" *Los Angeles Times*, April 25, 1990: E-1.

9

Making Alternate Deals

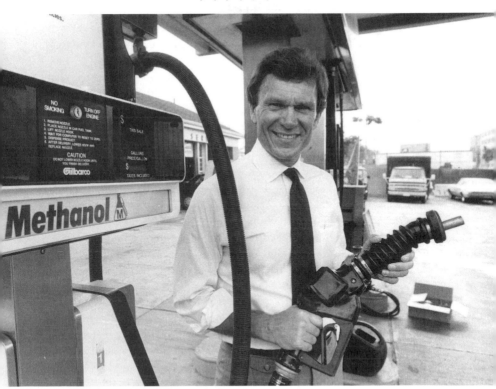

Sen. Tom Daschle pushed relentlessly to force more use by consumers of cleaner fuels for their cars. He was one of the few legislative outsiders with a major impact on the final clean-air bill.

Legislation can move in unexpected directions. We have seen how legislation can be affected by personalities like Dingell and Waxman. We have seen how it can be affected by interest groups. We have seen how it can be affected by secrecy. In this chapter, we will bring together these and other pieces to tell the story of one particular "miracle" provision: alternative fuels.

There is no precise definition, even among the experts, for alternative fuels. Generally, however, the term refers to the refining and blending of fuels that reduce automobile emissions and result in cleaner-driving vehicles. "It has been widely accepted by all segments of the automotive and motor fuels industries that alternative fuels have positive effects on [carbon monoxide] emissions from automobiles, especially during cold weather and at higher altitudes," according to a Washington-area lobbying group. Cleanliness, of course, is in the eye of the policy-makers and it became the subject of extensive debate in Congress.

Approval of the fuels proposal was a rags-to-riches story of a legislative orphan. Congressional support for a major shift toward alternative fuels had barely existed during the early years of the clean-air debate. President Bush's 1989 proposal mandating that one million cars be equipped for methanol fuel eventually led to the more sweeping action. But his own top aides and agency officials were badly divided on its merits and the White House essentially abandoned its own plan. That proposal had no major Capitol Hill booster when the debate began. And the leading environmentalists, who seemed like logical supporters, were lukewarm at best. Despite the lack of enthusiasm, however, the idea took on a life of its own. It would not die because the plan ultimately made too much sense to be excluded from clean-air legislation.

Its prospects were improved because some oil companies panicked after they learned that Bush intended to raise the issue. That panic became a vital development in the clean-air debate. Because the refiners preferred to control their destiny, they introduced amid great fanfare their own cleaner fuel in hopes that they could prevent the federal government from telling them what to do. That created a new dilemma, however. Once they conceded—after earlier denials—that they *could* change the formula for gasoline, they opened the door and lost control of the debate to the public officials in Washington. "The industry got a little bit pregnant," said a key House aide working on the bill. "Then, Waxman demanded more."

Understanding the alternative-fuels debate seemed like a daunting task, which most lawmakers and their aides preferred to sidestep. Few high-powered political insiders want to take the time to learn about products like "oxygenated fuels" or, especially, gasoline "aromatics," an unlikely-seeming term for synthesized chemicals. In fact, the technical details could be learned rather easily. It was the politics that proved more difficult to comprehend. Why, for example, did Bush's top aides walk away from both his campaign pledge to support cleaner fuels and from his own legislative proposal? Why did the environmentalists and many of their congressional allies display little enthusiasm—and, in some cases, outright skepticism—for one of the most convenient ways to reduce pollution? Why did major farm groups and grain dealers become the chief advocates of a proposal to promote cleaner air? And why did the automobile industry and its leader, Dingell, oppose requirements to reduce auto emissions that would have placed the new financial burdens chiefly on the fuels industry?

Some answers can be found to these questions. But perhaps the biggest mystery is why Bush, who set up business in Texas's Oil Patch after he graduated from Yale University, embraced a plan that was ardently opposed by his erstwhile business partners. The personality of Bush's legal adviser, Boyden Gray, and the politics of the January 1988 Iowa presidential caucuses provide the clues. Gray was such an enthusiastic supporter of alternative fuels that he drove a methanol-powered Chevrolet and kept a can of the fuel in his office. And Iowa, the site of the first contest in George Bush's presidential candidacy, produces the nation's largest supply of corn, which has become a major source of ethanol, another cleaner-burning fuel.

Ethanol and methanol are the two principal alcohol fuels. They contain more oxygen than the traditional carbon-based fuels such as oil and coal, which are used for most forms of energy. The higher the level of oxygen, the less carbon monoxide produced by the fuel. Although backers of these two fuels sometimes cooperate, they are also highly competitive. Ethanol is more expensive to produce. But methanol, which is a by-product of natural gas, has important disadvantages because it is more corrosive and can require the installation of new fuel lines in a car.

The political attractiveness of alternative fuels began to coalesce as far back as a February 1987 meeting at the White House. In attendance were Gray and Bill Rosenberg, the Republican businessman from Michigan who had advocated more use of grain by-products as fuel supplements to spur economic development in the Midwest. Rosenberg, an Ann Arbor friend of Bush political adviser Bob Teeter, was later named by Bush as his chief air-quality administrator at EPA. His initial contact with the Bush operatives led to preparation of a statement strongly endorsing grain-based fuels, which Bush delivered in Iowa the next month. "For years, [ethanol] has been touted as America's home-grown alternative to energy dependence," Bush said. "Never has its potential been fully tapped. I believe it's time to utilize this great resource."

Since 1972, when the Iowa caucuses first marked the start of presidential campaigns, they have become important for candidates and political insiders. That also can boost the influence of local economic interests. As it turned out, Bush finished a nearly disastrous third behind Bob Dole and evangelist Pat Robertson in the Iowa caucuses in 1988. Nonetheless, Bush had formed his alliance with Rosenberg and his commitment to support alternative fuels.

When Bush advisers began to prepare his clean-air proposal in early 1989, Rosenberg advocated that they include a mandate for the use of ethanol in metropolitan areas with the worst air quality. But Rosenberg met strong opposition from fiscal-policy experts at the Office of Management and Budget and from White House economists. They had long held reservations about ethanol because a large tax credit supporting its development costs the federal Treasury more than a half-billion dollars annually. The Energy Department also strongly opposed alternative fuels because its officials doubted that the public would buy the products at an unsubsidized price.

After many heated meetings, the group settled on what became known as a performance standard that alternative fuels would have to meet, and they mandated one million annual sales of cars that burn such fuel. In addition to Boyden Gray, who favored methanol in large fleets such as those operated by delivery companies, some high-level EPA career officials were methanol enthusiasts.

But Bush's plan only started the debate. "There were a lot of problems with the proposal," OMB's Robert Grady said. Among them were the automobile industry's complaint that there was no guarantee that anybody would buy the new cars and the Energy Department's opposition to what it claimed was an EPA power grab to make the program work. "The proposal was more aggressive in promoting alternative fuels than the political sphere of reality warranted," said the Energy Department's Linda Stuntz. And, although the administration claimed that the proposal did not favor any form of alternative fuel, its standard was pegged to M 85, a fuel that is 85 percent methanol and 15 percent gasoline.

Some private alternative-fuels experts said that, even with the encouragement it received from Boyden Gray, the methanol tilt in the formula may have been unintentional. Regardless, the administration's lack of consensus meant that Capitol Hill critics could drive wedges into the support for its plan. Its backers responded that the result does not detract from the significance of their effort in giving credibility to the alternative-fuels debate. "We were focusing on the next generation of vehicles," Rosenberg said. "Ethanol focuses on cleaner cars in existing vehicles. But the result of our proposal was that we challenged others, like the oil industry, to do their share. We put the quality of the gasoline into play in the clean-air debate. That was fundamental."

Regardless of its merits or the political obstacles that the plan faced, the oil industry took Bush and his plan very seriously. Less than a month after Bush sent his plan to Congress, the Atlantic Richfield Company announced on Aug. 15 that it would introduce a "reformulated" fuel called EC-1 (Emission Control One) to replace leaded gasoline in southern California, where ARCO was the top gasoline marketer. The new product would reduce pollution in older cars and certain commercial vehicles by as much as 15 percent. An ARCO official said that the threat of new federal and state regulations gave the company incentive to devise the new formula. Other California-based refiners soon followed suit with similar announcements.

ARCO and the other companies had been secretly developing a reformulated gasoline long before Bush's announcement. After unsuccessful private lobbying of Bush to exclude an alternative-fuels program, they launched a public-relations offensive to counter the prospect of federal legislation. Alternative fuels posed several perils to their industry, they argued, each of which could be avoided by reformulated gasoline: Alternative fuels most likely would require the construction of new refineries and distribution systems; industries such as natural gas and grain would gain part of the market share for motor fuels; and the new fuels would reduce the net income for oil companies. In addition, oil lobbyists added, nearly all automobiles could immediately use the reformulated gasoline. From an environmental perspective, however, reformulated gasoline did not reduce emissions nearly as much as some of the alternative fuels.

If oil-company executives thought that their modification of conventional gasoline would reduce Washington's interest in more exotic fuels, they were sadly mistaken. "They verified that fuels could play a big role in the clean-air debate," said Rosenberg of the EPA. "They showed that cleaner fuels were feasible and economic. That cut the pins out from under the American Petroleum Institute's argument against stronger federal standards." ARCO's initial move was a reaction to Bush's plan, he boasted, an effort to cut added costs by promoting cleaner gasoline instead of alternative fuels. In a January 1991 speech to automobile-industry executives in Detroit, Rosenberg pointedly assessed the oil industry's "most remarkable" response to Bush's proposal. "I'm not now talking about the intense lobbying effort waged inside the Washington beltway against 'government gasoline,' but rather the immediate market response to develop and sell cleaner gasoline," he said. A clean-air expert in the private sector remarked that, from its narrow perspective, "ARCO said more in its EC-1 press release than it should have."

Although ARCO's initiative immediately caught the attention of participants in the clean-air debate, the response on Capitol Hill was not uniformly positive. "Reformulated gas," which did not previously exist as a term in the policy debate, suddenly became a topic of discussion. Members from states producing natural gas or corn felt fewer constraints on pushing their local alternative fuel. From Dingell's perspective, however, announcement of reformulated gasoline made it more difficult to hold together his fragile coalition of the oil and auto industries, whose goal was to minimize the new federal controls affecting auto emissions. His constant refrain was that those two industries needed to cooperate and that the environmentalists were trying to push technology too fast. His fear was twofold: On behalf of Detroit, he wanted to prevent Congress from mandating new fuels that might force an overhaul of the automobile. Legislatively, Dingell needed to keep the votes of oil-state lawmakers in his coalition to support a bill. But those tactics had become questionable in the wake of ARCO's advances. Many alternative-fuel advocates, in fact, suggested that Detroit should have led the parade on behalf of the newer fuels because, in the long term, that would reduce pressure on the automobile industry to make more expensive design changes in its engines.

Dingell's coalition held together, at least in the short term. After his October 1989 agreement with Waxman on tailpipe emissions, the committee chairman abandoned his newfound California partner. Instead, he supported an amendment by Democrat Ralph Hall and Republican Jack Fields, both Texans, that gutted Bush's alternative-fuels plan. The Hall-Fields proposal, prepared with help from the auto and oil industries, weakened the methanol-based standard and removed the million-car mandate. In its place, it permitted other clean-fuel alternatives, including reformulated gasoline, and required only that the auto manufacturers "certify" that they could produce cars running on newer fuels. Waxman's subcommittee, over his strong opposition, approved the substitute on a 12–10 vote.

The outcome was preceded by one of the more comical features of the clean-air debate. Prior to the vote, EPA administrator Reilly called Waxman from a pay telephone in Chicago to assure him of the Bush administration's continued support for its original proposal and its opposition to Hall-Fields. But Lent had a short time earlier received a phone call from Sununu at the White House, who said that the administration had no position on Hall-Fields. The mix-up resulted from "a communications glitch," Rosenberg later said: Sununu merely was indicating the administration's "willingness to negotiate" on its proposal so long as another option was environmentally acceptable. But the embarrassing phone-booth interlude was an early sign that, when the crunch came, the White House would swing to Dingell and the industry coalition rather than stand by its position.

The fact that industry opposed the stronger alternative-fuels plan was no big surprise. Less obvious was why many environmentalists and their congressional allies did not sign on. At the Senate Environment and Public Works Committee, the environmentalists' citadel, the administration's plan was scuttled in favor of tighter tailpipe standards. The only alternative-fuel provision that the committee included was a modest proposal setting standards for the use of alternative fuels in new cars in cities with the worst air quality. It did little more than pay lip service to alternative fuels, according to a critic of the committee.

"The environmentalists could never make the transition from tighter regulation of gasoline-powered cars," Waxman said. "They locked themselves psychologically into this position and they were not as interested in alternative fuels." Waxman said that he could not explain this attitude. Mitchell and Baucus "thought that alternative fuels were for funny cars" and they gave the subject little attention in committee, said an aide to the Senate panel. The senators also initially viewed alternative fuels as an extraneous energy-policy issue. Some aides also feared that more use of the potentially hazardous natural gas-based methanol, for example, would mean less use of natural gas as a fuel; that, in turn, could accelerate burning of coal, which they opposed. In addition, the committee's geographic base largely excluded the interests of senators from states producing corn and natural gas.

But the rationale for their negative view was more complex. As shown during the extended acid-rain debate, the environmentalists who dominate the Senate panel have historically favored a "command and control" philosophy of strong federal regulation rather than marketplace solutions. Earlier, Mitchell and others were willing to mandate the more expensive solution of scrubbing high-sulfur coal by power plants rather than allowing utilities to switch fuel. Now they were wary of giving the fuels industry discretion to develop what they considered untested new automobile fuels. "The environmentalists had a hard time accepting our policy arguments on the benefits of alternative fuels for cleaner air," said Michael D. Jackson, a clean-air consultant to California agencies, who urged more congressional support for the new fuels. The California advocates generally favored methanol over ethanol; ethanol was dirtier and had a higher price because of transportation costs from the Midwest.

Legislative factors also help to explain why the Bush methanol-based initiative and ARCO's reformulated-gasoline alternative failed to stir much interest when the Environment Committee was set to send its bill to the Senate floor. Because the committee had spent so many years developing its comprehensive proposal, there was a reluctance—tending toward inertia—to make last-minute changes. Even after Waxman in late 1989 personally urged Mitchell and Baucus to support an alternative-fuels initiative, most members of the Northeast-tilted panel wanted nothing to interfere with their prime goal of acid-rain reduction.

The continuing close access and friendship of Leon Billings—Muskie's chief staffer during the 1970s who had become a successful Washington lobbyist—to several committee aides was another reason the panel preferred to reduce auto emissions through engine redesign. According to clean-air experts, the fact that a Billings client was the Johnson-Matthey Co., a chief manufacturer of the pollution-controlling catalytic converter, led many environmentalists both on and off that panel to prefer, maybe subconsciously, automobile changes advocated by that firm. Greater reliance on engine modification, rather than cleaner fuels, obviously served Johnson-Matthey's interests.

When alternative-fuels advocates tried to influence the month-long negotiations in February 1990 between senators and White House officials in Mitchell's office, they again met a stone wall from key participants and their aides. Tom Daschle, the South Dakota Democrat who would take the lead when the issue later reached the Senate floor, sent a letter to Baucus urging a reformulated-gasoline standard in the nation's most polluted cities. But he received no response. And Daschle said that when he held tense discussions of the issue with Roger Porter, Bush's chief domestic-policy adviser and the head of the White House negotiators, he was given the cold shoulder. "Boyden Gray was our strong advocate for alternative fuels but I took it that he was not able to override Roger Porter," Daschle said. As in Waxman's subcommittee, the White House appeared to show little interest in defending the development of new fuels. "People misunderstood what we were saying," Porter later said. "We wanted a market orientation, with a certain level of environmental benefit. Daschle tried to push it in one direction to benefit his farmers."

But Daschle, refusing to take no for an answer, would not abandon his cause. Over the formal opposition of Mitchell and the White House negotiators, and with the belated support of Dole, he used a floor debate to win Senate approval of major new requirements for the use of alternative fuels. The unexpected and little-publicized passage of the Daschle amendment became the political equivalent of ARCO's announcement seven months earlier. It was the first major legislative effort to reduce auto emissions by targeting the fuel instead of the engine. Senate passage virtually assured that some version would become part of the clean-air package approved by Congress later in the year. And, despite the marked differences between Bush's earlier proposal and the new plan, a good case can be made that one became a sine qua non for the other.

Although Daschle represented a major corn-producing state, his amendment did not explicitly favor the grain-based ethanol. Instead, he permitted the use of *any* formula for the reformulated gasoline that the proposal required. The plan was to start in 1995 for all drivers in the nine cities with the nation's worst air quality. Working with information from the Clean Fuels Development Coalition, which backs all environmentally safer fuels and is based in the Washington suburb of Bethesda, Maryland, Daschle aide Whitney Fosburgh drafted the amendment. The plan required that the weight of the fuel in the designated areas include at least 2.7 percent oxygen. It also required that refiners reduce to a maximum of 25 percent the "aromatics" in gasoline—benzene and two other toxic chemicals that refiners had added when they were required to eliminate lead from the fuel. An ARCO study showed that the increase in these chemicals proved "the danger of relying solely on vehicle-control technology for emissions reductions,"

Daschle said. "It does not matter how many levels of tailpipe standards were required if the technology cannot handle the gasoline." The Environmental Protection Agency had already sanctioned 11 additives, including both ethanol and methanol derivatives, to replace the aromatics. Despite the administration's later decision to oppose the amendment, the EPA's Rosenberg had assisted in drafting the language.

Daschle was invited to submit his proposal as part of the broader Wirth-Wilson amendment to reduce auto emissions. The sponsors of that package had hoped that inclusion of Daschle's plan would make their proposal more favorable to farm-state senators. But Daschle had a fallback plan. During debate on that proposal, which was defeated 52–46, "We made clear that if Wirth-Wilson failed, we would offer our amendment on its own," Daschle said.

His move came on March 29 as the Senate neared the end of the clean-air debate. Byrd's proposal to guarantee the salary of mineworkers left unemployed by the new acid-rain plan had been dramatically rejected a few hours earlier. Oil-industry lobbyists, having witnessed Mitchell's success in defeating all amendments that he said were inconsistent with his agreement with the White House, assumed that their work in the Senate was finished. As a result, they were not worried that Daschle's amendment would pass. "We probably miscalculated and we were worn out after a month-long debate," said Dale Brooks of Chevron, who coordinated the industry's lobbying in the Senate. "We never thought that it would pass. . . . We got blindsided."

Among the mistakes made by opponents of the amendment was their expectation that Minority Leader Dole, under White House and oil-industry pressure, would oppose the proposal. Instead, Dole changed signals and decided a few hours before the vote that he would co-sponsor the amendment, apparently in response to the strong support from Kansas grain companies that had moved into the ethanol market. He dismissed criticism by Baucus, the bill's chief sponsor, that opposition of the White House and Mitchell to the proposal automatically made it a "deal breaker" of their earlier agreement, which Dole had backed. In bargaining over the automobile provisions of that deal with Sen. Carl Levin, a Michigan Democrat, Mitchell and his staff had mostly steered clear of alternative-fuels issues, except to oppose Bush's proposed million-car mandate. "I am certain that definitions of reformulated gasoline were not discussed in the negotiations," Dole said. After a brief debate, the Senate passed the amendment on a 69–30 vote. The opponents were an odd mixture of environmentalists and oil-state senators. The outcome was the only vote that Mitchell and company lost on the floor during the Senate debate.

Mitchell's opposition to the Daschle amendment was accompanied by a symbolic wink to senators who cared about where he stood. The signal was that its passage would not threaten the broader deal. He remained off the Senate floor until the end of the vote and made no effort, as he had on earlier amendments, to keep wavering senators on his side. "We feared that its passage might open up Pandora's box for environmentalists," said Rosenberg. "But neither the White House nor Mitchell pulled out all of the stops to oppose the amendment." Daschle and Fosburgh had been quietly courting Mitchell's staff to inform them of the proposal, hoping to allay their fears. The fact that Daschle was a close political ally of Mitchell, who had named him as co-chairman of the Senate Democratic Policy Committee, may have been another vital factor in the outcome. And Mitchell perhaps determined that since the amendment likely would pass no matter what he did, he should avoid a precedent that might encourage the approval of other more harmful amendments.

Despite the political and environmental significance of Daschle's amendment, it had its limitations. Especially for California clean-air experts, who generally agreed that their state required more radical reduction of auto emissions than did most of the nation, the amendment fell short of their hopes for a major breakthrough on alternative fuels. "Reformulated gas will be good for the nation's air quality," Mike Jackson said. "But it does not do much for California or for our energy security."

Among the key congressional players, we have seen heroes and villains, cowboys and team players. But what happens when a previously quiet senator like Daschle enters the fray? Where does he look for help?

Daschle worked most closely with the Clean Fuels Development Coalition, whose members ranged from General Motors to the Edison Electric Institute and the Nebraska Corn Utilization Board. Although the Renewable Fuels Association (RFA), which has its plush headquarters on Capitol Hill, is far better known in congressional offices as the chief promoter of cleaner fuels, it gave Daschle little help until late in the game. A major reason was that the RFA, despite its all-inclusive name, was an ethanol booster. More specifically, it was committed chiefly to, and run by, the Archer Daniels Midland Co., the Illinois-based firm that is the nation's largest processor of farm products, including ethanol.

Although its officials publicly deny the connection, numerous news stories plus people familiar with the association have reported that a bitter battle within the RFA in the mid-1980s resulted in its takeover by officials dominated by ADM. The RFA's former president told a reporter that he left the trade group "in large part because of interference by ADM."[1] ADM, whose president, Dwayne Andreas, has been a friend of political leaders from Democrat Hubert Humphrey to Republican Bob Dole, has worked actively to cultivate its national image and to gain influence in Washington. Its political action committee has contributed hundreds of thousands of dollars to congressional candidates. Although it claims that its interest is to encourage more use of grain to produce ethanol, it has been less enthusiastic in promoting a newer combination of ethanol and natural gas known as ethyl tertiary butyl ether (ETBE), which has become a popular additive in reformulated gasoline. This fuel, which has been produced by other large grain companies, has posed a real threat to ADM's one-time dominance of the ethanol market. The advantages of ETBE include that it is more easily transported and blended with oil to produce gasoline than is the traditional ethanol.

ADM worked closely with Dole and other supporters to enact in 1979 a significant federal incentive for ethanol production in the form of a tax credit. The new tax credit exempted purchases of ethanol-blended fuels from a share of the federal gasoline tax. As of 1991, the 5.4 cents credit (lowering the 14.5 cents per gallon tax to 9.1 cents) costs the federal government about $600 million annually. Ethanol producers justify that expense by pointing to an even greater amount that is saved from the federal budget because the increased purchases of corn have reduced the farm program's grain subsidy. But the cost, and ADM's aggressive lobbying, have given ADM a bad name in some parts of Congress. Daschle went out of his way at key points to make clear to other senators that he was promoting his clean-fuels amendment independently of lobbying by ADM and the RFA.

Despite the Senate's approval of the amendment mandating increased use of reformulated gasoline, action in the House was stymied by the coalition of oil and auto companies. Dingell and Waxman resumed their conflicts and bitterness in the spring of 1990, after having eased temporarily during their earlier agreement on tailpipe emissions. The alternative-fuels debate would witness a full flowering of the old antagonisms, replete with procedural ploys and hair-splitting disputes. Although each was bolstered by other colleagues and his aides, there was little doubt that the two titans were at the helm. In the end, it was left to House Speaker Tom Foley to stare down Dingell and Waxman and force them to reach an agreement in the heat of battle on the House floor.

Dingell's opposition to federal mandates for cleaner fuels had been a matter of public record for many years. He objected to the costly federal subsidy for ethanol and to ADM's political muscle. "Many so-called oxygenated fuels were supported on the basis of their political influence," Dingell said. "The figures used by ADM and others are only slightly related to reality." He feared that the use of grain could jeopardize the nation's food supply if the farm surplus turned to shortages. He also was skeptical that many members truly understood the issues or had cared strongly before Bush's 1989 initiative about requiring more use of the new fuels. Mostly, of course, he worried that an expensive program posed perils for the automobile industry, which already was on the financial ropes as its market share decreased at the hands of more efficient Japanese-manufactured vehicles. He especially opposed federal mandates requiring Detroit to produce cars for which there were no certain buyers.

For Waxman, his interest in alternative fuels was motivated chiefly by the needs and politics of California. At a time when the increasingly dense cover of smog was forcing state regulators to talk about regulating the use of items such as barbecue grills and lawn mowers, state officials and other experts were demanding every possible step to reduce auto emissions. Unlike most clean-air issues, Waxman was not receiving much pressure on alternative fuels from the environmental lobbyists in Washington. But the Senate approval of Daschle's amendment injected the farm community as a new element into the debate that Waxman could turn to his advantage. And once administration officials fumbled the issue by backing off Bush's plan, the politically shrewd Waxman also saw the opportunity to score partisan points.

The Energy and Commerce Committee was so divided on alternative fuels that it abandoned the format by which it had handled all of the other issues on the clean-air bill. Instead of seeking consensus in endless back-room meetings of members and staff, the fight was waged in the open with all 43 lawmakers forced to take one side or the other in front of the swarms of lobbyists. Three separate blocs—environmentalists, farmers and the oil-autos coalition—sought different vote combinations for an alternative-fuels deal. The oil interests on the committee tried to find a formula with an acceptable oxygen level to satisfy the ethanol backers. The environmentalists worked with the farm-state members to find a compromise on a cleaner reformulated gasoline than the oil refiners were willing to accept. Even the arch-enemies from the environmental and industry camps struggled to find common ground. Waxman, in fact, won the support of some of Din-gell's Midwest allies, including Democrats Sharp and Eckart. But they were not enough for a majority.

In the end, as had happened in Waxman's subcommittee six months earlier, Dingell carried the day by a slim margin in the full committee. First, the panel defeated on a 22–21 vote an amendment by Bill Richardson, a New Mexico Democrat, that was similar to Daschle's plan to increase reformulated gasoline but required less spe-cific numbers. Then, Louisiana Democrat Billy Tauzin proposed a modified version mandating the use of alternative fuels for large fleets of commercial vehicles; he lost, 24–19. Finally, the committee ac-cepted, by 24–19, another version of the relatively weak Hall-Fields amendment, backed by Dingell, which encouraged the dirtiest cities to offer cleaner fuels; critics said that it was filled with loopholes. Ironically, the crucial votes came on March 29, at virtually the same time that the Senate unexpectedly approved Daschle's plan. "If the votes had come an hour after Daschle, instead of an hour before, we might have lost," an oil-industry lobbyist later said.

But those votes did not settle the issue. Even after the Energy and Commerce Committee formally approved the complete bill on April 5, the Dingell and Waxman staffs continued their negotiations. Despite his victory, Dingell was forced to contend with the prospect that Waxman likely would win if he offered an amendment on the House floor. Despite industry lobbyists' assurances that they could defeat Waxman, such a showdown remained daunting to Dingell following his unexpected 1987 loss to Waxman on the largely symbolic issue of extending the local air-quality enforcement deadlines. For the next six weeks, while Finnegan and other aides coordinated the complex task of drafting the 686-page committee report accompanying the bill, nego-tiations continued on alternative fuels and several other less contro-versial issues that the members instructed their staff to resolve.

The fact that Dingell and Waxman controlled the final talks was no coincidence. "Dingell kept alternative fuels on the side until the other issues were resolved," said Rep. Synar, whose continuing sup-port for a strong natural-gas-oriented fleet program had placed him in the chairman's doghouse. "It became a reward-and-punishment system for members. . . . He played 'br'er rabbit' and was looking for sympathy because he said he had been 'so badly hurt' on the rest of the bill." Synar, an active promoter of deals, had supported increased use of natural-gas products, which would help his home state of Oklahoma.

Once the committee approved the bill, however, an important new force entered the debate. Speaker Foley, the Washington Democrat who had replaced Jim Wright of Texas following his ethics-tarred resignation one year earlier, insisted that the House pass a strong clean-air bill. Foley was mindful that he could cite it as a proud accomplishment of Congress and his own leadership. But he also feared partisan attacks from the White House if the Democratic-controlled Congress failed to complete action on his bill before the 1990 election. And Foley clearly wanted to avoid a fractious Democratic bloodbath in full public view on the House floor. Knowing of Dingell's hostility to key parts of the bill and his penchant for endless delay, Foley and his chief legislative aide George Kundanis closely monitored the bill's progress and made clear that they would tolerate no shenanigans. As a former chairman of the House Agriculture Committee, Foley was familiar with both the procedural prerogatives available to chairmen and with the political pressures that could force their hand. Using emissaries from the Dingell and Waxman camps, the Speaker became both a prod who kept the pressure on both sides, and an honest broker who tried to help them settle differences in the last-minute negotiations.

In a key move that forced the committee's hand, Foley set a deadline for the House to complete action on the bill before the Memorial Day recess. Given the busy schedule facing the House in its remaining months before the election, Foley did not want to allow the possibility of delay to strengthen either side. "There were two very strong characters [Dingell and Waxman] involved," said Rep. David E. Bonior of Michigan, a high-ranking member of Foley's leadership team. "To the extent that they could work out their problems, that was important. . . . We deferred to them but we did not want to have a protracted fight." Although it was likely that Wright would have shared those goals if he had remained in office, his closer friendship with Dingell and his less enthusiastic support for environmental goals might have made the former speaker a less effective mediator.

With the deadline for House debate only a few days away, the Dingell and Waxman staffs finally reached agreement on a formula and the rules for using reformulated gasoline. It followed the general outlines of Daschle's amendment, requiring the cleaner gasoline in the nine cities with the worst smog. Even at that point, however, several technical details remained unresolved on the clean-fuels provision. Although Waxman had abandoned Bush's proposed million-car mandate, he had developed an alternative for what he called a California "pilot program." Under Waxman's modified plan, 300,000 light-weight vehicles meeting tighter emission standards would be annually produced and sold to auto dealers in California by 1997. Waxman, on behalf of his home state, had wanted more use of clean fuels such as compressed natural gas in automobiles. Experts have said that CNG is widely available from domestic sources; methanol, by contrast, which Bush had recommended a year earlier, is mostly imported.

Finnegan and Waxman's PP&G team bargained through the night of May 22 and until dawn. Only hours before the bill was set for final House action, they appeared to have finally resolved all of the details. Waxman failed to get as much of a mandate for the required sales of cleaner-fuel cars as he preferred; Dingell was forced to concede a state-of-the-art program, if only because California regulators were already pushing in that direction. The discussions had been held in such secret that even the oil-industry lobbyists were unaware that they were taking place. Eckart continued to play his role as babysitter to the staff on both sides during the final all-night sessions. But, as day broke, Finnegan told Waxman's staff that the proposal was unacceptable to the auto industry. Eckart telephoned Dingell at his home to discuss the details. During the same conversation, Dingell agreed to stop by Eckart's home in nearby McLean, Virginia, to pick up a change of clothes for him. Meanwhile, Eckart briefed the House Democratic leaders on the overnight developments.

When Dingell arrived on Capitol Hill in the morning and consulted with House leaders, he decided to make another bid to close the alternative-fuels deal. More negotiating was required. At issue were a series of details, including a mandate for sales in California of lower-emissions cars and the extent to which the provision would cover buses and heavy-duty trucks in the affected areas. Even as the antagonists worked to resolve the precise language with Pope Barrow, one of the House's elite corps of legislative counsels, the House began to debate the bill. Because the months of negotiations in the committee's back room and among the staff aides had resolved virtually everything, only one amendment other than alternative fuels remained in controversy between Dingell and Waxman. It dealt with the relatively minor issue of the duration of coverage for auto-emission warranties; Waxman's side won, 239–180. The House was ready for the vote on the bill's final passage later that day, May 23. But still the deadlock continued.

An impatient Speaker Foley approached Dingell and Waxman on the House floor to inquire what the new problem was that had stymied the tentative agreement. Seated between them in the theater-style cushioned chairs in a back row of the chamber, Foley listened as the two principals and a crowd of staffers surrounding them explained the technical issues. Foley did not suggest or explicitly demand a solution. But through his body language and his tone of voice, he made it clear to the participants that he wanted the conflict settled then and there. In effect, Foley would not leave until the two sides had made their final deal. The message got through. Each side made its final concessions and the exhausted players had an agreement. With quiet strength, Foley provided the last push needed to reach a compromise.

Was the final melodrama a real conflict or was it a statement by each side that it was pushing the debate until the final possible moment? Dingell, Waxman and their teams insisted that the remaining issues were significant and that they took time to resolve. But a top House aide who witnessed the final talks said that they were "pre-wired" and that both sides simply wanted Foley to share in both the decision making and the accountability for a bill that ultimately would cause hometown grief for both Dingell and Waxman. "The issue was less important than the tactics," the aide said.

Who won the House debate on alternative fuels? Both sides blinked. Given how far the debate had moved, however, Waxman had to be pleased on both that issue and on the broader bill. He had decided to accept a certain 90 percent victory rather than to risk the bitterness and possible loss that could result if he pushed for 100 percent. According to an appraisal written immediately following the House outcome, "Waxman may have lost the battle with Dingell over the auto industry, but thanks to the rising tide of environmental interest, he won the Clean Air Act war in the House."[2]

The EPA's Rosenberg, whose enthusiasm for ethanol had triggered the push for cleaner fuels more than three years earlier in Iowa, was gratified by the outcome. "The bill that emerged will produce more clean air than what we or anyone else had proposed," he said. "But that success was because of the administration." In effect, he said, the president led and Congress followed. But the handling of the alternative-fuel section made it clear that once the president submitted his proposal, he lost control of the details that are at the heart of the legislative process. Whether the final language made more sense than Bush's original proposal may be left for the technical experts and history to determine.

Endnotes

1. Michael J. Weiss, "Ethanol Lobby," *The New York Times*, April 1, 1990 (Magazine, Part 2): 18.
2. Margaret E. Kriz, "Politics at the Pump," *National Journal*, June 2, 1990: 1328.

10

Reaching Common Ground

Rep. John Dingell (*left*) and Sen. Max Baucus (*right*) cooperated behind the scenes to make sure that a House-Senate conference committee agreed to a clean-air bill before the 101st Congress adjourned.

151

Following Senate and House passage, all that remained was to settle the differences between the two chambers. Given the similarities in the outlines of the respective bills and in many of their details, that should have been an easy task. Like most other aspects of the 1990 Clean Air Act, however, the final act became an ordeal. It was time consuming and exhausting. It revisited many of the same battles encompassed by both houses. It was controlled by the legislative technicians. But it ultimately succeeded in strengthening the bill that was sent to President Bush.

The Senate-House conference committee has historically been among the least-examined and understood facets of the legislative process. Sometimes referred to as "the third House," this final bill-drafting committee usually operates behind the scenes, with control centered among a few senior lawmakers from each side. The designated members of each chamber meet separately to cast a vote. A majority from each side must agree on all details.

Given the history of the clean-air bill, it was no surprise that the traditional conference-committee secrecy dominated its final stages. It was also no surprise that the House members ultimately controlled the pace and outcome of the proceedings since they and their staffs had a better grasp of the politics and issues. Having done a better job of defining and exploring the ramifications of most disputes, the House side was better prepared to examine all issues in the conference committee. What was unexpected, however, was that the House members' deliberations revived the same roundtable style that had marked the House Energy and Commerce Committee's earlier debate. Weeks were consumed as House aides and a few members met in the committee's hearing room to prepare their offers to the Senate conferees. They settled the details of some issues that had not been fully resolved before House passage. They reopened other issues, by mutual agreement. The end-game dynamics also extended the jousting between Dingell and Waxman, the leaders of the two sides throughout the decade-long struggle.

The House members did not dominate solely because they knew more about the issues. One other major cause of their superior influence was an unusual agreement by Dingell and Waxman to keep their bond on most issues throughout the conference committee. Their earlier negotiations had been strenuous and often bitter. But now, by joining forces, they represented such a broad cross-section of the House that they strengthened their collective hand in dealing with the Senate. Although the two principals and their aides continued to bicker on some issues, their pact meant that they usually presented a unified front in the broader negotiations.

The chief Senate conferees, by contrast, were the same Environment and Public Works Committee members who had seen much of their earlier proposal undercut during the month-long negotiations in Mitchell's office. Although unified, they felt less commitment to the final Senate bill and therefore little hesitation about abandoning important pieces of it. And they continued to depend heavily on their committee aides, most of whom were less adept than their House counterparts in manipulating the high-stakes political gambits of a conference committee. On many issues, the Senate's most important role was to support Waxman on issues where he differed with Dingell. "Not much of our Senate deal survived," said Boyden Gray, the White House counsel.

The chief part of the final package on which the Senate did prevail was the acid-rain section. In that case, the Senate version was a more coherent plan and was closer to the Bush administration's proposal, which had played a vital role in breaking the years-long deadlock on acid rain. Because of the give-and-take nature of any negotiating process, the Senate's concessions on so many other issues increased the Senate's leverage to assert its authorship on this section.

The Senate conferees' decision to concede to the House on many of their differences had one other important source. At the close of the Senate-White House negotiations in February 1990, Mitchell had offered to bind the newfound partners to their deal through the conference committee. At the time, his suggestion had even taken his own staff by surprise. But White House domestic-policy aide Roger Porter turned down the proposal because he and other administration officials wanted to preserve their flexibility. They believed they could win important concessions from the House. "I think that was a mistake for them," Mitchell shrewdly predicted immediately after the Senate passed the bill in April.

Administration officials later agreed that their failure to commit themselves to their deal with Mitchell was a tactical blunder. "I thought that it was a good idea to support our agreement through the conference committee," said the EPA's Rosenberg. "But others in the administration thought that they could not commit the House and that they did not want to take that philosophical approach" to the relationship between the two branches—that is, they did not want to offend the House by allying with the Senate. Most especially, in one of the odd alliances that Washington creates, they did not want to offend John Dingell, who had introduced Bush's original bill in the House.

"Sen. Mitchell told me that I would not get a better deal from the House," Porter said. "But I told him that was not the reason for our decision. . . . In hindsight, we might have been better off with certain parts of the Senate bill. But that would have evidenced a lack of good faith with the House." Thus, a Republican president who postured himself as pro-environment chose to pacify a Democrat opposed to most clean-air proposals, who had himself only introduced the bill in order to control and weaken its contents. Another high-ranking official said in retrospect that the White House decision to abandon the Senate deal was "a grave mistake." That action was to blame, he added, for major shortcomings in the final bill sent to Bush.

The error of the administration's decision to reject the Mitchell offer quickly became clear. Dingell sided with Waxman in barring the presence of administration officials from both the House's bill drafting and the final dealing with the Senate. The House Democrats' decision may have been solely a partisan maneuver against Bush. The House often shows greater loyalty to tradition, which in this case dictates a "members only" conference. But the fact that the Bush administration became "irrelevant" to the process, by its own officials' admission, caused serious second-guessing and internal sniping among them.

The modest role of administration officials from the Senate-House conference committee was a disappointment for Porter and the OMB's Bob Grady, who wanted to help complete the process that they had begun in early 1989. Several Republican conferees at the start of those sessions had urged the Democrats to allow Porter to attend, but that request triggered an angry exchange. "I don't know how you can possibly go forward without having information from the president of the United States," Sen. Simpson of Wyoming said at a July 25 meeting of the conferees, which was one of their few public sessions. Chafee and Lent, the senior Republicans on the Senate and House committees that handled the clean-air bill, echoed Simpson's view. But Baucus said that the conferees already had received the administration's views in a letter. Porter got into more trouble when he was asked to move from the front row of the audience to the conferees' tables to answer a question. Waxman then strongly objected to giving a seat at the table to any administration official. "This is a conference between the House and Senate," he said. In any case, Waxman added, any statements should come from Reilly, the EPA administrator, not from a White House aide.

Dingell, who frequently made clear his low regard for Reilly and Rosenberg, agreed with the Republicans that the White House should be allowed to select its own spokesman in the deliberations. But he squashed the July 25 discussion by saying that the conferees were spending a lot of time "on a matter that is not really before us" because no formal request had been made on Porter's behalf. That, in effect, ended the matter. Republicans informally advised the White House a few days later that, because of the Democrats' objections, they should drop the request.

Porter's limited role resulted in another humorous episode in the clean-air story. At an important bargaining session, Porter met with Republicans in their caucus room adjacent to the Energy and Commerce Committee's main room, where the negotiators were meeting. But when he later was kept out of the secret sessions with the Democrats, Republicans asked him to remain in their anteroom to listen to the debate through an open door from the committee room. While seated on the floor, the president's top domestic-policy aide sometimes strained to listen.

As a result of their limited access, the unhappy White House officials sought to influence the Senate-House conference committee by preparing two wide-ranging letters on the economic impact of the clean-air measure. Michael J. Boskin, the chairman of the president's Council of Economic Advisers, sent the memoranda to Dingell, who then circulated copies to the other conferees. Bush's original proposal, Boskin wrote, was "carefully crafted to make significant progress toward solution of important environmental problems" while keeping the costs to industry and consumers at about $20 billion and assuring compatibility with economic growth. From this viewpoint, Boskin added, the $25–35 billion cost of both the Senate- and House-passed bills was too high.

Although the White House had voiced similar warnings earlier during the year, Boskin's letter on Sept. 21 refocused the conferees' attention on the marketplace impact of the legislation. The letter, whose contents became holy grail for a few administration loyalists on the conference committees, gave a detailed breakdown of the cost of dozens of provisions in the bills. The biggest single increase in 1995 would be the $1.6 billion addition for the reformulated-gasoline program. Other administration officials signaled that congressional failure to reduce these new costs could make the clean-air bill the target of a Bush veto. A separate letter, which was co-signed by Porter, Reilly and Energy Secretary Watkins, objected to the clean-fuels requirements: "Unless these provisions are changed, they will result in unnecessary increases in the price of gasoline to consumers and in potential supply disruptions, without producing commensurate environmental benefits." The impact of these efforts, said another administration official, was to "lay down a marker," which proved especially important to congressional Republicans working on the bill.

Some House members had their own difficulty in gaining entry to the conference committee sessions. But, unlike the White House officials, two Energy and Commerce Committee Democrats finally entered the fray as a result of well-placed help from Speaker Foley. Although the appointment of House conferees is the formal prerogative of the speaker, he usually ratifies the recommendations of the committee chairman with authority over the bill. On the clean-air bill, Dingell had disbursed those highly valued invitations in part on the basis of who had been most helpful to him.

Like Santa Claus at Christmas, Dingell had his own list of who was naughty and who was nice. The chairman wanted to make sure that he had a firm majority of the House conferees on his side. As a result, he sought to exclude Democrats Mike Synar of Oklahoma and Gerry Sikorski of Minnesota because they historically had sided with Waxman on critical points of the alternative-fuels and acid-rain disputes. But that led to a conflict within the committee that delayed for several weeks the formal appointment of the conferees. A leading Dingell foe called his action "mean and gratuitous." Finally, Foley held a private meeting with Dingell, in which the speaker stood up to Dingell and ordered that the two junior members be included on the list of conferees.

Although the House passed the bill on May 23, it took until June 28 for the House conferees to be formally appointed. Dingell was not the only complication. In a decision that senators later said was "intimidating," Foley selected 130 conferees to represent seven committees that asserted a formal interest in the bill. That turf-grabbing showed what Speaker Foley described as the proclivity of committees to seek jurisdictional imperative "with the dedication of medieval monks." The House Merchant Marine and Fisheries Committee, for example, helped to craft a section of the bill controlling air pollution from offshore oil-drilling facilities. Several other panels also had played bit roles in the prior debate, and most of the 130 conferees would be on the sidelines during the real work of the conference committee. But the nine Senate conferees representing two committees complained that the sheer numbers on the House side made it more cumbersome for them to negotiate with their counterparts.

The five-week delay in the selection of its members became standard fare for the conference committee. Its first formal meeting took place on July 13. When Congress adjourned for a month-long recess on Aug. 3, after having held two more sessions, the conferees had approved a less publicized section of the bill phasing out the use of ozone-depleting CFCs. With Congress preparing for its usual election-year adjournment in mid-October, time was running short. Some members of the conference committee and outside lobbyists started to raise doubts about whether Congress would have enough time to finish the clean-air bill.

The growing concerns about the bill's fate were fueled by events on the other side of the world. On August 2, Iraqi president Saddam Hussein invaded neighboring Kuwait and took control of its government. It would take seven months and the efforts of more than 500,000 U.S. troops to oust the Iraqis. In the meantime, however, some business lobbyists and House Republicans briefly explored whether the invasion might give them an unexpected and long-shot opportunity to turn the tables on the clean-air bill. They suggested to some lawmakers and to Bush administration officials that the economic and energy perils posed by the threatened loss of Persian Gulf oil outweighed the environmental gains from the clean-air bill. Dingell weighed, in effect, whether the invasion could be used as a pretext to kill or substantially weaken the legislation. But he determined that the bill had gone too far to be stopped and he quickly dropped the idea. Most likely, Dingell also realized that he had made too much of a personal investment in the bill to let it die. "It was the opponents' last hurrah," a Bush administration official later said. Reilly sealed the issue by releasing a report that showed that the new Clean Air Act would save one million barrels of oil a day, which exceeded the total imports from Kuwait and Iraq before the war.

As with the earlier work by the House and Senate committees, the long periods between public sessions were filled with endless private meetings among numerous staff aides and a few members. Many of the aides, by now, were physically and emotionally drained by the legislation. The biggest problem was the exhaustion of Dingell's top policy aide Dave Finnegan, who was forced to rely increasingly on other Dingell aides who did not share his deep knowledge of the clean-air issues or of the deals that already had been cut. With his expert drafting, the chief House Republican aide Chuck Knauss also helped Dingell and Finnegan survive the final trying weeks. Often, however, it took Finnegan and Knauss long periods to reach agreements between themselves and with sympathetic industry lobbyists before they could take their proposals to the staff for Waxman and other environmentally minded members. "The drafting became more ambiguous as time went on," said a senior Senate aide who worked on the bill. "The agreements often were compromises, whose meaning was in the eye of the beholder."

Another important factor in the conference-committee dynamics was the less intensive role played by Baucus, the chairman of the Senate Environmental Protection Subcommittee, who led the Senate negotiators. He remained inexperienced in coping with both the broad range of issues and the intense pressures of the setting. At several critical points, Mitchell was forced to intervene to protect his own and the Senate's interests in the bill. Although Baucus had been first elected to Congress in 1974 as part of the Watergate class, which also included Waxman, the clean-air bill was the first controversial environmental legislation on which he played a major role. Baucus made no serious blunder during his baptism by fire. But he was no match for Dingell or Waxman during the final maneuvering and his constant pleas for the negotiators to finish their work became something of a joke among the participants. "Baucus wanted speed; Dingell wanted control," according to an analysis published at the start of the conference committee. "But observers say Baucus is untested in an arena as big as the clean air conference, and some contend that he is overmatched by Dingell . . ."[1]

The two chairmen tested each other, especially at the start. Baucus got into a flap with Dingell, for example, on what seemed a procedural issue that threatened to derail the conference committee. Dingell, on behalf of the auto manufacturers, feared that many states would follow the example of California and establish their own auto-emission standards. The issue moved to the forefront during the conference committee when New York State environmental boss Tom Jorling adopted the California standards for his own state. Fearing the impact on Detroit of similar steps by other states, Dingell wanted to clarify a section in the existing law that allowed California to set its own standard. Dingell demanded federal "pre-emption" of other states that might want to create what became known as a "third vehicle." That is, he wanted the federal government to control whether or not states could set their own standards. But Baucus and the Senate conferees resisted. Sen.

Daniel Patrick Moynihan, a New York Democrat who served on the Environment Committeee but had not played an active role during the 1990 debate on the bill, said, "This conference is in trouble if [Dingell's] provision stays in place."[2]

As often happens during a legislative crunch, the lawmakers were taking their cues from lobbyists with a strong interest in the bill. On the pre-emption issue, the Senate conferees were especially attentive to Jorling because he had been the chief Republican aide to the Environment and Public Works Committee when Congress passed the 1970 Clean Air Act. And Leon Billings, who was Jorling's partner on Muskie's staff at that time and had remained a close friend, was the Washington lobbyist for southern California's chief clean-air enforcement agency. Billings, a Montana native, had long been a friend of Baucus and the two of them had become confidants on the 1990 clean-air bill. But the Jorling-Billings effort failed when Waxman decided to maintain a unified House front. In return, Waxman won from Dingell an agreement permitting only California to continue to set separate motor-vehicle standards and making it easier for other states to adopt those standards. After some additional jockeying, including a threat by Finnegan to close his briefing books and walk out of the negotiations unless the Senate side dropped the issue, the senators and their aides backed down and agreed that the modified federal pre-emption resolved their concerns.

Most differences between the Senate and House during the conference committee were relatively narrow disputes over details, not over broad policy. But the resolution of those conflicts often carried a major impact for one region of the nation over another, or one industry over another. As the leading conferees moved toward agreement on what they knew would be a law with wide-ranging impact on business, consumers and the economy, they became increasingly mindful that they needed to give special care to seeking the clearest and most sensible legislative language.

The clean-fuels provisions became another example of how this careful approach led to some unusual procedures in drafting the clean-air bill. Sen. Daschle, the original sponsor of the provision encouraging more use of reformulated gasoline, was not a conference committee member. Because the chief Senate conferees were not interested in the issue, control again shifted to the House. The key players there were Democrat Waxman, who saw the toughest-possible provisions as a plus for his smog-choked Los Angeles constituents, and Republican Madigan, who viewed the increased use of the corn-based ethanol products as a boon for his rural Illinois constituents and local grain-processing companies. In a separate corner were the oil companies, represented by Texans Ralph Hall and Jack Fields; they wanted to retain as large a share of the auto-fuels market as possible and to assure that the final deal did not pose intolerable burdens on their refineries.

Dingell, who had reasons to keep the Los Angeles, Illinois and Texas camps happy, sought to keep above the fray and to encourage agreement. But that was not easy. Every increase won by Illinois and the Corn Belt in the required percentage of oxygen content in the fuels was money taken from the pockets of Dingell's Detroit and the Oil Belt. The political dealing became so intense that the grain and oil interests at one point tried to make a deal, which would have guaranteed certain levels of the by-products in the gasoline. But the environmentalists objected.

After the House Members and aides finally moved toward the outlines of an agreement, they convened what became a two-day, around-the-clock meeting to resolve the final details with several chiefs of the U.S. oil industry. Included were top officials from Exxon and Mobil plus lobbyists from Amoco and the Washington-based American Petroleum Institute. Meeting behind closed doors in an Energy and Commerce Committee room, they held several sessions to agree on the final details. Much of it was highly technical language concerning the formula for cleaner fuel and its use in metropolitan areas with the worst air quality. They agreed, for example, to define gasoline with legislative language that included the following:[3]

SPECIFICATION OF BASE GASOLINE USED AS BASIS
FOR REACTIVITY READJUSTMENT:

API gravity	57.8
Sulfur, ppm	317
Color	Purple
Benzene, vol. (percent)	1.35
Reid vapor pressure	8.7
Drivability	1195
Antiknock index	87.3

The final agreement also included the more ambitious House provisions requiring that certain commercial fleets of cars use still cleaner alternative fuels. These standards were those that California regulators had already set for the late 1990s. The deal retained the House-passed plan for the annual sale in California of 300,000 clean-fuel vehicles. But the conferees gave more flexibility to the auto companies by extending the original 1997 deadline until the 1999 model year. The agreement was less dramatic than the million-car mandate in Bush's original plan. But lawmakers hoped that the reformulated gasoline provisions and the California-based programs would be more realistic alternatives that, in the end, would accomplish far-reaching objectives.

As the House-Senate negotiations continued, the meetings—both the relatively few formal sessions among members and the many informal discussions dominated by staff—alternated between the hearing rooms of the Senate Environment and Public Works and the House Energy and Commerce Committees. In the final hectic days, as senior lawmakers were dashing from one meeting to another, some clean-air sessions moved to a large room in the Capitol that was a half-minute walk from Majority Leader Mitchell's office. There, the negotiators engaged in the final major round of high-stakes poker on acid rain, the issue that had been the most divisive during Senate and House deliberations.

They largely retained the Senate's acid-rain agreement, which was based on Bush's innovative plan for allowance-trading and a 10-million ton annual cut from the 1980 level of sulfur dioxide emissions. In addition to the Bush-Mitchell link on acid rain and the fact that the House had prevailed on most other issues in the conference committee, the decision to take most of the Senate plan reflected more practical considerations. It was the final major issue facing the conferees and the congressional session was running out of time for full-fledged bargaining. "It was distressing that much of our work in the House got lost," said Rep. Sharp of Indiana.

Sharp and other Midwest lawmakers worked during the final days of the congressional session to salvage a form of pork-barrel aid: additional allowances to ease the pain for their local coal-fired utilities that would be hardest hit by the new rules reducing their acid-rain emissions. Their continuing effort, led by Sharp, to achieve a more direct form of national cost sharing to finance the clean-up never had much chance of success. But Sharp kept the faith for his region. He rejected on principle, he said, a Senate proposal that was designed to placate him with aid narrowly targeted to his local Indiana utility in lieu of the broader Midwest.

The Midwesterners among the House conferees settled on a last-gasp proposal to give 200,000 additional credits to Illinois, Indiana and Ohio utilities each year until 1999. Because each credit permitted the emission of another ton of sulfur dioxide, the change would allow some of the dirty utilities to meet the new requirements without spending $50 million or more to scrub their emissions. The plan had been developed when EPA staff recalculated the nationwide acid-rain total, including emissions from Energy Department plants. But when the proposal was presented on Oct. 20 at a private, late Saturday-night meeting of the key conferees, the initial reaction was not positive. "It resulted in a Midwest-bashing speech by Max Baucus, who told us that we didn't know what was good for us," said Rep. Eckart of Ohio. "He and I had an exchange that was not friendly."

Eckart then walked the Midwest's proposal to Mitchell's office, telling him that the talks were at an impasse and that the region badly needed help. "George Mitchell suggested that if I put together an acid-rain offer that was a balance, he would go along with the 200,000 credits," Eckart said. After some additional shuttle diplomacy that produced minor concessions by the Midwesterners, Mitchell secured a post-midnight deal and Baucus yielded, despite his initial opposition; Eckart then won the House conferees' okay. "The Westerners, in their mood and language, felt that they could do a bill without us. . . . In the end, Sen. Mitchell broke the logjam," Eckart added.

A conflict within the administration added further spice to the Saturday night deal. When the negotiators asked for White House approval of the added 200,000 credits, Sununu and Porter agreed. But other administration officials, including Reilly and Rosenberg, reportedly were unhappy and refused to process the letter that Sununu had ordered. A story in the *Washington Post* outlined what happened next: "On the morning of Oct. 20, as conferees focused on acid rain, Reilly argued against the letter in a talk with Porter, and the decision whether to send it was left open." Reilly then reportedly left for his weekend home in rural Virginia and was virtually incommunicado until the conferees resolved the acid-rain issue.[4] Months later, Dingell fumed about the incident. "Mr. Reilly and Mr. Rosenberg were not well esteemed here," he said. "On acid rain, they were lacking in competence and integrity. . . . Sen. Mitchell agreed to the 200,000 tons but no one could find Reilly or Rosenberg."

On another issue related to acid rain, the Midwesterners scored little more than a Pyrrhic victory. After the Senate defeated by one vote the Byrd amendment for generous unemployment benefits to coal miners who lost their jobs because of the new acid-rain controls, the House added a more modest benefit plan covering workers in all industries who were unemployed because of the new law. Despite a presidential veto threat, the House approved the amendment by coal-state Democratic Rep. Bob Wise of West Virginia on a 274–146 vote before passing the clean-air bill in May. Opponents objected that despite Wise's low $250 million pricetag, the plan could become a raid on the federal Treasury.

When Wise's amendment reached the conference committee, White House officials demanded to scale it back further. In the face of the renewed veto threats, the lawmakers virtually conceded the issue. As enacted, the "job displacement" section was revised to "encourage the Labor Department to provide technical assistance" for job searches by individuals left unemployed by the new law. The $800 maximum allowance for each eligible person was less than 1 percent of the total amount that had been envisioned by the Byrd amendment. The law also provided additional money for training and education of workers who become unemployed. Even its supporters agreed that the compromise was a pale shadow of the Wise amendment. But its supporters, including Dingell, contended that the result affirmed Byrd's earlier point that the clean-air bill had adverse economic consequences. "It makes a political statement that environmental regulation costs jobs," one supporter said. Symbolism, in short, can be an important rationale for legislative actions.

The conferees failed to resolve fully some other peripheral issues in the clean-air debate. Steel-industry officials, for example, convinced key lawmakers that they could not afford the huge cost of reducing toxic emissions from their often antiquated coke ovens. Although the Senate had included requirements that the steel industry clean-up start by 1995, the House language was more stringent. (Dingell had a special interest in the issue because a National Steel Corporation plant was the biggest employer in his auto-based district.) The conferees agreed to allow 30 years for steel companies to meet the law's stiffest requirements, even though they acknowledged that they have no idea whether the required technology will be available.

"The issue kept getting put off because it is very esoteric and very narrow," said Eckart, whose home state of Ohio is the nation's second-largest steel producer. "When chairman Dingell, Mr. Waxman and I negotiated at the end, we agreed to give the industry more time but required them to meet standards. It is uncertain whether they will have the money to pay for it."

On their final contentious issue, a proposal to restrict air pollution in national parks, the conferees decided simply to punt. In this case, it was the House that used stringent language that most Senate conferees and some House members found objectionable. The conferees addressed the dispute during a meeting held after midnight on Oct. 22. The pressure to settle was intense. A formal meeting of the conference committee was scheduled for that afternoon to ratify the entire package. Rep. Ron Wyden, an Oregon Democrat, explained that his House-passed amendment to impose new rules on pollution at national parks was designed to limit further "visibility degradation" in the public lands. But Wyden encountered hostile opposition from Sens. Baucus and Simpson, who represented states with big national parks and were prominent members of the conference committee. Adoption of Wyden's language would kill the bill, they said flatly. Consistency, of course, is not a priority for legislators. The same two senators earlier had fought hard for acid-rain controls elsewhere in the nation that would increase mining of their states' low-sulfur coal.

"There was a vehemence in the senators' opposition," said Rep. Sharp, who attended the final meeting. "We debated for 45 minutes in the middle of the night. There was no time to look at alternative proposals." Wyden, who received little help from Dingell, emerged with noncommittal statements from the conferees that he had raised an important issue that they would attempt to address in the future. And the conferees retained the Senate provision for five years of federal research on the problem.

Their decisions finally completed, the weary conferees opened a few bottles of champagne at 5:02 a.m. But they had little time to savor their accomplishment. Most quickly went home and prepared for their afternoon meeting, where they would formally conclude the conference committee and sign the report accompanying the massive bill.

The final six days of legislative action on the clean-air bill moved into the public forum, where it attracted far more press attention than had the intense deliberations of the previous year. But the final act had little significance. The work was done. All that remained were the efforts to take credit and to characterize what had been achieved.

We began our tale in the Cannon House Office Building with an exhausted Dingell holding his head in his hands. This hardly seems surprising, considering that the final session began at 2:30 p.m. after the 5:02 a.m. conclusion of the deal cutting. The conferees formally convened in the Cannon Building's large caucus room for their final session. The brief public meeting was filled with congratulatory statements. There was virtually no discussion of the complex issues and the bitter disputes that had consumed the attention of many of them for as long as a decade. Dingell and Mitchell conveyed the prevailing mood combining exhaustion and relief. Rep. Al Swift, the Washington Democrat, was more boastful. "At a time when members of Congress and the media are raising questions about whether Congress can deliver, we demonstrated that, yes, this institution does work," Swift said. Before and after the meeting, many of the key players held press conferences or issued statements praising their own actions.

The lobbyists flocked to the meeting room to distribute their views. "America's skies will—literally—be bluer because of this legislation," said Dick Ayres, the leader of the environmentalists. But more remains to be done, he added. "Congress was unable to overcome the objections of the auto and oil industries to produce a bill that will assure healthful air quality in our cities in this century." Bill Fay, the leader of the business coalition that had opposed tough new controls, had a different view of the same picture. "Americans will see continued progress in their efforts to improve the nation's air quality," Fay said. "But they will also pay the price of those efforts through job losses and dislocations, higher consumer product prices, increased electricity bills, reduced competitiveness, changed lifestyles and slower economic growth."

The final debates in the Capitol a few days later were also perfunctory. Most House members and one-third of the senators were in the midst of re-election campaigns and had long since grown tired of their legislative session, which had run way past its scheduled adjournment. Many were busy crafting the final deals to resolve the separate months-long deadlock over the federal budget. That controversy had been the chief reason why the session ran so late into October and why the public was growing even more negative about how Congress does its job.

When the conference report on the clean-air bill was discussed in each chamber, members took a few hours mostly to praise the result. Many made points for local consumption. "I am particularly proud of the positive impact that this clean-air bill will have on my own home state of Oklahoma," Rep. Synar said. Michigan Republican Rep. Carl D. Pursell, asked about the formula that the Michigan South Central Power Agency, a utility in his district, would use to determine its allowances for acid-rain emissions. Others engaged in the common practice of placing statements in the *Congressional Record* without reading them. In many cases, members or friendly lobbyists would later copy those statements—many of them written by lobbyists—and distribute them for any of a myriad of self-serving reasons.

On the final votes, the House passed the clean-air conference report, 401–25, in the early evening of Oct. 26. The Senate's approval came on an 89–10 vote at noon the next day, which was a Saturday. The negative votes came mostly from conservative Republicans and a few coal-state lawmakers. Sen. Byrd, the former majority leader, remained unreconciled to the end. He voted against the bill and delivered the final statement of the two-year congressional debate. "We have a responsibility to enact legislation that takes into account the interests of all of the regions of our country," Byrd told the Senate. "I cannot ask thousands of coal miners in West Virginia—men and women who daily risk their lives to provide our nation with much-needed energy—to sacrifice their jobs so that the nation might gain some uncertain benefit from reduced sulfur-dioxide emissions."

Byrd's speech was a stark reminder of the age-old congressional adage that all politics is local. Fortunately, for the Clean Air Act, Congress's job was done. There remained only the non-local issue of presidential approval.

Endnotes

1. George Hager, "Cannons of the Conference Room Draw Clean Air Battle Lines," *Congressional Quarterly*, July 21, 1990: 2291.
2. Keith Schneider, "As Session Nears End, Revisers of the Clean Air Act Deadlock Over a New Proposal," *The New York Times*, Oct. 9, 1990: A18.
3. House Report 101–952, "Clean Air Act Amendments of 1990," Conference Report: 119.
4. Michael Weisskopf, "With Pen, Bush to Seal Administration Split on Clean Air Act," *The Washington Post*, November 15, 1990: A23.

11

Clearing the Air
★ ★ ★

Surrounded by Executive Branch officials and Vice President Dan Quayle, President George Bush signed the Clean Air Act on Nov. 15, 1990. Key lawmakers were little more than props at the White House ceremony.

167

For two years, the clean-air debate had been largely non-partisan. The constant clashes that plagued the divided government of the Reagan presidency had been set aside. Republican George Bush and Democrat George Mitchell, both of whom had strong partisan instincts, had cooperated to achieve their goals. And they worked to overcome divisions within both the executive branch and Congress.

But that comity, ironically, seemed to collapse once Congress finished action on the bill. First, the Democratic leaders of Congress denied the Republican president his hope of gaining partisan advantage with the enactment of the bill. Then, Bush returned the favor by staging a White House ceremony where he signed the bill into law with flourishes that showed a notable disdain and disrespect toward congressional leaders. Because politicians' actions are rarely unintentional, some score settling obviously was at play. Washington's normal gamesmanship had reasserted itself.

The final steps in the clean-air drama showed that legislation and politics are inextricably linked, even when the players claim otherwise. When the Senate approved the conference report on Oct. 27, 1990, there were 10 days remaining until Election Day. That was more than enough time for each party to use the bill for its own partisan purposes. The Bush White House decided that it wanted the president to sign the bill into law in California, where voters were especially attuned to environmental problems and a hard-fought and close contest for governor was in its final moments. What could be better for Republicans than Bush applying the final flourishes to the clean-air legislation at an environmentally symbolic site in the Golden State with Pete Wilson, the Republican nominee for governor, at his side?

The move was not discussed publicly at the time. But some congressional Democrats guessed at the possibilities, and made sure that the election-eve spectacle did not happen. In the recesses of the Capitol, where computer-era clerks still perform the age-old ritual of writing formal documents with a fountain pen and parchment, Democratic officials passed the word that there was no hurry to finish the so-called "enrollment" and send the final clean-air document to the White House. As a result, Bush did not sign the bill until Nov. 15, which was 19 days after final congressional action and nine days after the election.

The presidential staff finally scheduled the stately signing ceremony for the East Room of the White House. Although Capitol Hill is usually a ghost town in the days immediately after an election, many important congressional players were in the front of the audience, to the left of the presidential podium. Senate leaders Mitchell and Dole entered with big smiles. Most senior members of the committees that had worked on the bill for so many years were there to join in the festivities—Baucus, Chafee, Dingell and Waxman, among others. Many were joined by their aides. Immediately in front of Bush were members of his own staff—Sununu, Gray, Porter and Grady—and other top administration officials. To the right, a flock of lobbyists had obtained coveted tickets and were jammed into the large room.

Flanking Bush at the podium was an unusual group—First Lady Barbara Bush, Vice President Dan Quayle, Energy Secretary James Watkins and EPA Administrator Bill Reilly. The first two had virtually nothing to do with the bill, and the role of Watkins had been modest. At other bill-signing ceremonies, it has been common to invite congressional leaders to surround the president. But they were not part of the picture that the presidential image-makers wanted for this day.

The proud president sought to prove his claim to being the environmental president. He reviewed his initial commitment during the 1988 campaign to clean-air legislation, highlighted the White House preparation of his proposal and took full credit for the outcome. "As we used to say in the Navy," Bush told his guests. "Mission defined. Mission accomplished." He barely acknowledged the countless hours consumed by the coterie of members of Congress to his side or the battles that they endured in drafting the several-inch stack of legislation on the desk before him. Reflecting the second-class status to which Congress is typically relegated in the public mind, Bush claimed and generally received much of the credit for the bill's broad principles, while Congress had slogged through most of the gritty details. He then signed the top sheet of the stack.

Immediately after the signing, in what appeared to be an awkward and unplanned move, he invited members of Congress to greet him. "Maybe we could have the symbolism," he said, according to the official transcript. "I don't think there's any protocol, but if I could just invite the front row here to come up with members of Congress, we'd at least show that this is an across-the-board . . ." A half-dozen lawmakers, led by Mitchell, lined up to shake his hand. Perhaps still smarting from the wounds of the earlier budget battle, Bush did not even stage the ritual of handing pens to the chief legislators responsible for the new law. By pointedly ignoring protocol, Bush and his aides further demeaned the congressional role in the crafting of the legislation.

The November 15 signing ceremony demonstrated another painful irony for Congress. The public focus on Congress that day was trained not on this important achievement but instead on the start of

Capitol Hill hearings into the celebrated activities of the Keating Five. Those five senators, accused of violating ethical rules by seeking favors for embattled savings-and-loan executive Charles H. Keating, came to symbolize what ailed Congress and why it was an object of public contempt.

Although Bush barely acknowledged Congress's handling of the new law, there are several ways to assess how the institution fared, how circumstances had changed since Congress passed the first major clean-air law two decades earlier, and who were the winners and losers on the 1990 Clean Air Act.

Performance: In substantive terms, passage of the new law was a positive statement that government can work. That was no small accomplishment at a time when stalemate and failure had become standard fare in Washington. "It was a real high," Baucus said. Democracy is "a painfully slow process but it works."

Responsibility for the legislation's passage was shared. Mitchell created a sometimes uneasy alliance with Bush in which they separately defined the policy framework for the bill and established a political course for Senate approval that made eventual enactment a virtual certainty. The House ultimately wrote most of the details within that broad framework. The expert's role on the vital minutiae of government has often fallen to the House because, as in this case, key senators and top executive branch officials lacked the requisite expertise or political skills to deal with those matters.

Even if Bush's own proposal was ignored, and much of it was, the fact that the president devoted his political capital to the goal of clean-air legislation could not be overlooked. "People in academe fail to understand that Congress is truly a 'deliberative' world," said Rep. Sharp, a former political science professor. "It is not the natural instinct of people to take on tasks that are not necessary. . . . Bush helped to force the agenda when he made his proposal. Everyone began to recognize that we were coming to the point of having to decide."

Mitchell's role may have been the most personally wrenching. He sacrificed much of the proposal from his own Environment and Public Works Committee and crafted an unusual alliance with the White House that reflected his pragmatic sense of power politics. In doing that, he found himself at odds with many in his own party, notably on Byrd's coal-miner amendment. And he bore the brunt of criticism from his former allies among the environmentalists for sacrificing principle, even though he believed that he worked far more than did the "true believers" to achieve their shared goals.

The two key House Democrats on the bill, Dingell and Waxman, scored a significant achievement that surprised many who had witnessed the layers of suspicion in their often bitter relationship. They convinced the many skeptics that they could do business on clean-air problems after having been at each other's throats for so long. Each could claim victory on his terms. By most accounts, Waxman skillfully drove the policy details in the bill that he had worked for a decade to achieve. Dingell's role was more elusive. Months after the bill's enactment, he remained bitter about the outcome. "Ask some of the jackasses who passed the bill," Dingell said, when asked why Congress tightened the auto-emission standards.

But, according to Energy and Commerce Committee insiders, Dingell also scored a real achievement. After having mastered delay tactics that postponed for a decade the financial day of reckoning for business, he kept control of a process that he was in jeopardy of losing when Bush took office. When, in Dingell's words, he "could not hold back the tide," he showed anxious House Democrats that he could exercise power, even if he did not embrace some of the result. "Henry was the leader of the catalysts for change," said Democratic Rep. Eckart. "John managed that change and shaped it." Former Republican Rep. Tauke said that Waxman was the bigger winner of the two and he enhanced his stature because "he got most of what he wanted." But Dingell, Tauke added, "prevailed on issues important to him and he kept control of the committee." Dingell showed, in effect, that his constituents at the Energy and Commerce Committee were at least as important to him as those in Detroit.

At issue was the exercise of political power—not by an individual, but by the institution. Congress faced the question of whether it could perform in the face of sometimes irreconcilable divisions and conflict. "It was political in a most intense way," Dingell said. "Issues only occasionally mattered. More often, it was politics—for regions, for the economy, for the environmentalists.... The bill was not an environmental decision. It was a political decision." In the end, Congress passed a far-reaching bill linking diverse issues and each side felt that it had gained as much as possible under the circumstances.

The achievement was all the more significant because doubts were widespread in 1989–90 that Congress could function in a meaningful way, for four chief reasons. At the top of its agenda during much of that time was the staggering and pervasive budget deficit, which had become a symbol for the futility of the legislative process. Although its results were dubious, a months-long budget summit between congressional leaders and administration officials garnered far more public attention in 1990 than did the clean-air debate. A second symptom of the legislative malaise was that government leaders had found it easier to deflect public problems or even to repeal a major law (in this case, the 1988 law to give the elderly improved insurance coverage against the cost of catastrophic illnesses) rather than to fashion a positive response to problems. Third, a proposed 50 percent pay raise for top federal officials triggered a national protest in 1989 and it was followed by an outburst of anti-incumbent sentiment as the biennial election neared. On an individual level, finally, 1989 was marked by the unprecedented resignations under fire of two of the top three House Democrats—Speaker Jim Wright of Texas and Majority Whip Tony Coelho of California. Both came under fire for the way they managed their personal finances.

Despite some inevitable shortcomings in the Clean Air Act, its outcome demonstrated that Congress can work, that private citizens with sensible ideas can have an impact on the system. The best proof of that was academic economist Dan Dudek of the Environmental Defense Fund. He helped the White House to add important details to its acid-rain proposal that, despite regional griping, largely withstood criticism. "The lesson is that government works," Dudek said. "I was able to turn an abstract idea into policy." That pride may be unfashionable amid typical modern public cynicism toward government. Even though few citizens can be as fortunate as Dudek, however, his success should serve as encouragement.

Process: The handling of the clean-air bill revealed significant changes in the procedures by which Congress transacts the public's business. Although defenders of the institution respond that the final substantive policy is all that matters, the process is important in other respects. How a nation conducts representative government serves as a statement that often directly affects the public's confidence in its leaders, both public and private.

First, virtually the entire clean-air bill was drafted behind closed doors—in the Senate, in the House and in the conference committee. Its provisions were so filled with scientific jargon that even the most knowledgeable members were forced to rely on the few congressional aides who understood most of its details and its potential impact. On the Senate and House floors, few votes affecting the product were cast.

If anything, most lawmakers were grateful that a relative handful of their colleagues had been willing to make the tough decisions on their behalf.

Was Congress, where closed doors have become common, supposed to work this way? True, the Constitution was written behind closed doors more than two centuries earlier. And public debate does prompt a large display of posturing that can be pompous or incendiary, or both. But as government becomes more complex and its impact more intrusive, and its workings become more secretive and mysterious, the danger increases that an uninformed citizenry will rebel against legislation that seems to arrive out of a black box.

Second, within Congress, the failure by most members to comprehend much of what they are doing can have a similarly corrosive impact. When legislation has become so complex that unelected aides handle many of the details, the representative process has been severely undermined. The often uncontrolled influence of committee staff meant that power was concentrated in individuals, no matter how public-minded, with inadequate accountability.

Third, the crumbling of committees during the past two decades, both in their influence within Congress and in their ability to operate in the traditional parliamentary fashion, is a worrisome development. No longer can Senate and House committees be trusted to provide the expertise needed to cool the passions and to temper the results. As shown by the clean-air bill, many committee members were not sharing the legislative responsibility. Worse yet, many proponents and opponents on the committees felt at liberty to engage in actions that pandered to regional or economic interests. They did more to make mischief than to produce consensus.

Knowledgeable and skillful lawmakers like Mitchell, Dingell and Waxman doubtlessly made positive contributions when they imposed some discipline on the unruly process and made many of the tough decisions. Sometimes, as in the House, influential committee members can take control. Or, as in the Senate, an astute party leader like Mitchell steps in. But an undue burden was placed on them. It is unrealistic to expect that these leaders, who might be unable to devote so much time and resources to a comparable bill in another conflict, will always come to the rescue.

Fourth, the erosion of the committee process and of legislative debate, generally, have made the job of congressional party leaders more difficult. "The loss of power by committee chairmen and the increased chaos in the use of Senate rules to promote a senator's views have required leadership to be more involved in keeping things going," said Robert G. Liberatore, a former top Senate Democratic aide who became a Chrysler Corp. lobbyist. Activist leadership can be desirable. But the party leaders run the risk of failing to chart an acceptable direction unless the rank and file has become fully engaged in the debate. Mitchell, for example, triggered considerable second-guessing among his troops. Although the more soothing style of a Speaker Foley may have given the needed incentive to resolve the House's internal conflicts, mere style cannot be expected to settle all deep-seated differences.

Finally, a surprising aspect of the bill drafting was the quick pace at which influence rose and fell among lobbyists. Leon Billings, for example, had been widely viewed as a deft congressional insider for two decades. As a lobbyist working on the 1990 bill, however, his harsh criticism of several decisions burned so many of his bridges that he became persona non grata in key offices. The former top Muskie aide, who played a critical role in drafting both the 1970 and 1977 clean-air laws, had long been allied with Mitchell and Waxman, but in 1990 he found himself virtually shut out of their offices.

Business lobbyists, for their part, appeared to have gained greater sophistication since the 1970s and made more effective use of their ample resources. By making the Clean Air Working Group into a well-oiled and publicity-conscious coalition, Bill Fay helped to level the playing field with the environmentalists. And the automobile companies, who were sideswiped in 1970, used their resources more effectively in 1990. They were helped, of course, by having Dingell in a position of considerable influence. But their lobbyists played their cards shrewdly not only in their advice to the House chairman but also in their willingness to accept middle-ground positions.

White House relations: For activist congressional Democrats, a majority of whom had never held their office with a president of their own party, Bush's ability to seek and gain credit for the new law was a sore point. "What's so frustrating about this administration is that it makes proposals, sometimes vague, and it doesn't follow through," Waxman said. "They jettisoned their own proposal on alternative fuels. . . . Franklin Roosevelt would convene people, prepare his own plan and then move it. A president should fight for his own bill."

The requirements of the new clean-air law mirrored the modern increase in mistrust and hostility between Congress and the White House. Lawmakers who had grown accustomed to battling bureaucrats at the White House and the agencies left nothing to chance. The Democrats knew that their influence started and stopped in Congress. Once the Clean Air Act was enacted, many years might pass before they would be in a position to govern the agencies that set enforcement guidelines.

One obvious difference between the 1970 and 1990 clean-air laws is their level of detail. The landmark 1970 law, which consumed 47 pages of the federal statutes, mostly set goals and left it to industry and the new Environmental Protection Agency to determine how to achieve them. In 1990 the new law ran 314 pages and was filled with requirements and timetables. The lawmakers wanted to limit the discretion of the Republican-managed regulators and Republican-appointed federal judges, so they mandated and set guidelines for more than 200 rule-making actions by the EPA in the next several years. "The specificity in the 1990 amendments reflects the concern that without detailed directives industry intervention might frustrate efforts to put pollution control steps in place," Waxman wrote in an overview of the law.

As conservative presidents have initiated fewer new programs and Congress has become more prescriptive in response, the shifting balance of power has left both sides unhappy. Presidents have complained that heavy-handed laws on the environment and other areas of federal regulation have produced congressional micromanagement. Many in Congress have responded that Republican bureaucrats ignore legislative directives. The clean-air conflict showed that divided government can become a recipe for years of legislative and regulatory battles.

Ultimately, the Clean Air Act showed that presidents matter. Once Bush was elected and decided to keep his vague clean-air campaign promises, the many constraints of divided government quickly disappeared. "What the Clean Air Act illustrates is that this genuinely was a presidential initiative," said Porter, Bush's chief domestic-policy aide. "He worked with a bipartisan group on the Hill to achieve the objective." Ironically, then, the clean-air debate, which raised so many divisive issues, may have proved easier to resolve because the political players astride the federal government represented a broad cross section of the ideological spectrum. Once there was a will to get the job done, a sense of inevitability quickly took control.

Public information: One area where Congress clearly fell short in passing the new clean-air law was in its responsibility to inform the public of its actions. One reason, of course, was that most meetings on the bill were held behind closed doors. But two other important factors were that the key legislative players had little interest in getting the complete story out and that the major news organizations largely accepted those conditions and made little effort to report much other than an occasional anecdote.

For the public, as a result, the story of the clean-air bill had a beginning and an end but no middle. From a congressional perspective, such an approach was welcomed by many. At the beginning, advocates of change were glad to use the press to tell compelling stories of the nation's poor air quality. Stories—better yet, pictures—of smog grab many readers' attention and can build public support for new legislation. At the end of the story, the lawmakers needed the press to give them credit for their accomplishment. But the vast middle of the story was not seriously reported. "Thankfully, there was not much coverage of the details," said a House aide who made a major contribution to crafting the bill. "I did not want news stories that we were doing well because it might have encouraged resistance by other people on other sections of the bill." An influential Senate aide, who agreed that press coverage of the bill was weak, voiced a similar comment: "It was not our job to explain the story." The problem, the aide added, was that "the bill was so complicated that you don't know where to start in explaining it."

The fact that a story is difficult to tell, however, should not have prevented the press from trying. The fact that the players were reluctant or unwilling to cooperate should have given reporters and editors all the more reason to uncover the facts. According to the aides who worked on the clean-air bill, however, weeks would often pass without a telephone call from the environmental reporters for *The Washington Post* or *The New York Times*.

While the print and broadcast media were largely ignoring the clean-air bill, they engaged in what appeared to be massive overkill in reporting the news—more often, the lack of news—in negotiations over the federal budget. Day after day, that deadlock was the page-one newspaper story or it received at least two minutes of precious time on the TV-network evening news. In contrast to the clean-air bill, the budget story had newsroom sizzle. For the same congressional Democrats who had low-keyed the clean-air bill, the budget deadlock became an especially good news story. They encouraged its coverage with daily comments attacking the Bush administration or presenting their own alternative. The success of the Democrats' press strategy can be seen in the numbers. The three television networks devoted a total of 20 on-site reports to the clean-air story in their nightly news broadcasts during all of 1990; in another nine cases, the network anchor read a brief report, usually no longer than 30 seconds. On the budget story, by contrast, the three networks devoted a total of 86 stories in the month of October alone.[1] The *Post*, the most widely read newspaper on Capitol Hill, was little better. Of the roughly two dozen stories that the *Post* published about the bill in 1990, nearly all were about public events and actions; the closed-door meetings were all but ignored. Contrast that with the budget summit, where at least one *Post* reporter almost always covered and wrote a daily story during the four months of usually fruitless private sessions.

The environment: Will the new law help to clean the nation's dirty and toxic air? Probably yes. But glitches surely will cause problems along the way, as happens with any new law. Years of testing and overhaul by industry plus enforcement by federal and local governments will be required to learn whether the law really works and what its shortcomings are. By that time, many members of Congress and their aides who helped to draft the law will have left Capitol Hill. They will have history, not the voters, to judge their accountability on the 1990 Clean Air Act.

Until then, beauty will be in the eye of the beholder. The members of Congress who invested so much of their time and energy in the law not surprisingly have sung most of its praises. But their varied levels of enthusiasm, some of which may reflect a self-protecting response, reveal the uncertainty among those closest to the law. "It was as strong as possible under the circumstances," said Mitchell, in typically guarded praise.

In Waxman's upbeat view, the historical record tells a striking tale. "Despite the fact that they are the product of extensive negotiations and compromise, the new programs in the 1990 amendments have comparable or greater stringency than the controversial legislative proposals under debate, and vehemently opposed by industry, throughout the 1980s," he wrote.[2] "Remarkably, in many areas, the amendments actually surpass in scope and stringency the earlier proposals." The EPA's Rosenberg agreed with Waxman that the bill had been strengthened compared with earlier versions. But he said that the Democrats failed to give Bush enough credit. "The reason that the bill was stronger was because of the administration," he said.

Dingell was more ambivalent when he discussed the new law. "In some instances, [Waxman's view] may be true," he said. "In my view, the bill should not be judged on whether it is tougher or easier. What is important is that it is better than the earlier proposals in its economic effect, its workability, its impact on jobs and industries. . . . Mr. Waxman is entitled to his view. He has difficulty proving his and I have difficulty disproving it."

Compromises were made at each stage of the process and with each major part of the bill. Leading environmentalists outside Congress were especially unhappy that the new law failed to require more reduction of automobile emissions. Billings said that the new law does little more than "get things moving again after the recent inertia." Several others criticized the absence of the type of technology-forcing requirements on the automobile industry that were included in the 1970 law. "They were very unwilling to take what the public health demands and to force technology to come up with answers," said Ayres, head of the clean-air coalition. But an auto-company lobbyist disagreed: "We are keeping all of our engineers at work to comply with the latest regulations."

Some environmentalists attacked the excessive delays extracted by Dingell for imposing new controls on industry, especially for autos. But Waxman responded that another few years of delay was an acceptable price for winning the support of Dingell and the Bush administration for the strict new requirements. White House officials responded, after they had reviewed the law, that it actually may be too strict. "I'm worried that some sections may be too demanding," said presidential counsel Boyden Gray. In the view of OMB official Bob Grady, the new anti-smog requirements on industrial facilities in the dirtiest cities were "unduly restrictive" and may hinder economic growth.

Critics from both the environmental and industry camps said that the new rules were especially tough for stationary sources because the automobile industry was allowed to get off too easily. But both Dingell and Waxman, whose October 1989 tailpipe deal set the framework for the new auto-emissions rules, strongly rejected that conclusion and its zero-sum premise. Waxman said that he especially welcomed the broad alternative-fuels requirements for California-based vehicles in the late 1990s.

The acid-rain section of the new law won the most plaudits for its innovation and required clean-up. "Acid rain was the strongest part of the bill," said Rep. Sikorski of Minnesota, an early advocate of federal action in that area. But some coal and utility-industry officials remained skeptical that the allowances-trading systems would work in the real world. "The jury is out," a coal-company executive said after closely examining the system for a few months. With acid rain, as with other parts of the bill, "the politics outran the science and Congress ignored the economic costs," another corporate lobbyist complained.

No after-the-fact analyses, a cottage industry in Washington, can change the reality that Bush and Congress passed a new law. Its policy and political effects will be subject to a host of largely uncontrollable factors, ranging from the nation's economy, to progress in research laboratories, to the skills of the EPA bureaucrats. But there can be little doubt that the 1990 Clean Air Act makes a broad attempt to live up to its name.

With the Clean Air Act completed, life in Congress returned to its usual pace. As energy legislation moved to the forefront in 1991, moves were quickly afoot to broaden—or to abandon—the new alternative-fuels program. The Senate and House committees that bore the major share of the clean-air work turned their attention to overhauling the less glamorous federal law that manages and seeks to reduce the nation's waste disposal.

Some more political changes also were under way. Aides to Max Baucus spread the word that the Senate Environment and Public Works Committee needed more effectively to manage its staff and internal operations. John Chafee, who had alienated some Republicans with his support for a strong new clean-air law, was stripped of his position as chairman of the Senate Republican Conference. Many observers considered that action a payback by GOP conservatives. On the House side, Dingell and Waxman resumed their bristling personal dealings on a host of issues. Dingell returned his focus to high-profile oversight hearings on universities that use research grants to rip off the federal taxpayer. Waxman resumed his long-standing campaign for a sweeping overhaul of the nation's health-care system.

George Mitchell joined Waxman in committing himself to leading the fight in the Senate over health care. "I said after the clean-air debate that a decade is long enough for any one subject," he said. "I would like to devote the next decade to another subject. I had in mind the health care issue. I hope it doesn't take me 10 years."[3]

Perhaps, in another decade, a whole new Washington will appear in a new book-length drama on the passage of national health insurance. Whatever details emerge in that or some other proposal, how Congress passed it into law will surely offer to another class of legislative students a story as exciting and as full of twists as that of the Clean Air Act.

Endnotes

1. Vanderbilt Television News Index and Abstracts, Vanderbilt University Television News Archive, 1990.
2. Henry A. Waxman, "An Overview of the Clean Air Act of 1990," *Environmental Law*, Lewis and Clark Law School, (forthcoming).
3. "On the Hill, Legislative War Goes On," *National Journal,* March 9, 1991: 578.

Index

acid rain
  alternative-fuels enthusiasts, 140,
    142
  Bush bill, reaction to, 60–61
  Bush's election politics, 46, 49
  Bush team prepares bill, 55–60
  Clean Air Act overview, 4
  conference committee overview,
    153
  Energy and Commerce negotia-
    tions, 126, 128
  Group of Nine discussions, 73
  House-Senate negotiations, 156,
    161–64
  industry lobbyists, 111
  issues summary, 23
  lobbying overview, 103
  1984–88 House maneuvering,
    33–34
  Senate Environment Committee
    bill drafting, 77, 79–80
  Senate in Reagan years, 36–38
  Senate negotiations, 91, 93
  Waxman's influence, 124
AFL–CIO, 101
Agriculture Committee, House, 126,
    147
Agriculture Department, 126
air-quality standards, 22
Alliance for Acid Rain Control, 107
alternative fuels, 178–79

Bush team prepares bill, 51, 59–60
  conference committee overview,
    156
  Dingell's leadership, 116
  Energy and Commerce negotia-
    tions, 126
  overview, 134–50
American Lung Association, 105
American Petroleum Institute, 138,
    160
American University, 97
Amoco, 160
Anderson, Glenn, 20
Andreas, Dwayne, 144
Annunzio, Frank, 20
anticrime bill, 67
Appalachian region, 38
Appropriations Committee, Senate,
    91, 98
  Agriculture Subcommittee, 98
Archer Daniels Midland Company,
    144–45
Atlantic Richfield Company, 137–41
Audubon Society, 50, 104–105
automobile emissions
  1970 Clean Air Act enactment, 15
  Senate debate, 95
  warranties, 149
automobile industry, 178
  alternative-fuels overview, 135
  alternative-fuels showdown, 145

181

automobile industry, *(Continued)*
   Bush bill, reaction to, 61
   Clean Air Act overview, 4
   Dingell-Waxman auto deal, 73–76
   Group of Nine discussions, 73
   industry lobbyists, 110–11
   issues summary, 23
   lobbying overview, 103
   1970 Clean Air Act enactment, 15
   1977 Clean Air Act Amendments,
      18
   1981–82 House debate, 29
   1984–88 House maneuvering, 33
   Senate in Reagan years, 41–42
Ayres, Richard E., 76, 87–88, 99,
      101, 104, 107, 165

Baker, Howard H., Jr., 16
Baker, James A., III, 60
Ball State University, 19
Bangor, Maine, 40
Barnett, Phil, 123, 126, 148
Barrow, Pope, 148
Baucus, Max, 151, 170, 179
   alternative-fuels enthusiasts,
      139–42
   back-room dealing, 130
   Bush signs the bill, 169
   conference committee approval, 2
   conference committee overview,
      154
   House-Senate negotiations,
      158–59, 162, 164
   initial Senate deadlock, 82–84
   lobbying overview, 100
   Mitchell's leadership, 88
   Senate Environment Committee
      bill drafting, 77–80
   Senate in Reagan years, 43
   Senate negotiations, 90
Becker, Bill, 108
Bentsen, Lloyd, 78
Berman, Howard, 122
Bhopal, India, 34
Biden, Joseph R., Jr., 97
Billings, Leon G., 15, 94, 140, 159,
      174, 178, 179
Blake, Frank, 50
Bliley, Thomas J., Jr., 75

Bond, Christopher, 92, 98
Bonior, David E., 147
Boskin, Michael J., 155
Boston Globe, 40
Boston Harbor, 49–50
Boucher, Rick, 71
Brady, Nicholas F., 47
Brenner, Rob, 55, 61, 92–93
Brooks, Dale, 142
Bruce, Terry, 71, 115
budget, 67
Budget Committee, Senate, 18
budget deficit, 172
Burdick, Quentin, 37, 78, 82, 98
Bush, Barbara, 169
Bush, George, 45, 81, 167, 170–71,
      174–79
   alternative-fuels enthusiasts, 142
   alternative-fuels overview, 134–36
   alternative-fuels showdown, 145,
      148, 150
   Clean Air Act overview, 5
   conference committee approval, 3
   conference committee overview,
      152–55
   congressional committee reforms, 65
   Dingell's leadership, 114, 116
   Dingell-Waxman auto deal, 73–74,
      77
   election, politics of, 46–50
   Energy and Commerce negotia-
      tions, 124–29
   environmental lobbyists, 105–107
   fuels industry, 137–38
   industry lobbyists, 111
   initial Senate deadlock, 83–84
   Mitchell's leadership, 85–90
   1981–82 House debate, 30
   1984–88 House maneuvering, 33
   preparation of bill, 50–60
   reaction to bill, 60, 62
   Reagan years overview, 29
   Senate debate, 96–97
   Senate Environment Committee
      bill drafting, 77, 79
   Senate negotiations, 91, 93
   Senate in Reagan years, 44
   signing of bill, 168–69
   Waxman's influence, 122

Byrd, Robert C., 18, 25, 29, 37–43, 58–59, 66, 82, 87, 91–98, 100–101, 127, 142, 163, 166

C-SPAN, 7, 100
California, 178
  alternative-fuels enthusiasts, 140, 143
  alternative-fuels overview, 137
  alternative-fuels showdown, 145, 148
  Bush's election politics, 48, 50
  Dingell-Waxman auto deal, 75
  House-Senate negotiations, 158–61
  industry lobbyists, 111
  1981–88 House debate, 31
  Reagan years overview, 28
campaign finance, 67
Canada, 4, 23, 38
capital gains, 85
carbon monoxide, 18, 22, 34, 135
Carson, Rachel, 11
Carter, Jimmy, 18–19, 26, 36, 43, 66, 86, 92, 118, 129
catalytic converters, 16
Chafee, John H., 78–80, 82, 84, 88, 100, 154, 169, 179
Chamber of Commerce, 109
Chappaquiddick, 14
Chemical Manufacturers Association, 109
Chevron, 142
chlorofluorocarbons (CFCs)
  Bush's election politics, 49
  Clean Air Act overview, 4
  House-Senate negotiations, 157
  issues summary, 23
  Senate Environment Committee bill drafting, 80
Chrysler Corporation, 30, 118, 174
Cicconi, James W., 60
Civil Rights Act (1964), 82
Clean Air Act (1970)
  House-Senate negotiations, 159
  issues summary, 23
  lobbying overview, 102
  1970 Clean Air Act enactment, 16
  1977 Clean Air Act Amendments, 17, 19
  Senate negotiations, 94

Clean Air Act (1977)
  environmental lobbyists, 104
  industry lobbyists, 108
  1981–82 House debate, 30, 32
Clean Air Act Project, 104
"Clean Air Facts", 121
Clean Air Working Group, 102, 108–12, 174
Clean Fuels Development Coalition, 141
Cleveland Plain Dealer, 33
closed doors, 129, 172–74
coal, 38, 79, 140
  Senate Environment Committee bill drafting, 79
coal industry
  Bush's election politics, 48
  lobbying overview, 102
  1984–88 House maneuvering, 35
  Senate in Reagan years, 37, 39, 41–43
  Senate negotiations, 91, 92
coal miners
  Clean Air Act overview, 5, 8
  final congressional passage, 166
  House-Senate negotiations, 163
  1984–88 House maneuvering, 35
  Senate debate, 96
Coelho, Tony, 70, 74, 123, 172
Cohen, William S., 86
Columbia University, 58
Common Cause, 129
compressed natural gas, 147
conference committee, 152–66
Congressional Government, 7
Congressional Record, 5, 166
Congressional Research Service, 40
congressional staff, 78–79, 120, 157, 173
Conservation Foundation, 47
Conte, Silvio O., 35
Cooper, Jim, 71–72, 104, 107, 127–28, 130
Council of Economic Advisers, 155
Council on Environmental Quality, 12–13
Curtis, Charles, 92

Dach, Leslie, 50
Dannemeyer, William E., 3
Darman, Richard G., 52
Darwin, Charles, 9
Daschle, Tom, 85, 133, 140–44,
145–46, 148, 159
Defense Department, 56
Democratic Caucus, 20
Democratic Policy Committee,
Senate, 143
Democratic Senatorial Campaign
Committee, 39
Detroit, 5, 19–31, 121, 138, 145, 158
Detroit News, 76
Dingell, Deborah, 29, 74, 119, 124
Dingell, John D., 171, 173–74, 178,
179
alternative-fuels overview, 134–35
alternative-fuels showdown,
144–49
back-room dealing, 131
Bush's election politics, 49
Bush signs the bill, 169
Clean Air Act overview, 5–6
conference committee approval, 3
conference committee overview,
152–55
congressional committee reforms, 66
Dingell-Waxman auto deal, 73–76
Energy and Commerce negotiations, 124–29
environmental lobbyists, 106
final congressional passage, 165
fuels industry, 138–39
Group of Nine discussions, 69–72
House-Senate negotiations, 156–64
industry lobbyists, 108–11
leadership of, 115–20
lobbying overview, 102–103
1977 Clean Air Act Amendments,
18–19
1981–82 House debate, 29–32
1984–88 House maneuvering,
33–35
Reagan years overview, 26, 29
Senate Environment Committee
bill drafting, 77
Senate in Reagan years, 41
Waxman's influence, 121–23

Dingell, John D., Sr., 30
divided government, 21, 27, 44
Dole, Robert, 83–84, 89, 97–98, 136,
141–42, 144, 168
Domenici, Pete, 78
Domestic Policy Council, 60
Duberstein, Ken, 118
Dudek, Daniel J., 58, 61, 105, 172
Dukakis, Michael, 46, 48–50, 65
Durenberger, Dave, 80

Eagleton, Thomas, 16
Earth Day, 11, 102, 106
Eckart, Dennis E., 33, 70–71, 117,
128, 146, 148, 162, 171
Edison Electric Institute, 38, 111, 143
electoral college, 48
electric utilities
alternative-fuels enthusiasts, 140
Bush team prepares bill, 56–57, 59
Clean Air Act overview, 8
House-Senate negotiations, 161
industry lobbyists, 111
issues summary, 23
1970 Clean Air Act enactment, 17
1981–82 House debate, 32
1984–88 House maneuvering, 33
Reagan years overview, 28
Senate in Reagan years, 38, 40
emissions-trading
Bush bill, reaction to, 61
Bush team prepares bill, 57–58
Energy and Commerce negotiations, 128
House-Senate negotiations, 161
Senate negotiations, 91–93
Energy and Commerce Committee,
House, 171
alternative-fuels showdown,
145–46
back-room dealing, 129
conference committee approval,
3
conference committee overview,
152, 155
congressional committee reforms,
67
Dingell's leadership, 115–17, 120
Dingell-Waxman auto deal, 73

Energy and Power Subcommittee, 128
environmental lobbyists, 106–107
Group of Nine discussions, 69–70
Health and Environment Subcommittee, 2, 19, 31–32, 34, 70, 74, 122
House-Senate negotiations, 156, 160–61
industry lobbyists, 112
lobbying overview, 100
negotiations, 125–29
1981–82 House debate, 30
1984–88 House maneuvering, 35
Reagan years overview, 28–29
Senate Environment Committee bill drafting, 80
Senate in Reagan years, 42–43
Waxman's influence, 123
Energy and Natural Resources Committee, Senate, 68
Energy Department, 39, 59, 84, 136, 155, 162, 169
enforcement, 23–24
Environmental Defense Fund, 58–59, 91, 105, 172
environmentalists, 6, 135, 145–46, 178
Environmental Protection Agency, 175, 177, 179
alternative-fuels enthusiasts, 142
alternative-fuels overview, 135–36
alternative-fuels showdown, 149
Bush bill, reaction to, 61
Bush's election politics, 47
Bush signs the bill, 169
Bush team prepares bill, 53–55, 58–59
Clean Air Act overview, 4
conference committee overview, 153–54
Energy and Commerce negotiations, 124
environmental lobbyists, 105
fuels industry, 137, 139
Group of Nine discussions, 71
House-Senate negotiations, 162
initial environmental efforts, 12
initial Senate deadlock, 83

issues summary, 22
Mitchell's leadership, 90
1970 Clean Air Act enactment, 13, 16
1977 Clean Air Act Amendments, 17, 19
1981–82 House debate, 32–33
1984–88 House maneuvering, 34
Reagan years overview, 26
Senate in Reagan years, 36
Senate negotiations, 92–94
Environment and Public Works Committee, Senate, 170, 179
alternative-fuels enthusiasts, 139–40
conference committee overview, 153
congressional committee reforms, 68
Dingell's leadership, 118
Energy and Commerce negotiations, 127
Environmental Protection Subcommittee, 2, 18, 37, 43, 76–77, 85, 185
House-Senate negotiations, 159, 161
initial Senate deadlock, 82, 84
Mitchell's leadership, 88–89
Senate debate, 95–96, 98
Senate Environment Committee bill drafting, 77, 80
Senate in Reagan years, 36
Senate negotiations, 94
ethanol, 5, 135–44, 149, 160
Ethics Committee, House, 67
ethyl tertiary butyl ether, 144
Exxon, 160

farm groups, 135, 145
Fay, Bill, 99, 102, 109–110, 165, 174
Fazio, Vic, 70
Federal Energy Regulatory Commission, 92
Federalist Papers, The, 21
Fields, Jack, 138–39, 146, 160
Finance Committee, Senate, 79
International Trade Subcommittee, 79

Finnegan, David, 6, 113, 117–19, 123, 125–26, 146, 148, 157–59

Fisher Body Corporation, 29

Foley, Thomas S., 3, 6, 145, 147, 149, 156, 174

Ford, Gerald R., 47, 53

Ford, Henry, 29

Ford Motor Company, 30, 118

Fosburgh, Whitney, 141, 143

Fowler, Wyche, 98

Gardner, John, 19

Garn, Jake, 18–19

gasoline station, 5

gasoline tax, 144

General Motors Corporation, 16, 29–30, 74, 118–19, 143

Goffman, Joseph, 58, 61, 105

Gorman, Theresa, 125

Gorsuch, Anne, 26, 32–33

Grady, Robert E., 48, 52, 56–57, 84, 89–90, 136, 154, 169, 178

grain industry, 137, 160

Gray, C. Boyden, 46–50, 53, 56–61, 84, 87, 89, 124, 135–36, 141, 153, 169, 178

ground-level ozone, 22, 34

Group of Nine

  Dingell's leadership, 115

  Dingell-Waxman auto deal, 73–74

  discussions, 70–73

Hahn, Robert W., 54

Hair, Jay D., 100–101

Hall, Ralph M., 75, 129, 138–39, 146, 160

Hawkins, David, 40

Health and Education Department, 11

health care, 68

Health, Education and Welfare Department, 15, 19

Heinz, John, 58

House of Representatives, 172–75, 179

  alternative-fuels showdown, 144, 147–49

  back-room dealing, 129–30, 132

  Bush's election politics, 47

  Clean Air Act overview, 4–9

  conference committee approval, 2

  conference committee overview, 152–55

  congressional committee reforms, 66

  congressional reform, 20, 22

  Dingell's leadership, 114, 118–19

  Dingell-Waxman auto deal, 74, 76

  Energy and Commerce negotiations, 124–29

  House-Senate negotiations, 157–64

  industry lobbyists, 108

  lobbying overview, 102

  1977 Clean Air Act Amendments, 18–19

  1981–82 House debate, 30

  1984–88 House maneuvering, 35

  Reagan years overview, 27

  Senate in Reagan years, 42

  Waxman's influence, 122–23

Houston, 4

Humphrey, Hubert H., 13, 104, 144

Hussein, Saddam, 157

hydrocarbons, 18, 22

ICF, 40

Illinois, 8, 48, 162

inaugurations, 46

Indiana, 162

Inouye, Daniel K., 66

Interior and Insular Affairs Committee, House, 12

Interior Department, 26, 32, 36, 118

Interstate and Foreign Commerce Committee, House, 19

Iran-Contra, 27, 65

Jackson, Henry M., 12

Jackson, Michael D., 140, 143

Johnson, Lyndon B., 11–12

Johnson-Matthey Company, 140

Johnston, J. Bennett, 66

Jones, Charles O., 13

Jordan, Michael, 95

Jorling, Thomas C., 94, 158–59

Judiciary Committee, House, 67

Kean, Thomas H., 47–48, 52

Keating, Charles H., 170

Kennedy, Edward M., 14
Kennedy, Robert F., 14
Kerry, John F., 95
Kimball, Kate, 6, 38–40, 42, 92
Klinefelter, Bill, 101
Knauss, Chuck, 117, 126, 158
Kolstad, Allen, 79
Kopechne, Mary Jo, 14
Kundanis, George, 147

Labor Department, 163
Lautenberg, Frank, 80
Lavelle, Rita M., 33
League of Women Voters, 105
Leahy, Patrick J., 98
Lent, Norman F., 125–26, 139, 154
Levin, Carl, 142
Lewis, Jerry, 28, 120
Liberatore, Robert G., 174
Lieberman, Joseph I., 95
lobbyists, 6, 16, 35, 90, 100–103,
    169, 174
Los Angeles, 4–5, 31, 120–21
Los Angeles Times, 76

Madigan, Edward R., 30, 126, 160
Madison, James, 20
Maguire, Andy, 19
Maine, 14, 38
Mallick, Earl, 109
Management and Budget, Office of,
    52–53, 62, 84, 89, 94, 136, 153,
    178
Mansfield, Mike, 20
"Massachusetts Miracle," 50
Mathews, Rusty, 38, 41–42, 91–93
media, 175–76
Melcher, John, 79
Merchant Marine and Fisheries Com-
    mittee, House, 156
methanol, 5, 135–36, 140, 147
Metzenbaum, Howard M., 91
Michigan, 8, 17, 48
Michigan South Central Power
    Agency, 166
Middleton, John, 15
Missouri, 48
Mitchell, George J., 81, 170, 173–74,
    177

alternative-fuels enthusiasts,
    139–43
Bush bill, reaction to, 62
Bush signs the bill, 168–69
Bush team prepares bill, 56, 58–59
Clean Air Act overview, 5, 9
conference committee approval, 3
conference committee overview,
    153
congressional committee reforms,
    67
Dingell's leadership, 114, 119
environmental lobbyists, 104, 106
final congressional passage, 165
House-Senate negotiations, 161
industry lobbyists, 111
initial Senate deadlock, 82–85
leadership of, 85–90
lobbying overview, 100–101
Reagan years overview, 29
Senate debate, 95–98
Senate Environment Committee
    bill drafting, 77–80
Senate in Reagan years, 37–43
Senate negotiations, 90–94
Waxman's influence, 123
Mobil, 160
Moffett, Toby, 19
Montana, 2
Moore, W. Henson, 59
Motor Vehicle Manufacturers Associ-
    ation, 109
Moynihan, Daniel Patrick, 159
Mulroney, Brian, 57, 60
Murtha, John P., 35, 74
Muskie, Edmund S., 10–20, 22, 37,
    86, 88, 159, 174

Nader, Ralph, 14, 19, 58
National Association of Manufactur-
    ers, 109
National Clean Air Coalition,
    101–110
National Coal Association, 109
National Council of Churches, 105
National Environmental Policy Act
    (1969), 12
National Governors' Association, 107
National Journal, 116

national parks, 2, 164
National Steel Corporation, 163
National Wildlife Federation, 100,
    102–105
natural gas, 137, 144
Natural Resources Defense Council,
    104–105
Nebraska Corn Utilization Board, 143
New England, 4, 36
New Jersey, 48
New York Times, 7, 176
Nicaragua, 65
nitrogen oxide, 18–19, 22–23, 37,
    49
Nixon, Richard M., 12–15, 43, 47
North, Oliver, 86

Ohio, 8, 48, 162
oil-autos coalition, 145
oil industry, 109–11, 134, 137, 142,
    146, 160
O'Neill, Thomas P., Jr., 66
Orlando, John, 110

paper industry, 14
Paster, Howard, 118
pay raise, 67, 172
Porter, Roger B., 45, 51–56, 60–62,
    84, 89–90, 105, 124, 141,
    153–55, 162, 175
Preyer, Richardson, 122
Princeton University, 55
Public Works Committee, Senate, 11,
    20
    Air and Water Pollution Subcom-
        mittee, 12
Pursell, Carl D., 166

Quayle, Dan, 167, 169

Randolph, Jennings, 36
Reagan, Ronald, 25, 171
    Bush bill, reaction to, 61
    Bush's election politics, 46, 47
    Bush signs the bill, 168
    Bush team prepares bill, 54
    congressional committee reforms,
        65, 67
    congressional reform, 22

Dingell's leadership, 118
environmental lobbyists, 104–106
era, overview of, 26–29
industry lobbyists, 108
lobbying overview, 103
1981–82 House debate, 30, 32
Senate Environment Committee
    bill drafting, 78
Senate in Reagan years, 36–44
Waxman's influence, 122–23
reformulated gasoline, 138, 140–44,
    146–47, 155, 159
Reilly, William K., 47, 53, 59, 83,
    139, 154–55, 157, 162, 169
Renewable Fuels Association,
    143–44
Republican Conference, Senate, 179
Robertson, Pat, 136
Rogers, Paul G., 19, 31
Roosevelt, Franklin, 174
Rosenberg, William G., 53, 55–56,
    59, 84, 135–36, 139, 142–43,
    149, 153, 155, 162, 177
Rowland, Roy, 75
Ruckleshaus, William D., 47
Ryan, Tom, 118

Samuel, Bill, 40
Scheuer, Jim, 115
Schiliro, Phil, 123, 126, 148
Senate, 172–73, 179
    alternative-fuels enthusiasts, 140,
        141–43
    alternative-fuels showdown, 144
    back-room dealing, 129–30
    Bush team prepares bill, 55–56
    Clean Air Act overview, 5–9
    conference committee approval, 2
    conference committee overview,
        152–55
    congressional committee reforms,
        65–69
    congressional reform, 20–22
    debate, 95–96, 98
    Dingell's leadership, 119
    Dingell-Waxman auto deal, 74
    Energy and Commerce negotia-
        tions, 124–29
    environmental lobbyists, 106

Environment Committee bill drafting, 77
House-Senate negotiations, 156–64
industry lobbyists, 110
initial Senate deadlock, 82–83
lobbying overview, 100
Mitchell's leadership, 85, 89
negotiations, 92–94
1977 Clean Air Act Amendments, 18
overview, 26–29
Reagan years , 36–44
seniority, 8, 20, 31
Sharp, Philip R., 19, 71, 77, 106, 127–28, 130, 146, 161, 164, 170
Sheehan, Jack, 101–102
Sierra Club, 102, 104
Sikorski, Gerry, 62, 67, 70–71, 107, 156, 178
Silent Spring, 11
Simpson, Alan K., 87, 154, 164
Slattery, Jim, 71
smog, 46, 60–61, 71, 95, 176
Stafford, Robert, 36–37, 40, 78–79
STAPPA/ALAPCO, 107
State Department, 60, 86
state implementation plan, 16
steel industry, 17, 29, 35, 163
Strauss, David, 78
Stuntz, Linda, 54, 84, 136
sulfur dioxide, 23, 38, 40–41, 49, 56, 60, 128, 161
Sununu, John H., 55, 60, 61, 84, 90, 97, 106–107, 139, 162, 169
Swift, Al, 28, 70–72, 112, 165
Symms, Steven, 96–97
Synar, Mike, 70–72, 120, 146–47, 156, 166

Tauke, Thomas J., 75, 112, 125, 130, 171
Tauzin, Billy, 71, 146
Teamsters, 101
Technology Assessment Office, 121
Teeter, Robert M., 47–48, 55, 135
Thomas, Lee, 61
Tower, John, 56

toxic chemicals
Energy and Commerce negotiations, 126
House-Senate negotiations, 163
issues summary, 23
1984–88 House maneuvering, 34
Senate Environment Committee bill drafting, 80
Train, Russell E., 13, 47, 105–106
Treasury Department, 47, 136, 163
Trumka, Richard L., 39–42, 93

Union Carbide, 34
United Auto Workers, 19, 109
industry lobbyists, 109, 111
United Mine Workers of America
Bush team prepares bill, 57, 92–93
Senate in Reagan years, 39–43
Senate negotiations, 92–93
United Nations, 47, 120
United Steelworkers of America, 101, 103, 105
University of California (Los Angeles), 22, 122
USX (formerly known as U.S. Steel), 109

Valdez, Alaska, 46
Van Buren, Martin, 46
Vanishing Air, 14
Vietnam War, 11

Warner, John, 73, 77
Washington Post, 7, 30, 162, 176–77
waste disposal, 179
"Watergate," 19–20, 129–30, 158
Watkins, James D., 54, 59, 155, 169
Watt, James, 26, 32, 36, 118
Waxman, Henry A., 64, 171, 173–78, 179
alternative-fuels enthusiasts, 139–40
alternative-fuels overview, 134
alternative-fuels showdown, 144–49
back-room dealing, 131
Bush bill, reaction to, 62
Bush signs the bill, 169
Clean Air Act overview, 5–6
conference committee approval, 3

Waxman, Henry A., *(Continued)*
  conference committee overview,
    152–55
  Dingell's leadership, 115–20
  Dingell-Waxman auto deal, 73–76
  Energy and Commerce negotia-
    tions, 126–29
  environmental lobbyists, 107
  fuels industry, 138–39
  Group of Nine discussions, 69–72
  House-Senate negotiations, 156,
    158–63
  industry lobbyists, 108
  influence of, 121–23
  1981–82 House debate, 31–32
  1984–88 House maneuvering,
    33–36
  Reagan years overview, 28–29
  Senate Environment Committee
    bill drafting, 77
  Senate in Reagan years, 42
West Virginia, 8, 38
Wetstone, Greg, 123, 126, 148
Wilson, Pete, 95, 168
Wilson, Woodrow, 7
Wirth, Timothy E., 19, 58, 95
Wise, Bob, 163
World Wildlife Fund, 47, 105
Wright, Jim, 66–67, 142, 172
Wyden, Ron, 164

About the Author

As congressional reporter for *National Journal* since 1977 and staff member since 1973, Richard E. Cohen writes about both legislative and electoral politics and deals regularly with a broad cross-section of members of Congress. He has been a frequent contributor to other publications, including the Sunday "Opinion" section of the *Los Angeles Times, The Baltimore Sun*, and *The Baron Report,* a political newsletter. He has also been a regular guest on the C-SPAN cable network. In 1981, he wrote *Congressional Leadership: Seeking a New Role,* a lengthy monograph published by Georgetown University's Center for Strategic and International Studies. He has served four terms as a member of the executive committee of the congressional periodical press galleries and chaired the committee from 1987 to 1989. Cohen was the 1990 winner of the Everett McKinley Dirksen Award for distinguished reporting of Congress.

Cohen graduated in 1969 from Brown University, where he was publisher of the *Brown Daily Herald*, and in 1972 from Georgetown University Law Center. During law school, he was an aide to U.S. Sen. Edward W. Brooke of Massachusetts. A native of Northampton, Massachusetts, Cohen and his wife, Lyn Schlitt, who is general counsel to the U.S. International Trade Commission, now live in McLean, Virginia; they have a five-year-old daughter.